# Forsaking Our Children

Bureaucracy and Reform
in the Child Welfare
System

# Forsaking Our Children

## Bureaucracy and Reform in the Child Welfare System

BY JOHN M. HAGEDORN

LAKE VIEW PRESS • CHICAGO

Lake View Press
P.O. Box 578279, Chicago, Illinois 60657


Library of Congress Cataloging–in–Publication Data.

Hagedorn, John M. 1947–
        Forsaking Our Children : bureaucracy and reform in the  child
welfare system / by John M. Hagedorn
                p.        cm.
        Includes bibliographical references and index.
        ISBN 0-941702-41-3
        ISBN 0-941702-43-X (pbk.)

        1. Child welfare--Wisconsin--Milwaukee County. 2. Milwaukee County
(Wis.). Dept. of Social Services--Reorganization.
I. Title.HV742.W5H34   1995
362.7'09775--dc 20                                    95-31317
                                                      CIP

*to my mother, who passed away*
*as this book was being finished*

*her unconditional love for her children*
*has been my inspiration in struggling*
*for reform of the social services*

# TABLE OF CONTENTS

PREFACE                                                                    xi

ACKNOWLEDGEMENTS                                                           xv

1    THE CHALLENGE OF REFORM                                                3
     The Basketball Game *3*
     The Rhetoric of "Reform" *7*
          In Search of a "Hill of Beans" *9*
          Reforming Social Services *13*
          The War on Poverty Revisited *15*
     Conclusion: Reforming Street-Level Bureaucracies *18*

PART I   THE MILWAUKEE COUNTY
         DEPARTMENT OF SOCIAL SERVICES                                     21

2    THE CORE TASKS OF SOCIAL WORK                                         23
     Investigating Child Protective Services *23*
     Social Work Routines *25*
          The Domination of Child Welfare by the Courts *29*
     Child Abuse and Bureaucratic Expansion *31*
     Conclusion: Social Service Bureaucracies
          Gain by Punishing the Poor *36*

3    THE FRAGMENTED STRUCTURE OF SOCIAL WORK                               39
     Shedding Some Light on a Family's Problems *39*
     The Child Protective Labyrinth *41*
          How Social Service Bureaucracies Became Fragmented? *45*
          The Structure of Work *49*
     Blaming the Workers *50*
     Conclusion: Making a Plan *55*

**4  UNDERMINING POOR NEIGHBORHOODS**                                57

  The Colored Maps *57*
  Where is Social Service Money Spent? *62*
  Support Networks and Social Work *67*
  Conclusion: Neighborhood and Bureaucracies *73*

**PART II  THE HISTORICAL CONTEXT OF THE REFORM
OF SOCIAL SERVICE BUREAUCRACIES**                                    75

**5  THE FRUSTRATION OF REFORM**                                     77

  The Emergence of Bureaucracies *79*
    Scientific Reform=More Supervision *80*
    The More Things Change... *83*
  The New Deal and the Segmentation of Labor *84*
    Common But Separate Purposes *86*
    A New Deal for Some and a Raw Deal for Others *88*
  Conclusion: Expanded Bureaucracies Minorities
    and Institutionalized Divisions *89*

**6  REFORM AND PUNISHMENT**                                         93

  Contingency Theory and Structural Reform
    in Business and Social Welfare *94*
    The Institutionalization of Public Bureaucracies *97*
    Social Welfare Expands Its Social Services Component *99*
    Response by a Threatened Institution *101*
    Social Service Bureaucracies in Search of a Mission *103*
  The Reagan Revolution and Business Reform *104*
    Welfare Bureaucracies Help Swing the Reagan Budget Ax *107*
    The New Authoritarianism *111*
  Conclusion: Social Service Bureaucracies in Need of Reform *113*

**PART III  THE DIRECTION AND MISDIRECTION OF REFORM**               115

**7  WHAT IS REAL REFORM**                                           117

  Six Hundred and Seventy Five Easy Answers *117*
  Altering Core Tasks *120*
    The Importance of Organizational Structure *123*
    Family, Preservation Services as Structural Change *125*
  Empowering Poor Neighborhoods *129*
    Decentralized Pilot Units *130*
    Neighborhood Councils and their Service Delivery Plans *132*
  Conclusion: Ideals and Reality *136*

**8 SYMBOLIC REFORM VERSUS
REAL REFORM FOR SOCIAL SERVICES** 139

The Story That Hasn't Ended *139*
Lesson One: Reform the System—Don't Give Up! *142*
Lesson Two: Beware of Symbolic Reforms *145*
Symbolic Reform Number One—
Reform as "Adding On" *146*
Symbolic Reform Number Two—Reform as Diversion *148*
Symbolic Reform Number Three—Reform as
Phony Participation *150*
Symbolic Reform Number Four—
Reform Without Evaluation *152*
Lesson Three: Get It While You Can *154*
Conclusion: Reform Local Bureaucracies *158*

**APPENDIXES**

**APPENDIX ONE
INVOLVED OBSERVERS AND ACADEMIC RESEARCH** 161

Getting Started: The Problem of Taking Sides *161*
Involved Observers *163*
Practical Problems *166*
Gathering the Data: The Problem of Bias *167*
Post-Positivist Research *170*
The Bias of the Paycheck *172*
Understanding the Data: The Problem of Analysis *174*
Writing It Up: The Problem of Audience *178*
That Reminds Me of a Story *180*
Conclusion: Inciting Change *181*

**APPENDIX TWO
AFRICAN AMERICANS IN MILWAUKEE: 1963–1987** 183

**APPENDIX THREE
FOUR STAGES OF ORGANIZATIONAL THEORY** 186

**NOTES** 187

**REFERENCES** 205

**AUTHOR INDEX** 229

**SUBJECT INDEX** 233

# PREFACE

This book was born out of the frustrations of a struggle to reform the Milwaukee County Department of Social Services. I was not only an observer of this struggle, but worked with a dedicated group of people as the coordinator of the reforms. At first I had no intention to write a book. But as with a fresh cut, the pain of the efforts that went into reform wouldn't let me think of anything else. I put aside my sociological research on gangs and wrote my doctoral dissertation on bureaucracy and reform. I returned to my work on gangs, but I couldn't let the social services go. I was driven to explore the lessons of our reforms for myself and then to summarize them for others.

This book is not only a work of scholarship for sociologists. I have written it for anyone who cares about our children. But first of all, it is written for those who have seen with their own eyes how the child welfare system doesn't work for poor families. This audience includes social workers and taxpayers, policymakers and parents, lawyers and judges, as well as students and faculty in social welfare and sociology. Fundamentally, *Forsaking Our Children* aspires to give direction to the reform of the public social services.

Many people think that social workers are lenient bleeding hearts who crack down on abusive parents only when it's too late. Public opinion today seems to lie squarely behind removing children more quickly from troubled families. Important public figures have called for some of those families to be replaced by orphanages. This book sails against that harsh tide and paints a very different picture of today's "child protective" system. For example, you will discover in these pages that social workers spend most of their time in court and doing paperwork, and provide very few services for families.

But although this book argues that the social service system should provide more services, it is not the familiar liberal plea for "more money" or "more staff." It shows how welfare bureaucracies, by their very nature, have used demands for more resources to strengthen themselves, often at the expense of the poor. Applying the literature on organizations, it provides an historical context to explain bureaucratic resistance to real reforms which would benefit the poor. Since the 1970s, I argue, the public social services have adapted to a more punitive political climate by making child abuse investigations, rather than supportive services, their prime function.

*Forsaking Our Children* constructs a new theoretical framework to look at social service bureacuracies. The book, however, is not abstract theorizing, but a narrative of our reform, using the words of social workers themselves to discuss what they really do and how they are organized to do it. It also examines how welfare bureaucracies have neglected and harmed poor minority neighborhoods by investing millions of dollars in agencies located far from the neighborhoods where their clients live. The book ends by applying lessons learned from restructuring modern businesses to the reform of welfare bureaucracies. It argues that most changes made by bureaucrats are more symbolic than real, yet significant reforms are indeed within our reach.

I've also done something a little different. I've tried to give life to my message by introducing each non-historical chapter with a brief anecdote from my experience of reform. Sometimes, I think, we learn more from stories than we do from coldly analyzing "the facts." I firmly believe social science should be as readable as possible for any educated woman or man. For those who wonder how a reformer can also do good research, I explore the role of the "involved observer" in an appendix.

Another audience for this book is everyone who is interested in broader social change. To them I argue that reforms of public bureaucracies, like our Youth Initiative, must be an essential part of any progressive social movement. I suggest there are more tasks for activists than marching in the streets, rejuvenating unions, or getting out the vote. Educational, welfare, and criminal justice bureaucracies, where many of us work, play a major role in regulating the poor.

It would be socially irresponsible not to attempt to reform them.

It can be argued, as Piven and Cloward do, that fundamental changes in welfare and other public bureaucracies can come quicker as a result of outside pressure from mass movements. I agree. Much of my own life has been spent on such grass roots organizing. Where popular movements arise, those of us who work in bureaucracies can and should link with them. A key lesson from my two historical chapters is that many reforms forced by mass movements have been coopted by adaptive bureaucracies. I argue that changes set in motion by outside pressure have proved to be ephemeral in part because new structures of work were not created to consolidate reform. This means that there need to be reformers "inside" working to reshape our social institutions in a way that is compatible with the demands of those "outside" banging on the doors.

These are times, unfortunately, when the poor are not in motion, loudly demanding change. On the contrary, the public mood is angry and impatient with those of us who would defend support for troubled families. Using the analysis in this book, we can predict that child welfare bureaucracies will accomodate to this angry mood in order to secure continuing resources. For example, I'm certain welfare bureaucrats will maneuver to control funding for orphanages. These same bureaucrats will also insist that if only we gave them sufficient resources, they could really crack down on abusive parents.

On the other hand, the welfare institution contains benevolent as well as punitive goals, and there are many humane bureaucrats who advocate less dismal policies. I believe real support for poor families requires commitment to an alternative, pro-family agenda. This book argues that we need to couple with this developing agenda practical reforms which can demonstrate, here and now, how public institutions could be reorganized. Where reforms are successful those local bureaucracies can, to some extent, become islands of humanitarian relief. At the very least, when the national mood finally swings in the other direction, a blueprint for structural reform will be available for others.

*Forsaking Our Children* begins to sketch that blueprint for the future of the social services. As an unrepentant sixties radical, I've written this book as a contribution to rethinking the meaning of reform.

# ACKNOWLEDGEMENTS

A book is never the sole property of an author, but more like an accumulation of debts. The trick of writing is to reshuffle that stack of debts into a playable hand. The next paragraphs acknowledge some of those debts.

When I first began at the Milwaukee County Department of Health Human Services, it was Sue Hansen who started me off on the right track. She convinced me that significant change within the bureaucracy could take place in six weeks, if only the will was there. Sue, I still think you were right. We spent many wonderful evenings plotting, scheming, and dreaming, trying to get that "six week plan" started.

If Sue pushed me from outside the Department, it was Kay Krall who showed me how changes inside the bureaucracy could take place. She had the insider perspective and argued against giving up... most of the time. Many of the "brilliant" ideas I came up with were really Kay's. Both Kay and Sue knew the system and hated what it did to children. This book in many ways merely gives expression to what I learned from them.

Sharon Schulz was my immediate supervisor and confidant. Together we died a thousand deaths trying to get the pilot units up and running and establishing family preservation programs. It would have been impossible for me to have stayed on the path of reform without her support. Thanks, Sharon. I hope I didn't cause you too much trouble and gave you as much support as you gave me.

Then there was my friend Howard Fuller, who hired me, and with whom I share a passion for change. By summarizing the lessons of our struggle, this book is in a way a repayment of my debt to Howard. If those lessons cause you any pain, Howard, rest assured they hurt me as well.

There were many others. There was Elvira Villarreal, who did miracles making the school collaborative "happen." I could always count on Elvira to share with me ideas and frustrations. Faye Camps taught me how the child protective system really works and was a consistent fighter for reform, though it cost her. Ardelia Mitchell is the epitome of what a "neighborhood coordinator" should be. I should also mention my old friend Paul Reinelt who knows how to make social work…work, Judy Herro who always had a balanced perspective to add to her love of children, child welfare lawyer Deborah Schwartz, whose enthusiasm and dedication to children I deeply respect , and Carol Latham who tried early on to move an immovable system. There were others whom I can't really name since they are still vulnerable to retaliation within the bureaucracy. I learned that our Department of Social Services, like other departments around the country, is filled with social workers who fervently desire change. They aren't the problem. It is more often we cosmopolitan "reformers" who, in the end, fail them.

In academia, I have to thank my dissertation committee, especially the chair, Joan Moore. Joan has been a friend and my invaluable teacher in gang research. Stan Stojkovic, Marc Levine, Howard Fuller, and Walter Trattner were also members of the committee. Walter Trattner subjected my dissertation to withering criticism. Thanks. I revised my argument based on your suggestions, but I didn't change my basic perspective. I'm sure you're not surprised.

My staff at the Drug Posse Project put up with my split days working on gang research and then frantically taking time off to write a piece of the dissertation or book. Jerome, Lavelle, Clint, Pops, Papo, and Rita: thanks. Thanks also to Veronica Emja and Steve Percy at the UWM Urban Research Center for making it possible for me to lead such a schizophrenic, but productive, life.

Paul Elitzik is my best friend and also my editor and publisher. He told me to take this book to a "big" press but it was too hard to imagine writing a book without him. It was Paul who took my raw skills and taught me how to write.

Debbie Schwartz from Chicago transcribed my field notes. Kathe, my "ex," suffered throughout the long days and pain of reform. I'm sure the stress of those times contributed to our divorce.

Finally, there is Mary, my partner, and love of my life. I hope I can give her the kind of support to write that she has given me. She also taught me to be more giving to our children, even though I'm engaged in "important stuff," like writing a book. I hope Tracey, Bryna, Katie, Marty, Zach, Jess and all children will be better off for this book being completed.

# Forsaking Our Children

Bureaucracy and Reform
in the Child Welfare
System

# 1

# THE CHALLENGE OF REFORM

## THE BASKETBALL GAME

There were three of us watching the Milwaukee Bucks playing basketball at the Bradley Center in April of 1988. First there was Howard Fuller, who as "Owusu Saduaki" had been national chairman of the African Liberation Support Committee and founder of Malcolm X Community College. For the past year or so he had been working as dean of General Education at the Milwaukee Area Technical College. Second was Michael McGee who had been a Black Panther Party leader, community organizer, and at that time was an alderman in Milwaukee's central city. Finally, there was me, John Hagedorn, a white activist and social scientist who had just finished a book on Milwaukee youth gangs.

We had just won an election: the city had elected a new mayor and county voters had thrown out the old county executive. Earlier that year we had finally gotten rid of the school superintendent, thanks in no small part to ten years of organizing by Fuller. All three of us had also contributed to ousting the police chief a few years back. A new day was dawning in Milwaukee.

But we were a study in contrasts. Michael McGee was exuberant, nearly ecstatic. "The revolution has come," McGee repeated over and over as we talked at our courtside seats. "All we fought for for so many years. Now we have it." He went on to list the things he had been promised by the new mayor. "We can get our people into top jobs. We've finally made it."

Howard and I were a bit less cheerful. To tell the truth, we were a whole lot less cheerful. Fuller had been offered the directorship of the county's Department of Health and Human Services (DHHS), which spent half the county's budget. He would run the county hospital, medical complex, oversee all welfare payments, and be in charge of social services. The thought of taking on an entrenched bureaucracy like DHHS was frightening. I asked Howard if he really wanted to run the "plantation": DHHS was white on the top, and gradually changed color as you went down the organizational chart until you got to a mainly black clientele. He laughed nervously.

In a way, though, this is what we had fought for. Like Pogo, we woke up one day to find out the enemy was us: we were "in charge." But while McGee was as high as I've ever seen him, Fuller was quiet, and I was scared. Much of our lives had been spent as revolutionaries, propelled by the sixties and our deep revulsion of injustice. We lived lives of dedication to the people, organizing the grass roots, demanding the system change. But we were getting older. And Fuller and McGee at least, more successful. I had begun to use the tools of social science to push for changes in public policy.

And now the elected leadership of Milwaukee actually wanted us to take over! We knew reforming a huge bureaucracy like DHHS would take all our energy for the next several years. And we were suspicious. Could it really be done? Could we do anything but put bandaids on gaping wounds? Was it a setup? Would we fool ourselves into believing we had accomplished something when we really had only minimal impact? Worse, would we change, would we become apologists, defenders of a new status quo, turncoats to our principles...and maybe not even be aware of what we'd become? Could we "make a difference" as we were asked? We really didn't know. As we watched the game—I'm sure none of us can even remember who the Bucks played that night or who won—there was no doubt we would try. Howard said, "After all these years of talking garbage about the system, now we have to put up or shut up. We just don't have any choice."

We went ahead and took on the bureaucracy. Fuller became director of DHHS and I was hired to design a "fundamental reorientation" of services for youth. My pain grew by the day. It was the most difficult thing I had ever attempted in my life. I thought my years of working with the gangs were hard, but gangs are much easier to deal with than the social service bureaucracy.

And McGee? His euphoria lasted only a few months. Disillusioned by the mayor and the politics of incremental change, he took again to the streets. He bitterly denounced Fuller as an "Uncle Tom" and founded the "Black Panther Militia." By 1995, he promised, if things didn't really change, he and his followers would begin guerrilla war. McGee had summed up the lack of reform and had chosen the sixties road of protest and threats. He believed the only way things could change would be to strike fear into the hearts of those with power.

Fuller and I took another road. Not that we were sure it would work, but we had to try...to see if we could "make a difference" in how these bureaucracies treat people. A lesson of the sixties, it seemed to me, was that while threats got attention, by themselves they had not brought lasting change. In fact, the repression that followed often left things even worse. Given the worldwide collapse of socialism, I asked myself whether the social institutions of capitalism could be reoriented to drastically reduce the sufferings of the poor? We were to be given the opportunity to run Milwaukee's health and human services system. How much could we get done? How far could we go? Would we become part of the problem, or be part of the solution?

This book is the story of our struggle and what I learned from it. Like all good stories, the reader may find more ambiguity in these pages than clear cut answers. But there is an argument I think our experience justifies: Given the opportunity to run these monstrous bureaucracies, we have to try. They are too important in the lives of the poor; too harmful when they are supposed to help; they've had too many resources dumped into them—honest people just can't ignore them. We have to struggle, to experiment, and then sum up our experience for others. This is what I've tried to do in the pages that follow.

In June of 1988, I accepted the job as coordinator of Milwaukee County's "Youth Initiative." David Schulz, the new county executive, had been elected as a candidate of "change" and had promised to shake things up. Schulz, unfortunately, had no concrete plan for how to accomplish what he boldly called a "fundamental reorientation" of services for youth. The appointment of Howard Fuller, an African American activist, as Director of Health and Human Services, was his way of showing he was serious. Fuller hired me to translate Schulz's vague campaign slogan into "real reform."

All I knew then was the social services bureaucracy didn't work very well—it was "broken," in the words of one friend. The following excerpt from my field notes, dictated into my recorder after a meeting early in our administration, sets the rather surreal scene in 1988 of former revolutionaries taking over a human services agency.

> One interesting thing about Fuller. How many Directors could say to a meeting of bureaucrats that those of us who are engineering this Youth Initiative are people who tried for a decade to make revolution in this country? Now we've realized that possibility had passed, so we're settling for militant reform. And nobody blinked an eyelash! Can you imagine that statement being said ten years ago? Utterly incredible!
>
> *Field Notes, November 17, 1988*

The bureaucracy we were trying to reform touched the lives of most children in Milwaukee. In 1990 our department received over 10,000 child abuse referrals, more than double the total of five years before. Researchers found that approximately 60% of all Milwaukee county youth under eighteen years old (121, 321 children) were our clients: they were either on AFDC, had an open case in Children's Court, or had been investigated by the child welfare system (Pawasarat 1989).[1] In some central city zip codes, more than three quarters of the African Americans and Hispanics who lived there were tied in some way to our Department of Health and Human Services *(see Appendix 2)*.

If you're poor, there's at least one bureaucrat for every problem and for some problems you literally get bombarded. In fact the three "p's"— police, public schools, and public welfare—dominate the lives of the urban poor. Lipsky (1980) calls them "street-level bureaucracies" because the line staff in these systems deal directly with clients and appear to have great discretion over how to treat them. Police, teachers, and social workers are the main ongoing contact points between the government and the nation's poor.

In Milwaukee alone there are more than 11,000 public school employees, about 2000 police officers, and my own Department of Health and Human Services had nearly 5000 employees, including social workers, nurses and nurse's aids, and financial assistance workers. Then there are public defenders; state, county, and city corrections staff; judges and judicial employees; probation and parole workers; district attorneys; public health employees; housing project staff; and so on.

I once called a meeting of all the social workers we could find who were involved in serving a single troubled family. It might be a good idea, I reasoned, for everyone to get together and talk. We ended up sending out more than forty letters to various county, city, state, school, and private agency staff who were directly involved with this one family's problems. And of course at the meeting, we discovered there were even more social workers involved we hadn't known to invite. "Real reform" of our social service bureaucracy would have a big impact on many people's lives, if we could only figure out what "real reform" meant.

## THE RHETORIC OF "REFORM"

The "Youth Initiative" came on the scene with press conferences filled with "radical" words promising "sweeping" changes. But to social workers and managers who had heard that kind of talk before, the Youth Initiative "really" meant new people coming into their turf, making a few waves and then departing. Social workers expressed their candid opinions on the Youth Initiative to evaluators one year after it was launched:

> There was an election and Dr. Fuller came in and if there's another election he'll be gone. That's all political on that end of it. #108

> There's another thing about these things...They spring up, they drop out, they spring up, they drop out. They tell us work takes priority and workers miss meetings about new programs, but they don't last. #409

I mean, I honestly have to say with all these other efforts, with the Youth Initiative. We've done all these things before. I think its a nice thing to try, and maybe if we try something different and I think we energize people to try things differently...We still got problems galore. #306[2]

To veteran social workers and long time bureaucrats, Fuller, I and the rest of his team were "cosmopolitans" appointed because of outside political connections. We arrived on the scene only to make cosmetic media-oriented changes while nothing would "really" be any different for staff. Our meddling would inevitably irritate the hard working "locals" who would remain long after the reformers left for other challenges (see Merton 1968; Gouldner 1957). Despite my optimistic predictions, one year into our administration, line workers looked at the impact of the Youth Initiative and our reform rhetoric in the simplest of terms:

Fuller's Youth Initiative hasn't meant a hill of beans to my job. #107

But what would a "hill of beans" be? What does it mean to "fundamentally reorient" services for youth? What constitutes "making a difference" or "real" reform? Reform has typically meant "adding on" for liberals or "cutting back" for conservatives (Galper 1975, 2–3). But does simply adding more staff or cutting the "fat" really change the conditions of work for social workers, or improve services for clients? Lipsky (1980), among others, argues persuasively that they don't. As we began the Youth Initiative, I admit I didn't understand what reform really meant.

Our main goal, as we loudly and nobly announced, was:

to stop losing ground in the battle to save a generation of young people. We intend to measurably impact on the multi-faceted problems facing the lives of Milwaukee's young people.

*(Internal Task Force, August 1988)* .

But what did that mean? While line staff remained skeptical, I insisted the

Fuller administration meant business. "I'll bet things will be different in a year," I said to anyone who would listen. A year? Boy, was I naive. I lost every bet I made.

## In Search of a "Hill of Beans"

Soon after I started work I interviewed social workers to try to find out what "a hill of beans" would be. I began by asking staff what they thought the real problems were. Here are a few examples from my field notes of what I learned. One of the first complaints I heard was the lack of training given new child abuse investigators:

> After listening all morning to caseworkers discussing their problems concerning child abuse intake, I just had to take a break. This job is an emotional roller coaster. Most of the time I'm "up," excited about change. Other times I'm so "down" I can't even speak to my wife.

> After listening today to how screwed up the child abuse intake process was, I was down. One of the points made by two workers who dropped by my office was that child abuse workers at times receive no training at all before they are sent out to investigate referrals for child abuse.

> And that wasn't all. A sexual abuse supervisor had explained to me that her ill-trained workers sometimes commit in effect a second sexual assault on the child by the way they conduct their investigation. No mechanisms exist to evaluate staff...or supervisors, for that matter. Sexual abuse workers receive no specialized training before being assigned to cases.

> But it was the lack of initial training that really stuck in my mind. How could anyone send an untrained worker off alone to a home, for example, where it is alleged that a father, brother, or another relative had

sexually assaulted a small child?

I went to lunch trying to get my mind off the lack of training. Coming up to my table at Big Boy's was my waitress and a second waitress followed, obviously being trained. I watched the experienced waitress stand next to the new trainee, both young women no more than 18 or 19. After a few moments I called over the more experienced waitress and asked her how much training the new waitress would be given. "We work nine hour shifts," she said. "After four days my trainee will be allowed to wait on tables by herself." I couldn't finish my lunch.

*Field Notes, July 16, 1988*

The comments of "a second sexual assault" by social workers requires additional explanation. The lack of training and support can make the difficult job of sexual abuse investigations bizarre. Listen to the words of one former social worker on how it affected her:

I knew initially when I started I would have nightmares of sexual abuses occurring, and I didn't know. It wasn't a descriptive abuse. It was sex, it was like I was morbidly sexually abusing this child. But it was like no, how could I. I don't believe in that. And I could just see myself in my nightmares, you know, always being the perpetrator of sexually assaulting a kid. Or whenever I would see an adult male with a child. He could be walking the kid to school, or whatever. I'd wonder what does he do with that kid. Because we've got referrals that a man was taking a child to school. Took the kid to the bathroom in the basement and assaulted the kid. And then we would get the referral. The child would go to school, to the classroom late. The teacher would say where were you? And then the kid would start crying. And then we find out that mom's boyfriend assaulted the kid at school. And then when I would see a man, I would question why is he with this child?

You know, just about everybody at some point became suspect. Especially when we started receiving referrals on priests as perpetra-

tors, judges, police officers, firemen....It's like everybody is guilty
until we prove them innocent. So a lot of times I think within the unit
we have been a support for one another. But the agency itself has not
offered us any type of support in terms of working out what we may be
going through personally as a result of working in sexual abuse. *#309*


My interactions with Child Protective workers were among some of the
more intense experiences of my life. The irrationality of the bureaucracy at
times seemed callous and inhumane. Again, here is a selection from my field
notes:

I went out on a sexual abuse investigation with one worker and it
turned out I knew the woman whose pretty little two-year-old girl had
gonorrhea. I knew the whole family from my gang research: the mother and her mom, the father, and the fellas the father hung with—one of
whom logically was the perpetrator. No one was ever charged.

It was on that case that I watched the worker use expensive "anatom-
ically correct" dolls to try to get two year old Dorothy to tell us what
happened. "Show me where he put it?" Dorothy was tenderly asked.
When it came time to leave, the worker reached out to take the doll
back and the look on Dorothy's face was enough to melt even a hardened observer. Dorothy badly wanted to keep that doll. The home was
sparsely filled with furniture which could best be classified as
Goodwill rejects. Cockroaches crawled alongside the cracked walls.
Dorothy and her two tiny sisters obviously had few toys. To have to
give this doll back hurt Dorothy and her sisters to their hearts.

Why doesn't our department give the workers other dolls to leave with
children? It had never been thought of, and when I brought it up to an
administrator, he said, "Oh yes that's a good idea." He told me later he
had got dolls donated. My last check with workers three months later,
however, showed not only no dolls, but no one ever told the workers

they would be coming. The management is so out of touch with the real work that ideas such as this...small things which are merely humane...never enter their minds.

*Field Notes, October 15, 1988*

I never did get those dolls for sexual abuse intake. They were not important enough for any manager to take the time necessary to get them donated. And then, because I had made such a fuss, they became too political, until even the line staff said they weren't needed. Working child protective intake is filled with stress and the workers didn't need being caught in the middle of a conflict between me and their managers. Consider a final excerpt from my field notes:

> One sexual abuse worker, Betty, came into my office. Her supervisor said Betty was her best worker, but couldn't take the pressure anymore and was transferring. Betty had gathered the opinions of all the workers in her unit of what should be done and was going to relay them to me. She was skeptical of reform, as were most staff. Prior administrations had asked their opinions too, and nothing had ever happened.
>
> What Betty told me was not as important as how she told it. I can still feel the waves of frustration and emotion as she described how hard it was to investigate sexual abuse cases day in and day out. After spending all day on a case which frazzles the emotions, she typically would return to the office only to find that another, perhaps equally disturbing case, had been assigned to her for the next day. She was routinely given a new case nearly every day, no matter what happened to prior cases.
>
> But not all workers get difficult cases. Some intake workers just never seemed to find clients at home and ended up closing the difficult cases as "not substantiated; failure to locate." Some "investigations," I was told, never left the lunchroom. Supervisors are aware of this and don't assign serious cases to slipshod workers, leaving a disproportionate number of difficult cases for responsible workers like Betty.

Finally, after an hour of talking to me, Betty broke down and said that she might have considered staying in sexual abuse intake if only she had "a week off now and then away from opening new cases so I could catch up on my paperwork." No procedures existed for giving workers any type of regularly scheduled break. The result is that most workers in this department transfer quickly, others turn off to doing their job responsibly, and the responsible ones, like Betty, burn out.

Two months later I saw Betty again in her new job. She told me that after she gets herself back under control, she probably will transfer back to sexual abuse intake because "not everyone can do that job." One conclusion I came to was that some of the line workers and supervisors in the Child Protective system were no less than heroines and heroes, doing good despite a bureaucracy that often made their jobs more difficult.

*Field Notes, November 26, 1988*

I learned from my investigation of child protective workers that reforms which would mean a "hill of beans" to Betty would be ones that changed her frustrating daily routine. I had a vague, but not yet understood, uneasiness about her demoralizing day after day experiences, her "core tasks" of investigating the poor, going to court, and doing paperwork. I was determined to improve conditions for workers while providing help, not just investigations, for clients. I was sure new structures needed to be left in place so when "hot shot" reformers like me are gone, things wouldn't automatically go back to business as usual.

## Reforming Social Services

The problems our administration set out to reform are not very different from problems faced by social services in other U.S. cities. There is nearly unanimous agreement from the experts that our system for protecting children and helping poor families is a mess. A major 1989 report on the state of social services, funded by the Annie E. Casey Foundation, surveyed 25 sites around the U.S. It found the situation alarming, calling social service reform "urgent"

(Kamerman and Kahn 1989, 307). They summarized: "...our major conclusion is that available delivery systems, intervention models, and line staffs are not equal to the legitimate and appropriate tasks which lie ahead for the social services" (269).

More broadly, the Midwest American Assembly (1990, 3), a diverse group of conservative and liberal officials stated categorically: "This system must be overhauled." The John D. Rockefeller-led National Commission on Children, concluded ominously:

> if the nation had deliberately designed a system that would frustrate the professionals who staff it, anger the public who finance it and abandon the children who depend on it, it could not have done a better job than the present child welfare system.
>
> *(Markowitz 1992, 29).*

For all the agreement on the need for reform there has been very little action. Problems like those in my field notes seem quite simple to solve, yet the reform story told in these pages will be painful, with even small victories proving difficult to attain. Larger attempts at nationwide reform have died stillborn. "Efforts in the 1970s to create service delivery systems that were more holistic and family oriented were generally not successful" (Kamerman and Kahn 1989, 65; see also Halpern 1991). Indeed, in Kamerman and Kahn's (1989, vi) definitive nationwide survey of social service systems they "found several exemplary components of delivery systems but not any model system."

Reform has been tied into an ideological straight jacket where the only options appear to be liberal solutions to "add on" or conservative cries to "cut back." Is "reform" really only a matter of begging for more money or wielding a mean-spirited budget axe? Lisbeth Schorr (1988) has raised the possibility of a new type of coalition for human services which can get beyond ideological stereotypes . She believes liberals, conservatives, and most Americans can be united around supporting programs that help more than harm people, are proven to be effective, and can strengthen families to carry on their traditional responsibilities. For Schorr, this goal too is "within our reach" (see Greenstein 1991; Specht and Courtney 1994).

But Schorr found one obstacle to developing effective programs is the large, fragmented, and inflexible human service bureaucracy. None of the effective programs impressively detailed in Schorr's book originated as part of a public bureaucracy.

> Many interventions have turned out to be ineffective not because seriously disadvantaged families are beyond help, but because we have tried to attack complex, deeply rooted tangles of troubles with isolated fragments of help, with help rendered grudgingly in one-shot forays, with help designed less to meet the needs of the beneficiaries than to conform to professional or bureaucratic convenience....
>
> *(Schorr 1988, 263–64).*

In other words, we may often know what needs to be done for troubled families, but just as often public bureaucracies interfere rather than help. While new programs, more resources, and responsible budgeting are important, might a key aspect of social reform be changing day to day practices of street level bureaucracies?

## The War on Poverty Revisited

My job was to come up with a plan for social service reform. I was concerned about the very real chance I would lose my bearings in such a difficult undertaking and get bogged down in making small, but insignificant changes.

> I am very worried as we try to fashion this Youth Initiative that we're going to be lost in incrementalism and small victories. The kind of bureaucratic structure that we will leave will be one that will be just as unresponsive to the real needs of people as the one we inherited. I guess my task in the next month is to try to look at the experience of the sixties, look at those programs, look at the literature on

decentralization, and sort out what is the direction that we have to go? What can we seize on that can make a difference in people's lives?

*Field Notes, November 22, 1988*

Aside from asking social workers themselves what was wrong, I read Lipsky's brilliant *Street-Level Bureaucracy*, and books on the war on poverty (e.g., Marris and Rein 1967; Moynihan 1969; Piven and Cloward 1971). I applied Lisbeth Schorr (1988) to issues of program and William Julius Wilson (1987) to the formation of an underclass. I read Clark's *Dark Ghetto* (1965). My studies made me think our tasks were hopelessly large.

But I also began to see our struggle as part of the legacy of the sixties. The war on poverty actually began as criticism of the recalcitrance of urban bureaucracies. Elites in the sixties were concerned that urban institutions were not responding well to the migration of blacks to northern cities.

> But though from the first, this movement of reform was concerned with poverty, it arose less from protest or moral indignation at injustice, than from a sense of breakdown in the institutions which should be diffusing opportunities to all....
>
> *(Marris and Rein 1967, 1)*

The Ford Foundation's "grey area" grants, the precursor to the war on poverty, declared a major effort at bureaucratic reform needed to be undertaken. Community agencies were funded to "encircle" unyielding urban bureaucracies and stimulate change (Piven and Cloward 1971, 262; 269). But a funny thing happened on the way to bureaucratic reform. The large bureaucracies weren't particularly enthusiastic about letting outsiders "participate" and tell them how to run the show. Listen to Marris and Rein tell the story of typical institutional responses to criticism from grey area project staff:

> Institutions would not in practice commit themselves either to the sacrifice of autonomy implied by the project's structure, or to its innovative spirit. The reformers supposed, for instance, that if the school system took part in the planning of changes in curriculum and teaching

practice, it did so out of genuine interest. But its participation seems often to have been merely defensive. To have rejected a grant, and refused its co-operation in a progressive community venture, would have incited a public opinion already critical of school performance. *But it did not at heart believe that short-comings sprang from unimaginative administration and insensitive teaching; it preferred to lay the blame on inadequate resources.* To the school system, the projects were a fund-raising resource, whose independent views on education practice were a tiresome impertinence, directing money into peripheral experiments. *(Emphasis added.)*

*(Marris and Rein 1967, 148)*[3]

Despite hundreds of millions of dollars and the best efforts of a generation of reformers, local bureaucracies today remain stagnant and ineffective. The critique we were making of social services in 1988 was essentially the same as the one made by activists in 1964: local bureaucracies were over-centralized, lacking lateral communication, fragmented, and ineffective.

Some point out the poor have not really won much, despite the huge expenditures of the Great Society. Francis Fox Piven (1973, 181; 200), in a short article, "The Urban Crisis: Who Got What and Why," argues that the real winners of the war on poverty were the heavily unionized street-level bureaucracies who captured most of the new funds. Sadly summarizing the entire period of the sixties, Piven laments, "the lower classes made the trouble and the other groups made the gains." Urban bureaucracies fattened up on programs funded by federal dollars, while successfully avoiding fundamental reform.[4]

Many who had led the charge in the sixties were co-opted into lower level management positions inside the very bureaucracies they had criticized.

If civil rights workers often turned federal dollars to their own purposes in the short run, in the longer run they became model-cities directors, or community action executives—that is they became government employees or contractors subject to the constraints of federal spending and federal guidelines.

*(Piven and Cloward 1971, 274)*

The demand for minority participation in bureaucracies saw perhaps the most progress. Piven and Cloward (1971, 276) concluded: "From the perspective of integrating blacks into the political system, the Great Society was a startling success." But participation does not equal power. The vision of those times has become lost in the struggle of the new minority bureaucrats to manage day-to-day routines.

The militants hired in the sixties had little power within welfare, education, and police bureaucracies to influence change. Marris and Rein (1967, 159–60) summarize that one of the weaknesses of the war on poverty strategy was the lack of committed leaders in positions of institutional power. "Reform must await the opportunity to promote its own supporters to positions of authority." It would be many years before the activists of my generation would be integrated into the existing bureaucracies and wield real power. Hmm. . . That, I believe, is where we came in.


## CONCLUSION: REFORMING STREET-LEVEL BUREAUCRACIES

This book, on its most basic level, is a narrative of our reform efforts in Milwaukee. It also places our story in the context of the history of reform of welfare bureaucracies. It is my attempt to answer the question: what does real reform mean for the social services?

The book is organized into three parts. Part I looks at the nature of today's public social service agencies. Chapter Two lets social workers themselves talk about what they really do. It shows how social service bureaucracies utilized campaigns for child abuse prevention to expand staffing levels. The "core tasks" of social work were consequently defined as child removal and foster care, not supportive services. Chapter Three describes the fragmented structure of Milwaukee County's Department of Social Services and demonstrates how it facilitates legal routines and paperwork, but not services. Chapter Four looks at the way in which the Milwaukee County Department of Social Services has contributed to undermining agencies and institutions within underclass areas and denying them meaningful input into bureaucratic policies which affect them.

Part II places this situation in context. Chapters five and six review the history of reform of social welfare bureaucracies, paying special attention to changes in social services. It shows reform has historically meant little more than adding resources to hungry bureaucracies. Neither clients nor social workers have benefited much by such incremental changes. I look at how public welfare agencies were reformed in similar ways as business organizations until around the middle of this century, when social welfare institutionalized as a set of self-interested bureaucracies. Then, after social services were separated from income maintenance, social work bureaucracies expanded and maintained themselves by accommodating to the anti-poor ideology of the times. Essentially, I look at the history of social welfare reform through the lens of organizational theory.

In Part III I apply the entire analysis to explore the meaning of reform. In Chapter Seven I argue real reform consists of: 1) changing the core tasks of social work from punitive to more supportive routines, and 2) altering the relationship between social service bureaucracies and client neighborhoods. I use our design of the Youth Initiative as a blueprint for structural reforms. Finally, in Chapter Eight, I predict welfare bureaucracies will adapt to the current punitive climate by continuing to emphasize investigation and foster care, not the reforms listed in the previous chapter. Still, I argue against pessimism and defeatism. I believe limited reforms are possible, though difficult, under present conditions. The book concludes with a research methods appendix which advocates combining activism with social science.

Unfortunately, the story you are about to read is not a true "success story." Much of what we accomplished was fragile, opposed by entrenched bureaucratic interests, and has been undone by the time you read this. While this book joins the national debate on the goals of the social services, I am essentially arguing there is an ongoing need for a city by city, bureaucracy by bureaucracy struggle to make social service agencies—and other public bureaucracies—less punitive and more supportive of poor families and the neighborhoods where they live. This was a central, if failed, mission of the War on Poverty. This book aims to challenge you, the reader, to continue that mission and improve on our modest efforts in Milwaukee.

So let's begin. What is it that social workers do, anyway?

# PART I

## THE MILWAUKEE COUNTY DEPARTMENT OF SOCIAL SERVICES

# 2

# THE CORE TASKS OF SOCIAL WORK

## INVESTIGATING CHILD PROTECTIVE SERVICES

It was my second day on the job. How in the world did I get myself into this mess? What did I really know about how a department of health and human services runs? I was hired to design the county executive's Youth Initiative, a "fundamental reorientation" of services for youth. Wonderful. I had seldom worked in a public bureaucracy, much less tried to figure out how to "reorient" one. My last few years were spent helping gang kids get out of trouble and doing research for my book, *People and Folks*. Much of my time was taken up by advocating for the kids in court and fighting with the schools and the welfare system. Me in the bureaucracy? There's no doubt I'd be voted "least likely to succeed."

I was so bad the first strategy paper I wrote brought Howard Fuller's deputies racing into my office telling me that I could never, repeat never, put things like that down on paper again. All I wrote was a memo analyzing who are our friends and who are our enemies...and named them. Howard commented it would take some time for me to get used to working in a bureaucracy.

But I was determined to do the job and I needed to figure out how to start. The county executive, who had won an upset election, wanted a "child-centered strategy" ready for release to the press in four months. Four whole months to figure out what's wrong with the system and how to fix it! What made things worse was Howard Fuller, the director, was also a newcomer to human services. His expertise is in education—he would leave DHHS three years later to become superintendent of the Milwaukee Public Schools. Neither of us, who were supposed to plan the reform, knew the human service system well. There was a great danger that all the hordes of bureaucrats who were surrounding us and so willing to help, might give us a snow job and we'd barely know it.

I was being counted on to be creative, to come up with some good ideas of what this "Youth Initiative" meant. Like other "creative" people, I seldom come up with ideas on my own, but I talk with people, "borrow" what they think, piece together an insight here and there, read a lot, and now and then come up with a winner. So I started to call some of my old friends, yelled "help," and tried to figure out what to do.

I struck gold after a few calls. Susan Hansen, an attorney friend of mine who specializes in child welfare cases, met me after work for dinner. I had expected to talk to her about delinquency problems, the area I knew best from my work with gangs. But Sue had a different idea. Juvenile Probation was a mess, she agreed. But Child Protective Services (CPS) was in even worse shape. She told me that CPS was bound by statute to investigate child abuse referrals within 24 hours but in practice that almost never happened. Days and weeks often passed before a referral was investigated. She also told me workers were burned out and were transferring in droves; there weren't enough minority social workers; there were almost no workers who spoke Spanish or Hmong; social workers had no time or resources to work with families who were not already extremely dysfunctional—and the dysfunctional families didn't get treatment, but got sent to court. She told me horror story after horror story of kids who got hurt because the system didn't work. If we did nothing else, she pleaded, we had to fix Child Protective Services.

The next day a top manager was in my office giving me the company line about how the system isn't perfect, but it works...you know, that kind of rap. I passively listened to him for about an hour and he never once mentioned any of the problems in CPS that Sue and I had spent the last evening discussing. It didn't take a genius to figure out that his not telling me about those problems was a sign there just might be something to hide. So as he was putting on his coat to leave I casually asked him, "Oh, by the way, is it true we're not in compliance with state law mandating 24-hour response to child abuse referrals?"

He reacted like a character in a silent movie. He did a double take with a panic-stricken look which had "What else does he know?" written all over it. He stood there, with one arm in his pinstriped suitcoat, frozen for at least a five count, not saying a thing, just staring. Then, gaining his composure, he slid his arm back out of his coat, hung it back up, and sat back down. He really didn't have to tell me anything after that. I already knew.

I was off on my white horse, investigating what was wrong at CPS.

Like other outsiders, before I took my job with Milwaukee County, I thought social workers helped families. I believed a social worker's job was to do things to help needy families get by. I expected social workers would be busy counseling and performing other unspecified "social services." But I quickly discovered, despite the good intentions of many social workers, their job is no longer primarily "helping" or "service."

While public opinion is occasionally outraged at the failure of a social worker to remove a child from an abusive home, that anger is often misplaced. Social workers today are not scurrying about doing what has been traditionally known as "social work." Performing family-oriented child welfare services today takes a back seat to police-like investigations, long days in court, and mounds of paperwork. Today there are few or no "services" in public "social services." This chapter explains how in the last decade or so, public social workers' day to day routines, their core tasks (Wilson 1989, 25–26) have revolved mainly around punishment: investigating child abuse or neglect, removing children from their families, and supervising court orders.

## Social Work Routines

What is it that social workers do? One child protective worker described a "typical day" to evaluators in detail. She related how in the morning she investigated a child abuse referral from a hospital. She had to decide whether a cocaine-using mother would be allowed to take her child home or whether the worker should take the child into custody and go to court to file a petition alleging abuse. She goes on:

> So that was the morning and there was just a lot of phoning back and forth which is real typical…I also had a court hearing pending that afternoon on a case that I had started four months earlier. I was asking the court to transfer custody and allow the children to remain with their grandmother…And in the afternoon I just made it to court for the one or one-thirty visit…And then I sat out in Children's Court for probably five hours, waiting to get into court which didn't happen until after working my normal working hours to get an order on this thing which I had started four months earlier. Oh, if the court's involved, that's real typical, the long waits, and trying to bring some paperwork with you. But that's real difficult to do….#405

A foster care worker concurs when asked what her job actually entails:

> Paperwork and court work. Court work is very frustrating. You go to Children's Court for a hearing to wait for hours. On one particular day, on one hearing, I had a hearing scheduled at nine o'clock in the morning. I got into court at five o'clock in the afternoon. So I wasted one whole day literally waiting to get into court. And the actual hearing when I got in at five or after five actually, lasted maybe a half hour. And I'm out at Children's Court which is approximately ten miles from here. I would have a difficult time taking my desk with me and…the work I need to do….It isn't quite that bad but I would say on the average if one waited two to three hours it wouldn't be unusual. #304

A social worker whose job is preparing "court studies" of families emphatically states what she would want changed:

> And I feel overwhelmed with all the work…that I was not really doing social work anymore. I'm more like an investigator, and putting

bandaids on everything. You know, if a relative is calling me that a mother is coming over drunk and harassing, I would normally, if I had the time, talk with the mother and try and get her not to do this. Now I'm just telling the ongoing worker that maybe the children shouldn't have visitation at grandmother's house any longer...And I feel kind of disappointed because I'm a social worker. I've been asked to do social work, and I would like to be doing more social work kinds of things. That's what I would like changed. #406

Another social worker points out how court appearances in themselves have become more important than client contact:

one thing I hate the most is having to go to court without having a chance to see the client first. Because the court gives us like a week and I get the case a day ahead, and I don't have time to study up on the client. And they [clients] get upset because they are expecting better service and they don't realize how [little time we have]. #102

The job of social worker has become so tied to the courts and legal proceedings that even the social workers begin to see their role more as carrying out investigations, not providing services. One worker, asked what type of changes she wanted to see, stated emphatically what her job really consists of:

We talk about this often. What we want is something that is very minor. We just want to be able to be given the time to do the job: a professional investigation. #309

Another worker adds that what she needs are not more service options, but more police powers:

And I also think that we're starting to realize that we are somewhat handicapped....It's kind of hard to deal with us not being policemen, it's kind of hard for us to deal with the cocaine, and the abuse of it. #103[1]

Another social worker insightfully comments that many of his colleagues have become used to the court routine and have given up on providing services.

> You know there's not a clear sense in this agency that the workers want to be relieved of the court responsibility...I think one of the reasons management doesn't choose to do that is that there's not a whole lot of support from staff for it. The staff sure don't want to get relieved of all of these court hearings. I think that would be helpful. I think if we got ourselves out of these courts some of these court hearings we'd have more time for clients...And I think sometimes some of our workers you know have given up, burnt out on clients. They just don't feel they can make an impact. #306

The core tasks of public social work have become even more centered on the courts as "services" have increasingly been "farmed out" to private agencies (Axinn and Levin 1982, 287). One worker sums up this widely noted trend:

> County employees are becoming more case managers. We're sending our clients...in foster care or whatever the program, to various system agencies...and then we monitor them. I've noticed that as a major change, not just over the past year but over the last few years. #303

When asked his opinion of this trend to privatization of services he spoke for most Milwaukee social workers about what they believe should stay as a county task:

> I do feel very strongly that the protective service (investigations)... should remain within the county. I think that as necessary because of the legal issues. #303

Public social workers' "job" today, their core tasks , are investigations of allegations of child abuse and supervision of court orders, not the provision of services. In reality, public social work today is a grim world of making decisions on whether to go to court, spending lengthy and often wasted time in court, carrying out court orders, and doing paperwork, often for the courts. There is literally no time left over for most workers to provide any "services." In fact, only one of the 28 workers and supervisors who were interviewed by evaluators described a "typical day" as consisting in any way of working with families, home visits, or anything that might resemble the commonplace notion of "services."

Families who need help are often ignored as social workers are too busy taking abusive or neglectful families to court. Rather than social workers preventing child abuse, they only act after the damage is already done and by then all they can do is remove the children. As I realized that public social work had abandoned prevention, I wrote an illustrated memo to Fuller comparing the Department of Social Services to a Fire Department. I drew a graphic where "DSS firemen" were leaving a house which had just caught on fire. They told the shocked resident, "call us back when it really gets going." Everyone had a good laugh, but it wasn't very funny.

## The Domination of Child Welfare by the Courts

Child welfare experts nationally concur with Milwaukee caseworker impressions. Kamerman and Kahn point out in their influential overview of U.S. social services: "Long time workers find themselves having been transformed from service providers...to investigators and paralegals" (Kamerman and Kahn 1989, 25). Leroy Pelton agrees:

> Indeed, it can be legitimately claimed that our public child welfare agencies, as currently structured, and under the weight of an avalanche of reports, do more investigating than helping.
>
> *(Pelton 1989, 141)*

Eminent therapist Salvador Minuchin (1991) adds that despite good intentions child welfare "has become a servant of the judiciary." Minuchin goes further: he dramatically indicts child welfare bureaucracies for "abuse and neglect of poor families." Investigating child abuse and documenting the case for court gets in the way of true social work with families, he believes, and services are de-emphasized. In an impassioned plea Minuchin demands the reintroduction of "human, social service concerns to our work with poor families... The problems of poor people and their children cannot remain within the realm of crime and punishment" (Minuchin 1991, 7–8).[2]

There are some objective measures which confirm this perspective. A computer-based investigation of "service events," activities of Milwaukee County child welfare social workers entered into the Department of Social Service's computer system, found that at least two thirds of all activities were tied to the courts and not related to any "services" (Pawasarat and Quinn 1990).[3] A follow-up report concluded: "Few social services are provided directly by the Department of Social Services (DSS)...most activity is focused on investigation and documentation of reported child abuse and neglect" (Pawasarat 1991, 2). A survey of Milwaukee County child welfare staff found that 93% felt their main problems were "too much time in court" and 85% cited "too much paperwork" (Hagedorn 1990).

As child abuse and neglect referrals have mounted, social service bureaucracies have become overwhelmed. Child protective services (investigations of allegations of child abuse and neglect) are "driving the child welfare system, often taking it over completely" (Kamerman and Kahn 1990, 9). In Milwaukee child abuse referrals tripled in the 1980s, paralleling a trend in other cities. According to the National Commission on Child Welfare and Family Preservation, nationally, over the past fifteen years, reports of child abuse and neglect have increased by more than 300% (National Commission 1990).

The sheer number of referrals and resulting increase in children placed in foster care have provoked a "national emergency" in social service bureaucracies. Hard pressed social workers have touched public sentiments with stories of impossible caseloads in excess of 100 or more. One typical headline, in the September 12, 1989 *Washington Post,* read: "Sitting on a Time Bomb: Waiting for Kids to Die. D.C. Child Welfare Services Overmatched" (Greene 1989). Social workers in this story and in similar ones from other parts of the country were portrayed as helpless amidst a torrent of referrals called in on drug crazed parents abusing or neglecting their children. A report by the U.S. Advisory Board on Abuse and Neglect drew the only seemingly logical con- clusion: "resources remain insufficient to reduce child abuse and neglect sig- nificantly" (U.S. Advisory Board 1990). That report and others concluded that many more social workers are needed to handle the flood of abuse and neglect referrals.

But wait! Doesn't this story ring a bell? Wasn't a lesson of the war on poverty from Chapter One that urban bureaucracies fattened up on additional resources but then didn't reform? Is the basic problem in social services the lack of resources? What about what we've already learned about what social workers do? Will more resources let them practice social work? Or would it allow them to go more often to court and pull more kids from their families?

Maybe we should take a closer look at the recent history of the child abuse and neglect crisis. Maybe we should look at how public social services have responded, as bureaucracies, to the increased problems facing our nation's children and their families. What impact has additional resources for social ser- vice bureauracies had on poor families?

## CHILD ABUSE AND BUREAUCRATIC EXPANSION

Public spending for social services first began to grow in the 1960s based on the belief that services would reduce dependency and counteract the expan- sion in the number of AFDC recipients. Social service expenditures jumped from $194 million in 1963 to $1.7 billion in 1972, nearly a 800% increase (Gilbert 1977). Welfare bureaucracies largely spent this new found wealth on expanding the number of caseworkers who would be counted on to help "indi- viduals change themselves in order to operate successfully in an apparently well-functioning economy" (Axinn and Levin 1982, 243).

But what social workers actually should "do" was unclear and sharply debated. When AFDC rolls shot up despite increased spending for social services, the role of public social work was thrown into crisis. Liberals assumed social work provided help to the needy and advocated more resources to hire more social workers. Conservatives argued for cuts, fearful that social services would provide incentives for the poor to stay out of the growing secondary labor market and "weaken moral fiber." A left-wing critique emerged that social services are no more than tactics to "cool out" the angry poor and are "functional" to maintain existing inequalities (Galper 1975, 2–3).

The actual tasks of social workers, however, had always been ill defined, varying widely between workers. Historically "social work" consisted of a vague notion of "counseling" along with the placement and supervision of children in foster homes or institutions (Kamerman and Kahn 1989, 41; Pelton 1989). Attacked from the left and right, social work was searching for allies while the Nixon administration was beginning to curtail the War on Poverty, decreasing spending for community-based programs (Moynihan 1969, 131). In 1967, a welfare reform act passed that contained punitive provisions aimed at pushing the "dependent" off welfare (Axinn and Levin 1982, 251). The provisions of the 1967 welfare reform act also separated social services from financial assistance. This provided a basis for welfare bureaucracies to aggressively seek federal and state funds specifically for expansion of their social service components. How could the newly separated social service bureaucracies best capture resources in a budget conscious and more punitive era? Enter the issue of child abuse, stage center.

The "discovery of child abuse" hit the national scene in 1963 with Dr. Harry Kempe's report on "battered child syndrome," the discovery that many children who were seen by physicians as the result of "accidents" were actually physically abused. The "discovery" became a national cause celebre. By the end of 1963, 13 states had enacted mandatory reporting laws and by 1973 every state had a law requiring doctors, social workers, and other professionals to report suspected child abuse (Pelton 1989, 23). This "informer approach," Pelton says, "contributed to the development of what can best be characterized as greatly expanded bureaucracies of investigators" (Pelton 1989, 140-1; cf Pfohl, 1977).

For example, Milwaukee County's Child Protective unit began as a federally funded demonstration project in 1962 with two social workers, a supervisor, and clerk-stenographer. By 1965 it had added six more social workers and a single intake worker (Herre 1965). By 1990, prior to the implementation of our reforms, child protective services had grown to a department of 245 social workers with 48 "intake" positions of social workers whose sole job it was to investigate child abuse. Increased staff was related to increased demand. Milwaukee County referrals for child abuse rose from less than 700 in 1968 to more than 2000 in 1978, more than 7000 in 1988 when our administration took over, and more than 9000 in the early 1990s.[4]

The reasons for the explosive growth in referrals and children placed out of their homes, however, may have as much to do with the dynamics of funding and the nature of the child welfare system, as with an overload of troubled kids. Pelton asserts that

> since the beginning of the twentieth century up until the mid-1970s, whenever child welfare agencies expanded and staff size increased, then the foster care population increased.
>
> *(Pelton 1989, x)*

As campaigns to prevent child abuse became more intense, social service bureaucracies added staff and promoted hot lines and other devices intended to increase reporting. Significant new funding for additional child welfare staff, which took place in the 1970s, was not prompted by skyrocketing referrals, which generally did not occur until the 1980s. Referrals increased only after additional staff were added due to the Nixon social service funding bonanza in the early seventies (Gilbert 1977, 625).

For example, in Milwaukee the number of child protective social workers reached their peak in 1973 with 358 funded positions. In that year only 1286 referrals were called in. It was only after this major expansion of staff, and corresponding pressure for budget cuts in the Carter and Reagan years, that child abuse referrals shot up, busting the 9000 mark in 1991. In other words, if social services could be compared to the laws of supply and demand for services, demand came after supply. Increased referrals did not prompt hiring more social workers, but more social workers were hired and then referrals increased. How can we account for this?

As conditions for poor families have deteriorated over the past few decades, social work administrators have found the child abuse and neglect campaign to be extremely functional as a means to resist demands for budget cuts. Promoting the horrors of child abuse led to increased public awareness, a corresponding increase in the number of referrals, and a convenient rationale to hire more social workers or to maintain existing staffing levels.

Kamerman and Kahn point out about the 1970s:

> In no time at all child welfare was to be dominated by the process of legislating, implementing, and publicizing child abuse reporting laws; large-scale public awareness advertising campaigns using all media; creation of centers for technical assistance, demonstrations, evaluations of demonstrations; widespread efforts and a center devoted to "prevention task forces and study groups.
>
> *(Kamerman and Kahn 1989, 51–52)*

They summarize: "Washington had successfully launched what was in the best and also questionable senses a growth industry."

So what's wrong with that, you might ask? Aren't such increases in social workers good for the poor? But as we've seen in the first part of this chapter, what these social workers mainly do is go to court, not provide services. The rise in federal spending in the early seventies, Derthick (1975, 2) found, was not for services, but appeared to be mainly for caseworker salaries and foster care payments, which support children who have been removed from their parents. By the end of the 1970s nearly three quarters of all child welfare dollars were being spent on foster care supervision and payments (Pelton 1989, 75). Federal regulations prohibit the use of AFDC foster care monies (Title IV-E) for placement prevention or family preservation services, mandating that dollars can only be spent on casework and payments for out-of-home placements (Center for the Study of Social Policy 1988, 4–5). In Milwaukee County a recent report found that 75% of the $59 million dollars spent on child welfare services is spent on out of home placements (Williams 1992). Kamerman and Kahn (1990, 10), in an article summarizing their nationwide research, lament that while foster care placements continued to rise they "failed to find a single state that provides enough family services to meet generally accepted standards of community responsibility."

The foster care population has risen sharply since Title IV of the 1961 Social Security Act provided almost unlimited federal dollars for court ordered placements (Pelton 1989, 9). On the other hand, Title IV-B moneys, for social services, have not increased in over twenty years (cf. Derthick 1975, 76). Thus states have a financial incentive to continue to place children out of their homes and not fund less expensive and less punitive diversion and prevention programs. In fact, Besharov suggests that if foster care dollars could be used for preventing the unnecessary placement of children, the foster care rolls could be reduced by from 30%–50% and taxpayers could save $1 billion per year (Besharov 1986, 29; cf. also Edna McConnell Clark Foundation 1990).

And what happens to children who are "protected" by the child protective system? The Edna McConnell Clark Foundation (1990), reporting on numerous government hearings, finds that most foster care placements bear no resemblance to the ideal short term stay on the way to family reunification. Rather, "the devastating norm for foster children is multiple moves, extended stays, and no stable permanent family ties." Besharov (1986, 11) points out that more than 50% of children are in foster care for longer than two years and more than 30% are separated from their parents for more than six years. African American children (55%) are more likely than white children (36%) to be in foster care for longer than two years and are also more likely to be placed for reasons of neglect, not abuse.

In 1991 a half million children were placed by courts out of their homes. One expert forecasts out-of-home placements may climb by 73% in the next four years—to 850,000—unless major reforms are adopted (Wells and Biegel 1991b). Our research discovered that two thirds of all boys and one third of all girls who first appeared in Milwaukee's child welfare system as abused or neglected later return to Children's Court as delinquents (Pawasarat 1991, 2). Not a very impressive success rate, by any standards. It's hard to argue that "child protective services" "protect" many children or offer many "services."

## GAIN BY PUNISHING THE POOR

In the more conservative post-sixties era, most federal social service dollars were actually going to create an expensive, punitively-inclined child protection apparatus which was to take over Departments of Social Services. Investigation of poor families and removal of children into foster care have crystallized as the core tasks of social work, those tasks which define what line workers do on a day-to-day basis. Even the traditional discretion given social workers has been altered from discretionary services to the discretion of whether to take a family to court or whether to do nothing.[5] As Pelton sadly points out:

> An increase in the number of caseworkers would not necessarily have led to more removals were it not for the fact that foster care was the primary resource that child welfare agencies possessed.
>
> *(Pelton 1989, 25)*

Doug Nelson (1988), in a balanced treatment of the social service system, summarizes three factors which have led to the current crisis. First states broadened the definitions of child abuse, increasing public sensitivity and therefore increasing reporting. Second, increased poverty has naturally produced an increase in the number of clients. He admits:

> the nation has been producing growing numbers of families—who by virtue of poverty, discrimination, family structure and other factors—are at increased risk of being unequipped to meet their parental obligations.

Third, Nelson concludes that while social problems have increased, social service bureaucracies grew or sustained themselves by adapting to the ideology of child protection, which in effect meant investigating child abuse and placing kids out of their homes. While in the past, social workers may have had a more variable relationship to poor families, often exercising discretion and finding time to provide services, the present structure of social service bureau-cracies almost completely prohibits such a "service" orientation (cf. also Nelson 1991).

The expansion of "social services" in the 1970s had little correlation to improved services for children and their families. Rather the chief beneficiaries of increased social service spending have been urban social service bureaucra-cies, who have used the funds to adapt to a punitive climate, expanding their capacity to investigate poor families and remove children from their homes.

This situation has been controversial within the social work profession (Wald 1988). Social work has long been conceptualized as a battle ground between those who advocate removing the children of the poor to "save" them and others who focus more on strengthening poor families, rebuilding the neighborhoods where they live, and expanding opportunities (Platt 1969). This historic contradiction is in some ways being played out today by advo-cates of "family preservation" versus those who support the traditional roles of child protection and foster care (Nelson 1988; Wells and Biegel 1991b; also cf. Katz 1989).

The tendency within social work toward investigations and child removal has been strengthened by changes over the past few decades in the structure of social service bureaucracies. Departments of social services have restructured in such a manner to facilitate investigative and child placement functions. Indeed, unless reform concentrates its local efforts on the structure of work in the social services, gains are doomed to be short-lived and any new resources will be diverted into more punitive practices. Let's continue our exploration of the core tasks of social work by looking at the bureaucratic structure of public social services.

# 3

# THE FRAGMENTED
# STRUCTURE OF SOCIAL WORK

## SHEDDING SOME LIGHT ON A FAMILY'S PROBLEMS

As part of the Youth Initiative we tried to subdue the long standing hostility between the Department of Social Services (DSS) and the Milwaukee Public Schools (MPS). We began a collaborative venture, targeting six schools where our two bureaucracies would work together to solve problems of troubled families. Getting the two bureaucracies to cooperate proved to be next to impossible—but that's another story. Late one night in 1989 I received a call from a Milwaukee alderwoman, who told me of a family who lived next door to her who was having serious problems. She had gotten a run-around from both DSS and MPS. She had heard of our collaboration. Could I get their school and DSS to work together to help this one family?

I called a meeting of the family's DSS social worker and the school's social worker and other MPS support staff. I asked that the family also be present to help all parties get a handle on the situation and figure out what needed to be done. The meeting began as each of the professionals listed the problems as they saw them: the DSS social worker saw the problem as the teenager being involved with a gang, having occasional run-ins with the police, and seeming to be generally out of control; the school social worker complained even the youngest child, age 7, did not regularly attend school; the school nurse chimed in that when the kids did attend school, they were often not clean. She once had to send the seven year old home, she was so dirty, the nurse complained, shaking her head for effect.

Through this whole scene the mother and two of her youngest children sat patiently at the very end of the table. Her English wasn't all that good, but she listened carefully to what each of the professionals were saying about her family. I figured she should have her shot at defining the problem so I asked her what she thought the main issue was. She barely hesitated before she answered "I don't have any electricity in my house." As this settled in, the quiet was broken by the DSS social worker, who piped in "that's right, you told me about it the last time I came by." I sat there a bit stunned at the realization that our social worker knew the family was without electricity, but had done nothing. The MPS social worker reported that he knew the family hadn't had lights for about six weeks!

"But that doesn't explain why the kids are dirty," the school nurse snapped, anticipating my reaction. "But the bathroom is on the second floor," Mrs. Hernandez quickly responded, not waiting for a translation. "There is no window, and the kids are afraid to go up there."

At that point I interrupted and said I thought we had a place to start. It was simple, someone should call the electric company and get the lights turned on. There was an embarrassed silence. No one offered to make the call. Our social worker finally looked at me and said, "Do you want me to get the lights turned on?" His job, he explained, was supervising a court order with the teenager, not dealing with electricity. The school social worker said he only dealt with truancy and the school nurse said her province was the student's health.

Turning to our social worker and using my non-existent, but perceived authority, I said calmly, "Read my lips. Get the lights turned on."

This story, reconstructed from my field notes, isn't a bad place to start to discuss the structure of social work today. While this family's problems went far beyond electricity, the point is it wasn't anyone's job to look at the family's problems as a whole. It's easy to blame these social workers for being uncaring...in this case they were. But the fundamental problem is much more complex and leads us away from bashing social workers. This chapter focuses on the relation of the structure of social service bureaucracies to what social workers do everyday.

We saw in the last chapter how social welfare separated into financial assistance and social service components. Social service bureaucracies since have themselves specialized. Their compartmentalized structure organizes social workers to investigate child abuse and place children in foster care as their core tasks. What the present structure of social service bureaucracies does not do very well is organize social workers to protect children and preserve their families.

But I didn't know this when we first embarked on our path toward reform. All I knew as we began the Youth Initiative was that the present system didn't work well and I had a hunch we should try some "pilot" programs. I read, but did not yet understand what Kahn and Kamerman (1989, 2-3) meant when they said "the typical situation in the field of social services has been, for some time, extreme and irrational categorical fragmentation."

## THE CHILD PROTECTIVE LABYRINTH

I spent the first several months investigating the child protective system and I was bewildered by what I found. Routines of child abuse investigation, court appearances, and monitoring court orders had become an end in themselves. While most social workers want to "do the right thing," all too often their job prohibits them from doing it. Here's how Milwaukee County's child protective system "worked."

A child abuse complaint or "referral," is taken by a unit of "phone workers," and after a stop at another set of workers for "clearing," or checking the computers to see if there is a prior abuse or neglect case, it is assigned to a specialized "intake worker." This social worker conducts only the investigation and concludes whether a complaint can be "substantiated" or not. Then his or her job ends:

> …as an intake worker, I'm through with it. Because all I do is investigate to see if service is needed or not needed. #407

The intake worker either closes the case or after a court appearance transfers the case to an on-going worker. The transfer takes time and paperwork and
any rapport the intake worker had developed with the family has to be regained
by the new worker. The ongoing worker has to take a second abuse or neglect
"narrative," the child and parent(s) telling their story all over again. If the case
goes to court, there is a court study worker, who represents the department
before a judge. This worker only sees the family right before court. The client
may have to go through the entire abuse tale a third time.

If a foster home placement is called for, a foster care licensing worker may
have to come to the foster home to decide if the home is "suitable" with the
licensing worker often asking the client to repeat a social history yet another
time. When the court places the child in a foster home, a foster care worker is
then assigned who theoretically takes the child's social history again. If an
adoption is possible, transfer to a separate adoptions unit is required. If the
child needs a medical card, another specialized worker takes over, from a separate "support" unit. Compounding matters, child protective social workers
typically have little communication with financial assistance workers, who often
have more contact with AFDC families than anyone else in the system. Of
course if delinquency is involved, probation is another distinct department
with separate probation officers.

The "case," that is, a parent or child, is passed between departments,
within the social service bureaucracy, each concerned with their specific
focus, with no one having the overall responsibility of assessing the needs of
the entire family. Each transfer between departments, of course, entails more
paperwork. And while the paperwork is being done, the client is often kept in
limbo, waiting on the next worker to take his or her turn. One worker explains
the process vividly:

> I don't know what a normal day would be. However, I could say with-
> out any emergency, it would be paperwork. It would be trying to get
> the files in order, and all the paperwork up to date, and all the neces-
> sary processes that you need in order to satisfy that case. And then, if
> you can, when you reached the end of it, you either close the case or
> transfer it to another department, like foster care, ongoing, something

of that sort. And then they would follow through.

But there's a whole process that you'd have to complete in order for the case to meet the requirements to be transferred. Everything has to be in a certain order, all the forms have to be in there in a certain order, in different section dividers. If they're not there it is possible for them to turn it down. And sometimes it takes time to get some of the forms, like disposition or orders from the district attorney, turnarounds from the person that does attend (the court hearing). If you don't have those forms to go into the file, you can't move the file.

The file sets there then something else happens in the case before you transfer it, then you've got to satisfy that before it moves. Understand what I'm saying? But the case is setting there gyrating, something is going on. (You) try to get it out of there. Before you do something happens and you got to hang onto it until you resolve it a lot of times. #103

I have a personal example. One day in October 1990, my thirteen year old daughter Tracey brought home a teenager. Typical of many troubled teens, Tracey's friend Daisy checked out our family and decided she'd like to stay, telling us we could get $324 per month foster care payment for her upkeep. Since the Department of Social Services finds teenagers nearly "impossible to place," teens in trouble or on the run often find a family for themselves and then get the family to apply to be foster parents. From October to December of 1990, Daisy had five different social workers from DSS, the first four of whom insisted she repeat to them her rather touchy story of abuse until I yelled "enough" the fourth time through. None of the social workers, as far as I can tell, ever saw her more than once. Finally, a fifth worker called me to tell me he would be Daisy's regular foster care worker, told me he had a huge caseload, and gave me his phone number. After a short silence after which he was about to hang up, I hastily interjected "She's doing fine." He said "Huh?" I repeated Daisy was doing well and was back to school. He said "Oh yes, I'm glad to hear it." End of contact with the overloaded foster care worker until Daisy returned to her family a year later. It is typical for DSS foster care workers to have no contact with most of their clients except when appearing in court.

This bureaucratic maze has little to do with service for clients, who are often unsure just who their social worker is at any given time. A public social worker's job is not to assess the overall needs of the family, but to perform a specific task related to the courts: investigating abuse, supervising a court order, licensing a foster home to place a child, and so forth. Lipsky (1980, 77–78) summarizes: "Divisions between intake and casework mean that interviews and fact gathering sometimes have to be repeated, which is inefficient." Rather than a more "holistic" approach, more difficult cases are often simply transferred so they become someone else's problem.

Even the legal requirement to report to the court on whether "reasonable efforts" are being made to reunify a child and his or her family (the "permanency plan") has added to the bureaucratic mess. Kamerman and Kahn conclude that PL96-272 which mandated "reasonable efforts" to reunify a child with his family must be documented, added a bureaucratic layer to an already fragmented system:

> There are in many places two staffs or two groups within one staff creating paper trails which are self-protective: documenting case investigations and recommendations, on the one side, and recording the activity of elaborate family reunification or permanency planning machinery, on the other. This is often an anxiety-dominated arena which generates rapid staff turnover, uncovered caseloads—and , then, more pressure for reports and administrative controls to avoid serious lapse and error.
>
> *(Kamerman and Kahn 1989, 56–57)*

Lizbeth Schorr (1988, 260) summarized the situation by pointing out that social service bureaucracies strive "for efficiency by deploying personnel to focus on sharply defined single problems…bureaucracies fragment services into absurd slivers."

# How Did Social Service Bureaucracies Become Fragmented?

How did public social services get to this sorry state? This is the central issue discussed in chapters five and six. But generally speaking, as organizations deal with an ever more complex environment they tend to become segmented to deal with specific environmental problems (Lawrence and Lorsch 1969, 8; 213). Wilensky and Lebeaux (1965, 58; 230) explain this process for social welfare. In a mechanistic version of Weber, they state: "To say bureaucracy is to say specialization" (235). Applying Weber's criteria of a bureaucracy to social welfare, Wilensky & Lebeaux claim that a drive for efficiency underlies the inevitable trend toward specialization (235-40).

Specialization in social welfare also has its disadvantages, Wilensky and Lebeaux admit. There are gaps in services, dividing the client between specialists, segregatng and stigmatizing the client, and duplicating services, among others (250-57). While these negative tendencies need to be combated, the "functional specificity" (299-300) of social work is inevitable: "Specialization itself, a prerequisite to professionalism, is the result of the underlying industrialization process." (285). In the final analysis, for Wilensky and Lebeaux, specialization is functional for the efficient operation of a modern welfare bureaucracy.

Rosenthal (1989, 298) captures this notion by comparing welfare bureaucracies to factory assembly lines, "high volume standardized processing that flows through a preset sequence of steps." Each worker on the line has a specific function and handles it with technical expertise with no occupational concern for the end product. Rosenthal was writing about financial assistance departments. But "high volume processing that flows through a preset sequence of steps" could equally refer to the present day specialized handling of child abuse and neglect referrals.

This extreme specialization, Robert Halpern (1991, 355) believes, is specifically a legacy of the "limited and ambiguous framework for social welfare" set by the New Deal and the "network of marginal programs" sponsored by the War on Poverty. He goes on to say that "each wave of service reform... had to contend with a more complex, inflexible, and fragmented human service system" (360). Indeed, Halpern concludes the present crisis of social services is the result of three constraining factors: American's ambivalence about the "causes, meaning, and most appropriate response" to poverty, an over-reliance on services, and an "ever-greater specialization, centralization, and bureaucracy within the human services themselves" (343–44).

This drive for specialization was given a major push with the 1967 separation of financial assistance and social services. That policy was intended to eliminate the discretion of welfare caseworkers to punish poor families for their child rearing practices by reducing their AFDC payments. It did this by setting up a separate social service bureaucracy which was, in Kamerman and Kahn's (1989, 49) words, "a legislative solution which was, again, narrowly categorical and unintegrated with the mainstream child welfare system."

The major rationale for the separation of social services from financial assistance was to give a client the "right to choose service voluntarily, when needed, without fear of losing a grant" (Axinn and Levin 1982, 252). In the atmosphere of the 1960s, legal safeguards and "due process" were promoted as a way to end the often racist practice of welfare workers insisting clients receive "services" as a condition of receiving financial assistance. Axinn and Levin point out that the Supreme Court's Gault decision and the separation of social services marked both "the end of the service approach to public assistance" and a "new concern for the rights of the poor."

But the separation had other consequences. While the threat of reducing the AFDC grant has been taken from the financial assistance caseworker, that threat was not eliminated, but rather transferred to the child protective worker. By placing a child away from his or her mom and with, say, grandma, the child protective worker now controls the amount of an AFDC grant, which would be automatically reduced if a child is removed from the home. Thus child protective workers, aside from being a threat to take children away from their parents, represent a financial threat to poor families. Discretion has been moved from a welfare worker who looked at the problems of the family basically from a financial perspective, to the child protective worker who is more narrowly concerned with violations of child abuse statutes (cf. Lipsky 1980, 197).

Besharov insightfully comments on this changed perspective:

The welfare caseworker [before the separation—JMH] saw the family as the client, and was inclined to view the poor child rearing as a correlate of poverty, requiring aid to the family as a unit. The child protective worker [after the separation—JMH], on the other hand, rightly sees the child as the client, with poor child rearing as a reason for coercive state intervention. And most significantly, the two caseworkers had an entirely different orientation to foster care and court ordered removal. Welfare caseworkers were rarely in court; they were not trained—nor deployed—toward easy access to court and court related removal of children from the home. Child protective workers are. In the context of heightened concern for the "abused" child, child protective agencies' responsibility for these poverty related cases and social deprivation inexorably led to more poor children being placed in foster care. In addition, federal funding for foster care, rather than for in-home services, created an added incentive to resort to foster care.

*(Besharov 1986, 18-19)*

Child protective workers became preoccupied with the courts to the neglect of broader client concerns. One expert points out:

few public workers inform welfare clients about the availability of services, diagnose problems during regular visits, refer those with particular needs to more specialized service workers or to emergency financial units, act as case managers, or advocate for clients.

*(Sosin 1990, 620)*

"Reforms" of social services since 1967 have basically entailed adding specialized layers to social welfare bureaucracies with few identified benefits for clients. Kamerman and Kahn (1989, 41-44) point out that the 1974 reform of the Social Security Act, which had a chance to develop a comprehensive service delivery system, left child welfare to stand on its own, fighting for resources, and far from "holistic."

Social service bureaucracies have built specialized hierarchical organizations which have had little freedom to dynamically respond to the complex, individualized, and ever changing needs of their mainly poor clients. Smaller neighborhood based programs or units, as organizational theory suggests (Lawrence and Lorsch 1969), would be structurally better suited to service families' complex needs. In the 1920s and again in the 1960s, such neighborhood-based services were a viable alternative to centralized bureaucracies (Halpern 1991).

But arguments for neighborhood-based, family-focused reforms did not prevail in the 1970s. The campaign against child abuse and neglect provided a better strategy for the expansion of public social service bureaucracies. Here was an area where the new social service departments could mark their turf and expand with little resistance. The core tasks of social work were redefined as "child protection." As Meyer and Rowan (1981, 311) point out, "Affixing the right labels to activities can change them into valuable services and mobilize the commitments of internal participants and external constituencies." Repackaging social services as "child protection" and "foster care" brought a massive influx of federal funds allowing for organizational expansion and public support.

Further, public social services could maintain a hierarchical organization, streamlined to fit the needs of the various legal bureaucracies with which it would be partners (Patti 1975). As studies of corporations have shown, a fragmented organization suited managers by facilitating bureaucratic control and keeping workers both divided and loyal.[1] Massive child protection bureaucracies also suited public service unions, whose interests lay in increasing or at least maintaining its civil service, dues-paying membership (Meyer and Zucker 1989). Here were expansion, employment for more professionals, legitimation, labor peace, and compelling arguments against budget cuts all rolled into one. Never mind that the social work tradition which stressed families and neighborhoods would have to be de-emphasized. That would be a small price to pay for maintaining jobs within the bureaucracy.

It is not correct to say that the true goals of social work were displaced by investigation of child abuse and removal of children. Contradictory goals are an inherent characteristic of social welfare. Both family preservation and child removal tendencies have long coexisted in every social service department.

Rather, in the more conservative post-sixties era, the best grounds for bureaucratic maintenance and expansion were found in embracing a more punitive rhetoric and practice. When this punitive agenda was combined with the needs of powerful public worker constituencies to survive in a more cost-conscious era, the die was cast.


## The Structure of Work

The myth that social services provide "services" is still useful to state legislatures who must provide funds, to a concerned public, and for internal morale. But, as we've seen in the last chapter, social service bureaucracies have recently been justifying their existence on the need to investigate "ever mounting" problems of child abuse and neglect and to protect children by "getting them away from their cocaine-using parents." Dangerously, social services today have sought legitimation from the public by stressing their punitive functions, often wrapping them in the garb of the "best interests" of the children.

While ideological differences are key, it is the structure of work, as Lipsky (1980) points out, that is a major barrier to solving the problem. The central thesis of Lipsky's brilliant *Street-Level Bureaucracy* is that reform of social services, and other public bureaucracies, must alter the structure of work faced by line staff, by its "street-level bureaucrats." The "dilemmas of the individual in public services" are dilemmas within the conditions of his or her work and the patterns of his or her practice: "the very nature of this work prevents them from coming even close to the ideal conception of their jobs" (xii).

Modern business theory stresses the same issue. When asked what they believe is the most important role in operating an ocean liner, corporate managers often tell MIT's Peter Senge the key role is the captain, the navigator, or some such position. The question is a "set-up." Senge quickly counters:

No one has a more sweeping influence than the designer. What good does it do for the captain to say, 'Turn starboard 30 degrees,' when the designer has built a rudder that will only turn to port, or which takes six hours to turn to starboard?

*(Senge 1990, 10)*

Nelson makes the same point specifically about social services.

Perhaps the most readily apparent illustration of the barriers to change
is in the existing job structures of most front-line family service and
child welfare workers. It is clear, for example, that the customary size
of worker caseloads, combined with their office-bound work routine,
preclude any real opportunities for the in-home locus and flexible
intensity of contact that appear indispensable to family preservation's
effectiveness. Realigning caseloads and job structures are thus obvious
prerequisites for any wider application of these practices. This, it
should be emphasized, is not a simple task...

*(Nelson 1988, 32–33)*

The problem is made clearer when we see how decisions are actually made
in organizations. Cohen, March, and Olsen (1972, 2) provocatively conceptualize organizations not as "problem-solvers" but as "garbage cans" of solutions.
Rather than looking for new ways to solve problems, organizations rely on a set
of stock solutions that are "looking for issues to which they might be the
answer." In other words, if social service bureaucracies are structured to provide mainly investigation and child removal as a solution, problems will
inevitably be defined in such a manner that investigation and removal are the
preferred response. To use Cohen et al.'s (1976, 26) words, investigation and
child removal are "an answer actively looking for a question." The question is
"what do social workers actually do?"

## BLAMING THE WORKERS

Some, particularly conservative theorists and managers, see the crux of the
problem not as how work is organized, but rather social workers themselves.
One critic, for example, chants a litany of complaints about civil service work-

ers: "the result is a system in which managers cannot manage, deadwood is kept on." If a "rational personnel system was set up, costs could be 20% lower (Osborne and Gaebler 1992, 127–78). Similarly, Chubb and Moe (1990, 154) attack the seniority system in education, saying "unions are large obstacles" to creating effective schools.

Whether to blame the workers or not is often simply a matter of perspective. Managers tend to see the problem as lack of worker productivity while workers themselves want to improve salaries and working conditions (cf. Lipsky 1980, 18). Interviews with DSS management as part of the Youth Initiative evaluation found widespread agreement that line workers were the greatest obstacle to reform (Devitt 1992). I could fill an entire book with "bad worker" stories from personal experience and from the lips of managers and line staff themselves.

Civil service has created lifetime jobs for many workers who have become "deadwood," ill-suited for the demanding, complex tasks of social work. Social work, most agree, is stressful. One worker complains:

> I think there's a burn-out factor. (Child protective jobs) are very stressful, frustrating kind of work. There's an awful lot of very difficult family situations.... And it leads to a lot of frustration, a lot of court work, a lot of situations that you really can't do anything about because of legal, and other related factors. #307

Another worker adds:

> There's very little gratification you can get from this job. The only gratification that you do get sometimes is from maybe your co-workers. #103

This situation is partially the result of the fragmented structure of social service departments. This fragmentation has created eagerly sought after islands of relief from the stresses of day-to-day contact with troubled families. As older, typically white social workers advance in seniority in the civil service, they bid for better and better jobs within the bureaucracy. High seniority workers, in Milwaukee almost all white, transfer to the nooks and crannies of the bureaucracy, to specialty positions like "purchase liaison," which entail little client contact and less stress. One high seniority worker who transferred to a specialty position puts it bluntly:

> This is the gravy train you know… People don't quit, people don't give up. This is the best paying social work job there is and yes, it is hard, yes it is demanding, yes it is depressing a lot of the times—not just some of the time, most of them—but we're paid well. What it is is the best paying social work job there is, or one of the best. #305

In Milwaukee in the late 1980s frustrated high seniority child protective workers bid into juvenile probation. One former foster care worker was asked what has changed the most in last few years.

> **A:** Two things happened, a few years back. One, the caseloads started to climb and the pressures were becoming much greater. Two, they let us transfer over to probation at the Children's Court Center which we couldn't do before.

> **Q:** Without losing seniority or anything?

> **A:** Right. All we had to do was put in the transfer and you could go. We got accepted. So a lot of people left here because the caseload out at Children's Court isn't nearly as demanding….The pressure isn't at all the same. And everybody that's gone over there seems to look healthier. Smile more….

> **Q:** What is the reason you transferred from foster care?

> **A:** Besides the fact that this is the job I wanted for ten years at least, and didn't have enough seniority to get it before. I was dying at foster care….It was just too much work. Too many needs to be met. And too many people pulling out of there. You can't adequately service that many

people and still do paperwork, and meet the court demands....#408

It's no wonder that a child protective staff survey, conducted for the Youth Initiative evaluation, found sharp differences in job satisfaction between workers with high and low seniority. A child protective staff survey summarized that

> among workers with more than eleven years seniority, there is a strong sense of job satisfaction and an overall belief present policy is effective. Workers with less than five years seniority are both less satisfied with their jobs, tend to not think their services are effective, believe stress levels are tolerable, and are evenly divided whether caseloads are too high.
>
> *(Hagedorn 1990)*

Thus the higher stress, client contact positions are filled by mainly newer staff, often transfers from other county agencies. Milwaukee County civil service procedures allow a worker to go one day from handling baggage at the airport or feeding animals at the zoo to the next day investigating sexual abuse complaints. Many of these new transfer employees wait their mandatory six months and then bid to a "better" job within social services. Thus the crucial jobs of client contact are held by a mix of highly committed, but frustrated staff, and staff who are "stuck" in those positions until they can bid out.

The extreme alienation of social workers to routines of court and paperwork has been generally met by management granting higher pay and benefit levels, and developing even more specialized job titles. Lipsky points out:

> Public service workers have increased their share of national wealth through higher pay and benefit levels, increased their collective bargaining power, and acquiesced in and often encouraged developments such as specialization, computerization, and fragmentation of responsibilities for clients. Street-level bureaucrats have enhanced their position in the political system to the neglect of aspects of service consistent with more humanistic models of client involvement, or at the expense of taking positions on clients' behalf.
>
> *(Lipsky 1980, 80)*

Lipsky instead makes an argument for structural reform which would benefit workers and clients alike (192–211). He argues there is a congruence between how social services are organized and the content of what social workers do. Change the structure and you begin to reshape the "solutions" to which problems are addressed and defined. If social workers have a supportive, service-centered structure of work, many of them can become less alienated and more helpful to poor families.

Structural reform, though seen by Lipsky and others as quite fundamental and radical, is not seen as all that important by other key stakeholders. I wrote in my field notes:

> The issues that are really important, the structure of work, are not that important to the county board. They do want change, except that they favor more punishment of the "undeserving poor." They will not see changing the structure of work, at least at first, as significant.
>
> *Field Notes, November 30, 1990*

This dirty work of restructuring bureaucracies is usually seen as a management prerogative and may not draw immediate fire from critics. But neither does it gain automatic support from human service sympathizers. Lipsky points out in an article on social welfare "disentitlements" that the "diffuse social welfare constituency is generally inattentive to program developments that fall below the waterline of high-level policy" (Lipsky 1984, 21). Senge points out that the

> functions of design, or what some have called 'social architecture,' are rarely visible; they take place behind the scene. The consequences that appear today are the result of work done long in the past and work today will show its benefits far in the future.
>
> *(Senge 1990, 10)*

Leadership, Kanter (1983, 61) points out, "consists increasingly of the design of settings which provide tools and stimulate constructive, productive individual actions." All this adds up to an opportunity for those who hold bureaucratic power to "fundamentally reorient" how services are delivered. Our reforms sought to alter core tasks by changing the structure of work.

## CONCLUSION: MAKING A PLAN

While the Youth Initiative was far from an experiment with a worked out theoretical perspective, we did make a plan. We mobilized a "Youth Initiative Committee" of prominent citizens and started them off with a bang: we had them read William Julius Wilson and Lizbeth Schorr. It may have been the first local citizens task force to begin its mission by reading theory, but we wanted to ground the task force in a new orientation.[2] Wilson's contribution will be fleshed out in the next chapter. We borrowed from Schorr the notion of what kind of human service programs work for families. We used this passage from Schorr's book as a theme:

> In short, the programs that succeed in helping the children and families in the shadows are intensive, comprehensive, and flexible. They also share an extra dimension, more difficult to capture. Their climate is created by skilled, committed professionals who establish respectful and trusting relationships and respond to the individual needs of those they serve. The nature of their services, the terms on which they are offered, the relationships with families, the essence of the programs themselves—all take their shape from the needs of those they serve rather than from the precepts, demands and boundaries set by professionalism and bureaucracies.
>
> *(Schorr 1988, 259)*

When Schorr met with our Youth Initiative Committee she pointed out that none of the programs she highlighted began in a large bureaucracy. She told us that in all her travels, she had not heard of as far-reaching a plan as what Milwaukee had in mind. In retrospect, I'm not sure that was a compliment.

Indeed, some analysts question whether large social service bureaucracies are even capable of meeting Schorr's criteria (Halpern 1990, 645; Schorr 1988, 79).

Undaunted, we plowed ahead. Our 1988 reform plan included both reform of the structure of social services along with a variety of reforms aimed at changing the relationship of our bureaucracy to residents in two targeted zip codes. The establishment of pilot units, neighborhood councils, and redirection of funding to Milwaukee's poorest neighborhoods was probably the most important lasting accomplishment of the Youth Initiative (Devitt 1992, 17–28). Let's turn now to examine the relationship of social welfare bureaucracies to poor neighborhoods.

# 4

# UNDERMINING
# POOR NEIGHBORHOODS

## THE COLORED MAPS

The setting was the University Club, picturesquely perched atop a bluff between Milwaukee's downtown and its fashionable east side. Gathered in one of its ornate meeting rooms on a winter day in 1988 were several dozen captains of Milwaukee's industry, financial barons, university presidents, and other upper class notables. Sitting demurely next to Milwaukee's Rockefellers and Fords was...me! What in the world was I doing in such obviously out-of-my-league surroundings? I was there to give Milwaukee's bourgeoisie a slide show on the Youth Initiative.

Now you have to appreciate the irony. Both Howard Fuller and I had graduated from the revolutionary movements of the sixties where we had considered my present company as our bitter "class enemy." I have to admit I have never given up my deep-seated hostility to those who have everything while so many others suffer. Staring into the eyes of Milwaukee's upper crust that day, listening in to their relaxed, but busy chatter, they seemed to me quite unlike the capitalist demons I had hated. They actually seemed quite ordinary—some were more energetic, others more bright, still others, I figured, wealthy only because of inheritance. But they did share one exceptional quality. All of them were obviously very comfortable with power. It was really nothing they said. It was more of an air about them, a quiet confidence they could "get things done."

I had been invited by the Greater Milwaukee Committee (GMC), the organization of Milwaukee's business leaders, to present our plans for social service reform. Fuller expected a favorable hearing, but didn't attend. Such affairs with the power elite were already "old hat" for him. I listened nervously as the opening discussion focused on the Milwaukee Public Schools (MPS). The business executives firmly placed themselves on the side of Bob Peterkin, then MPS Superintendent. They blasted the educational bureaucracy that got in the way of Peterkin's reforms. The key issue for reform, one CEO stated as if it were indisputable fact, is bold and decisive leadership. Unless there's change, he insisted, the schools would not produce a better quality of worker, and Milwaukee's business would suffer.

I was second on the agenda. The lights were dimmed after I was introduced. We had developed a series of maps of Milwaukee's zip codes and made them into color slides. What the maps displayed were the geographical distribution of Milwaukee County welfare cases, delinquency reports, child abuse referrals, and other "risk indicators." The overwhelming majority of all of these social problems, the maps showed, were from only six of Milwaukee's 34 zip codes.

Our reform plan centered on two zip codes: 53206, a very poor but stable African American area, and 53204, a polyglot of neighborhoods containing Hispanic, Native American, white, and Asian residents. The two zip codes, which contain only 8% of Milwaukee's population, accounted for more than 25% of all Milwaukee County AFDC and General Assistance cases, child abuse referrals, juvenile corrections placements, and teen births. These two areas, we were arguing, should be targeted for innovative programs, the organization of neighborhood councils to improve bureaucratic accountability, and investment of new resources.

The response to my presentation was luke warm, but supportive. One of the few African American GMC members pooh-poohed the maps, self-consciously saying, "You knew this before you started didn't you?" Others predicted union troubles if we moved to decentralize. All expressed confidence in Howard Fuller's leadership. Then the chairwoman asked me the $64 million dollar question: "Why don't we just write off those two zip codes and concentrate on fringe, more integrated areas where things aren't so bad? Doesn't it make sense to only tackle problems where you have a fighting chance at success and not throw good money after bad?" The room was quiet. I saw a few barely perceptible nods of agreement.

I wish I could report I responded with a brisk one liner or scored with a stunning repartee. Instead, the chair's question left me speechless as scenes from *Escape from New York* flashed across my mind. That was the movie where all of Manhattan is walled off to incarcerate a future New York City's criminals and deviants. Maybe, I thought, the GMC would like to build a Great Wall around Milwaukee's central city and forget about all the people who live there?

Write off the underclass? As I stood there it occurred to me that the policy of writing off the "undeserving poor" was probably an assumption for most of the GMC, resting comfortably in their leather chairs. If the underclass can't easily be trained to be our future workers, why waste money on them? If underclass males are going to be criminals, and underclass females welfare mothers, why reorganize social services to help? Why not just punish them or force them to work? "Getting things done" just did not include helping the underclass share in the American Dream. The business executives gathered there that day supported our reforms because they liked my boss, Howard Fuller. Most of them didn't really give two hoots about the people a welfare bureaucracy serves.

All this ran in a disorganized way through my head, and I couldn't form a coherent reply. The different worlds we lived in were just too far apart. Our reforms were aimed at empowering the very people and neighborhoods the Greater Milwaukee Committee would write off. All I could stammer out was "I don't agree with you, we have to try" and left it at that.

It's not a good ending to this story, but it's what happened. I went away unsettled, more conscious of how difficult our reform of social services would be.

The Youth Initiative Committee could only be described as "optimistic." Appointed by County Executive David Schulz, fifty-six concerned citizens, social service administrators, social workers, and minority community leaders gathered in September of 1988 to oversee a "fundamental reorientation" of Milwaukee County's services for youth. Howard Fuller, who had been a militant spokesman for the African American community, especially on issues of education and youth, was the newly appointed Director of the Department of Health and Human Services. There was anticipation, even hope, among African Americans and others on the Youth Initiative Committee that after countless past "task forces," this time real change was on the agenda.

Fuller and I were trying to reframe the mission of social work to be one of serving "children in the context of their families and families in the context of their neighborhoods." We distributed a review of Lisbeth Schorr's *Within our Reach* to the Youth Initiative Committee and used it as a theme:

> Crime, school dropouts, teenage childbearing, drug abuse-each of these and other major problem behaviors of adolescents can be studied separately, but in the real world they interact, reinforce one another, and often cluster together in the same individuals.....not only do the problems cluster, *but the individuals having these problems live in the same neighborhoods.* For them, the damage that begins in childhood becomes visible in adolescence and reverberates throughout a community as part of an intergenerational cycle of devastation.
>
> *(Dryfoos 1988, 2; emphasis added)*

We planned to operate our administration within a social work tradition of community organization and neighborhood-based services (Halpern 1991). From the settlement houses in the twenties to the funding of community agencies in the sixties, the importance of neighborhood has been a persistent, if often neglected, theme in social welfare. Our reform effort would stress environmental changes and strengthening families in contrast to social work's current psychological approaches. We based much of our philosophy on concepts from the war on poverty, especially the notion of "community control." For example, Janowitz points out:

> The welfare state, especially in the United States, emerged with the strong imprint of a bureaucratic organization insufficiently concerned with the elements of community, of social cohesion and group identity as they operate as welfare objectives. The demand for community control was an impulse to construct entities that would

combine a geographic base with ethnic, racial, and religious, or just local, sentiments.

*(Janowitz 1976, 127)*

Fuller and I had numerous discussions on the "lessons" of the War on Poverty. An important issue, I argued, was the question of the mortality of small neighborhood organizations. Most 1960s community action agencies had faded away while the survivors were often scraping by on crumbs from big institutions, preoccupied with maintaining their own funding (Marris and Rein 1967, 245–72). We generally knew that the old poverty agencies received very few contracts from our department, and few services were located in poor neighborhoods.

Two problems confronted us. First, unlike the 1960s, there was no social movement to press for reform. That meant, at best, we would be limited in what we could accomplish (Lipsky 1980, 210). The citizen-based Youth Initiative Committee, though they worked hard and with considerable enthusiasm for change, was a start—but still a poor substitute for rowdy demonstrations in the streets. We would have to find other means to create, stimulate, or provoke out-side pressure on ourselves.

Second, conditions in the poorest neighborhoods had gotten much worse over the past decades. We portrayed these worsening conditions and the con-centration of poverty in Milwaukee with a series of color maps and presented our plans to the Youth Initiative Committee. I had stolen the idea of color maps of risk indicators from William Julius Wilson after watching a presentation he made on Chicago's underclass several years before. The Youth Initiative Committee's "Final Report" used Wilson's terminology and discussed the "entrenchment" of an "underclass" in Milwaukee County.

According to Wilson (1987, 61) the central issue was "social isolation," that is, the effects of concentrated poverty. The flight of more conventional resi-dents of these areas of poverty had resulted in the loss of positive role models for the young. Conventional residents, Wilson added, were not only role models, but also the backbone of local institutions. Wilson contended the loss of jobs and the flight of African American workers and professionals from central cities had led to the deterioration and collapse of local social institutions like churches, schools, corner stores, and community-based programs.

> As the basic institutions declined the social organization of inner-city neighborhoods (sense of community, positive neighborhood identification, and explicit norms and sanctions against aberrant behavior) likewise declined.
>
> *(Wilson 1991, 138)*

This analysis led the Youth Initiative Committee to issue a final report October 10, 1988, which called for extensive pilot programs in two neighborhoods.

> In sum, the objective of the neighborhood pilots would be to strengthen existing institutions as Wilson recommends. Stronger local institutions means a stronger voice for the neighborhood in demanding accountability of service providers...In a word, this type of approach empowers a neighborhood and sees it as part of the solution rather than neglecting it or seeing it only as a problem.
>
> *(Milwaukee County 1988, 10–11)*

## WHERE IS SOCIAL SERVICE MONEY SPENT?

As we began implementing the Youth Initiative, we drilled the importance of "neighborhood" into the social service bureaucracy. The Youth Initiative looked at everything geographically: characteristics of clients, types and location of services, assignment of social service cases, etc. The Youth Initiative introduced a whole new vocabulary into Milwaukee: "I live in '04" (zip code 53204, pronounced "oh-four") or "my agency has an office in '12' next to '06'" ("one-two" next to "oh-six") became social service Newspeak all across town.

We began a process of intensive investigation of the two zip codes. We contracted for research to develop a needs assessment to propose changes in how to deliver services (Moore and Edari 1990b),[1] formed neighborhood councils who inventoried existing services, and hired neighborhood coordinators who staffed the councils and helped prepare resource directories and service delivery plans. I demanded and got print-outs from nervous managers of all our social service and income maintenance caseloads by zip code.

When I asked for the data on child abuse, the responsible manager, an easy-going white liberal, resisted. He had gathered that data a few years ago, he said, to demonstrate how child abuse affects all classes and all races. But when he found out that more than three quarters of all child abuse referrals came from the central city, he quickly and quietly suppressed the report.[2] Don't stir up racism, he begged me, by releasing that kind of information. Worse, making that information public might lose the support of upper and middle class white women's groups who were active in supporting the department's programs on child abuse.

Both Fuller and I had little patience for such deception. Child abuse across the U.S. has always been concentrated in areas of greatest poverty, where stress is more likely. Family income is still the best predictor of removal of a child from the home by a social worker (Fein and Maluccio 1992, 340). The "myth of classlessness" serves to divert funding from poverty related concerns like jobs and concrete services to "counseling" and other medical model gimmicks (Pelton 1989, 37–38).

But there is a more insidious consequence of denying that child abuse and other social problems are concentrated in poor communities. By claiming that child abuse is not a poverty problem, white-led traditional social service providers have gobbled up purchase of service dollars for "prevention" and "intervention" programs which often have served a suburban or more affluent clientele. Poor minority neighborhoods are thereby denied resources needed to deal with the much greater problems within their own communities. I was offended in principle about deceiving the public. But this manager sparked my interest in finding out where our department had spent its purchase of service dollars.

I began to carefully gather data from our managers on the geographical distribution of where we spent our annual $51 million of purchase of service dollars, or funds which are contracted out to private agencies. We funded about $25 million per year in youth programs, at least $21 million for out-of-home

# The Distribution of Youth Service Dollars by Zip Code: 1988

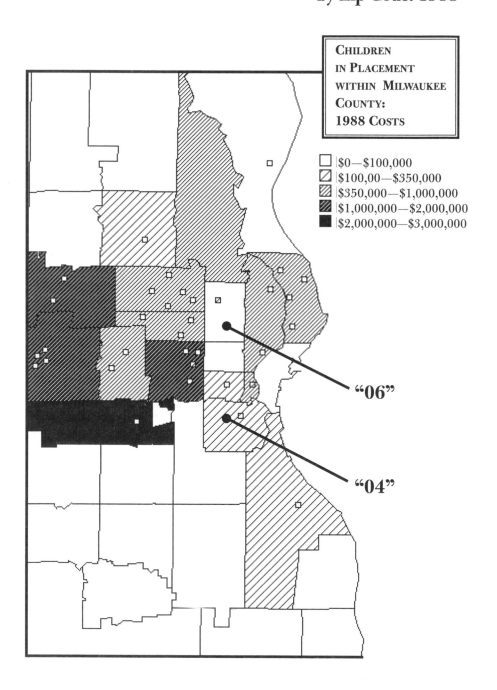

CHILDREN
IN PLACEMENT
WITHIN MILWAUKEE
COUNTY:
1988 COSTS

$0—$100,000
$100,00—$350,000
$350,000—$1,000,000
$1,000,000—$2,000,000
$2,000,000—$3,000,000

"06"

"04"

placements. The other $26 million funded various alcohol and drug programs and programs for the mentally retarded and developmentally disabled.

It took me a while to get these numbers from managers who were more than a bit nervous about what I would find. For good reason. On February 10, 1989, I burst into Fuller's office bubbling with excitement and armed with maps and charts. First, I told Fuller, we spent most of our juvenile purchase of service dollars outside Milwaukee County, a fact that might prove useful to our parochial-minded county board. But there was more. Less than $350 thousand of $25 million dollars in youth program contracts went to agencies located in our two targeted zip codes. None of the $26 million we spent on alcohol and drug and other programs went to fund agencies located in the 53206 African American community and only two small programs were funded in 53204. When I added it all up, less than 1% of our purchase of service dollars went to agencies located within our target neighborhoods, where 25% of our clients lived! I illustrated my point with the zip code map on the preceding page. Notice how the agencies which received youth service funding circle the central city areas, particularly zips "04" and "06."

Aside from the $51 million, all of our $1.3 million in contracts for agencies to arrange foster care placements (for mainly African American children) went to large, white-led, traditional providers not based in the central city. Minority run agencies, no matter where they were located in 1988 received about 9% of all our contracts, while minorities make up 23% of Milwaukee County's population and as many as two thirds of our clients (Planning Council for Health and Human Services 1990). What this added up to was a consistent policy to fund agencies which had no physical stake in our two zip codes or any of the neighborhoods where most of our clients resided. By investing more than $50 million annually in outlying areas, the Department of Health and Human Services made a decision not to invest that money in the central city. This decision, which translated into jobs as well as accessible programs, might have helped prevent these poor communities from deteriorating.

This situation is the result of maneuvering in the 1970s by family and youth service agencies. As the war on poverty wound down, federal dollars to public bureaucracies for purchasing social services doubled. These funds, however, were overwhelmingly funneled to private agencies which had few connections to minority communities. The minority-led war on poverty agency programs, which had been funded by the Office on Economic Opportunity (OEO), were almost completely left out of the purchase of social services business (Sosin 1990, 631 n.4). As OEO funds disappeared, neighborhood agencies began to decline while private agencies, which received money from a different federal pot, enjoyed a funding bonanza. A "good old boys" network was built between departments of social services and mainly white private agencies. Poor minority neighborhoods would see little investment in local agencies from public social service dollars.

My maps were icily greeted by nervous private providers who argued that minority or neighborhood-based programs were not effective, and that's why they got the money. Of course this assumes the traditional providers are effective in treating youth. So to counter their arguments, I did a study of youth released from traditional residential and group homes in 1988. The first thing I found out was that no data on outcomes were even kept by our department. In other words, we handed out millions of dollars in youth program moneys each year without gathering any data on outcomes or the effectiveness of those programs. When I did gather outcome data for 1988, I found that a majority of all youth placed in private agencies either ran away, were transferred to secure correctional surroundings, or turned 18 and were just released, for a disheartening "failure rate" of 55.7% (Hagedorn 1989).

Programs in minority communities also need to be evaluated. But my investigation revealed that there is no empirical basis for the large white-led providers to claim that they are getting the money because they are effective. Indeed, by any reasonable standard, nearly every one of Milwaukee's traditional agencies should have had their funds cut off for lack of success rehabilitating the youth they serve.

Other researchers have found the reason for refunding traditional providers has had little to do with quality of service. Private providers, Sosin (1990, 623) finds, "are not forced to change technologies" even if necessary and "governments provide few controls that might change their behavior." In Milwaukee, traditional programs are refunded year after year with little or no objection from the county board. Funding traditional providers based in outlying areas rather than neighborhood-based agencies is a political decision, and private agencies have considerable local clout. The reasons to fund neighbor-hood-based social service programs should in part be based, we argued, on cri-teria of how to help strengthen the neighborhood where troubled youth grow up.[3]

Thus, the Youth Initiative made a careful analysis of the damaging effects of our own social welfare bureaucracy's policies on the structure of poor commu-nities. It added a new dimension to Wilson's underclass concept, which cen-tered on changes in labor markets. An underclass, as I saw it, did not develop only from the loss of industry or the flight of the black middle class. Policies of public bureaucracies have also undermined the institutional infrastructure with-in poor neighborhoods. The urban underclass may have been created by macro-economic dislocations, but it is maintained through deliberately decided institutional arrangements.[4]

As an immediate result of our investigations, our department added a clause to many of our purchase of service "requests for proposals" stipulating that a program, if funded, must be physically located in "04" or "06." That stip-ulation brought howls from the traditional providers. Many quickly tacked on paragraphs to their annual proposals that "if funded" they would move "an office" into our targeted neighborhoods. Those proposals we carefully placed in the circular file as we funded only neighborhood-based programs. Such are the perks of power.

## SUPPORT NETWORKS AND SOCIAL WORK

The lack of funding of neighborhood-based programs has inhibited social ser-vices from playing a supportive role for poor families. One excerpt from my field notes gives an example.

As part of my investigation of what was wrong in the system, I accom-panied a child protective worker through a day's cases. The first home we went to visit was on the relatively affluent East Side, a case of sus-pected neglect which had not yet been confirmed by the intake work-er. The allegations of neglect were made by the divorced husband and the nine year old boy was the subject of a custody battle. The allegation was that the white 25-year-old lower middle class mother kept moving and never stayed in one home for more than a month or two.

There seemed to be some truth to these facts, but when we arrived at the home we were greeted by not only the mother and child but also a representative of a battered woman's organization who acted throughout the interview as an advocate. The mother was participating in group discussions and was being seen by a therapist associated with the woman's group. This group was helping her to find a job where she could support herself and one child. She also was apparently being helped by the woman's group to deal with the stress of a destructive relationship, making it on her own, and going through the custody battle.

The interview was pleasant with the advocate doing most of the talking. She recognized me from a "Milwaukee Magazine" article and photo and I was introduced by the social worker as a DHHS official looking into how child abuse cases are investigated. I asked no questions and happily I was ignored once the interview was seriously underway.

We left that home with the case not making a strong impression on me. This seemed to be a situation where the ex-husband was trying to get custody and the mother obviously had made some mistakes, but mainly needed a job, parenting classes, and therapy. Thanks to the advocate, those needs were being addressed separate from our intervention. The neglect case would be closed as "unsubstantiated."

Our next stop was in the central city at the home of a 25-year-old black mother. Her child's school had reported a suspected case of abuse several months ago. Unlike the first case where the east side mother responded to the child protective worker's call by setting up and keeping an appointment, it had taken the worker nearly three months to actually find the second mother. She was never home when he called and would not keep appointments. When she had finally been located about two months before I visited the home, she admitted a cocaine abuse problem and agreed to out-patient care for addiction at St. Anthony's Hospital. The children were taken by relatives while she was in treatment.

When we entered her house, she let us in and then screamed at her son to "get out of here" while we were talking. I was introduced the same way as in the first case and similarly ignored as the interview continued. She told us she had improved and didn't see the boyfriend who had introduced her to cocaine "very much." Her home was decorated a bit better than the first home we visited and was larger since there were several other children and relatives residing at the home as well. The child protective worker told me the most favorable thing about the woman was that she voluntarily sought cocaine treatment. She told us in the interview that cocaine had "made her a different person... someone I didn't know... I never want to do that again." However on the whole, the woman told us very little and except for a month's out-patient treatment, nothing had changed in her life to suggest she would necessarily be a different person. I left the home unconvinced that a crisis in her life would not send her back to cocaine and thinking that the child continued to be at risk. The worker concurred, but not having the time to deal with it himself, referred her case to "On-going" services.

Later that night I reflected back on those two visits. Comparing the two, I was struck by the support mechanisms that existed for the east side white mother that weren't there for the central city black mother. The white child protective worker had told me that he was aware of "no agencies within the black community which deal with abuse/neglect" and he made referrals only to agencies located outside the central city. The east side mother, on the other hand, lived close to the battered women agency that provided her with services. The advocate in the first case can be seen as a good example of the on-going support the east side mother might be expected to receive. A support network was being consciously built to help this mother deal with any problems as they might arise.

But what can the central city black mother expect if there are problems in the future? She can take a bus to a far away treatment program and try to resume therapy. But no one is monitoring her case (except for our Ongoing Services, who will try to check in at most once a month). No agencies have been mobilized to give her support. Those few agencies in the black community that do provide such services are underfunded and not known by the social worker. What will happen to her?

*Field Notes, November, 1988*

What was missing were not programs: there were plenty of alcohol and drug or parenting programs either mother could enter. But the central city mother did not have any programs within her community that could provide her immediate, reliable, and ongoing help. This leaves only support from kinship and friends for poor minority women.

Those kinship supports, however, were often very real. In our survey of residents of the two zip codes, we found that nearly half of all adult African American respondents saw their parents every day and over ninety percent visited parents and siblings at least monthly. Kinship ties in the other zip code were nearly as strong, even though many of the respondents were first generation immigrants with many relatives abroad. Finally, more than three quarters of all respondents belonged to families that held family reunions—and well over 90% regularly attend those reunions. Even child protective clients, who are among the most transient residents, had extensive kinship networks (Moore and Edari 1990a).

As the Youth Initiative Needs Assessment put it:

In sum, though there are clearly problems in many of these families, the family networks are in place for most residents, especially on the northside. And they are functional for most residents as well. These

are not isolated or anomic individuals, by and large, but are well integrated into functional social networks.

*(Moore and Edari 1990b, 28).*

It is those networks, and not social service agencies, which are used as the
main line of financial, household, and emergency support for Milwaukee's poor
families. We asked respondents whom they would call to get help with different types of problems. Almost two thirds of respondents would go to relatives
first for problems with money, half would go to relatives for help dealing with
problems with someone in their household, and about a quarter would even
turn to relatives for help solving problems in their neighborhood. As Stack
(1974, 107) describes African American families: "In times of need, the only
predictable resources that can be drawn upon are their own children and parents and the funds of kin and friends obligated to them."

It may be surprising to some that social work is nearly absent as a reliable
resource for Milwaukee's poor. After relatives, it is the police whom poor residents turn to most often for help. While it might be expected that police are
called most often for help with problems in the neighborhood, they are also
called to help with problems arising within the household. "Social workers"
were listed well behind "relatives," "friends," "police," "clergy," and "other" as
a resource to call in time of money, household or neighborhood trouble. Even
in cases of child abuse, twice as many respondents said they would call police
before they would call a social worker. The category "social worker" finishes
behind the category "nobody" as whom respondents would call in times of
almost every type of difficulty we listed in the survey. All this adds up to a rather
stunning lack of confidence in public social services.

Other studies have also found a tenuous relationship between poor people
and social services. For example, the literature review of one Chicago study
found families on AFDC were less likely than others to know about helping
organizations. General Assistance clients as well, while relying heavily on
friends and family, "had little connection to the formal social service network"
(Stagner and Richman 1986, 1–13). What do poor residents do when they
need social services? In the Chicago study, half of those surveyed didn't go to
any service agency and didn't ask for help from any formal system. Less than a

quarter of respondents ever used any public social services.

One reason for such under-utilization, we have seen, is social services' helping role has declined as investigatory and child removal functions have increased. Poor people are skeptical of the value of asking an agency for help when its prime function appears to be taking away their children. Another reason, however, is the location of any real services. Poor people logically utilize services that are readily accessible, respectful, and which effectively address real needs. A Milwaukee study concurred that program location was strongly related to utilization of mental health services by minorities (Planning Council 1986, 2).

The fragmentary nature of services compounds the problems of location. The Chicago study concludes, "Services are also less likely to be used if people must go to a different location for each specific problem they face " (Stagner and Richman 1986, 30). It suggests that if services were neighborhood-based and served multiple needs, they would be more likely to be used, an argument reminiscent of the war on poverty (cf. Janowitz 1976, 130).

It is precisely those local helping agencies that were stunningly absent in zip code 53206, our African American target neighborhood. Zip code 53206 is a 20 by 20 square block area with 40,000 residents in the heart of Milwaukee. When we began the Youth Initiative those neighborhoods had no large chain grocery store, not a single bank nor even a check-cashing store. Bars and drug houses were in plentiful supply and the area had the highest number of Milwaukee drug arrests. Still, this zip code area did not have a single alcohol/drug treatment facility. Service agencies are located on the outskirts of 53206, circling the neighborhoods where their clients live, but not a part of them.[5]

Milwaukee's "underclass," particularly in the poorest African American neighborhoods, are not so much socially isolated as they are cut off from access to both jobs and services. With no helping institutions to turn to, poor people rely on themselves and their kinship networks. When help is needed, it is the police who are the most often present and available. The job of the social services ought to be to provide accessible, effective support to everyone like those provided to the East Side mother in my field notes. It is not the absence of conventional families that defines Milwaukee's African American underclass areas as much as it is the absence of effective, non-punitive, social institutions.[6]

## CONCLUSION: NEIGHBORHOOD AND BUREAUCRACIES

One pillar of our reforms was to alter the structure of work to emphasize services, not punishment. The second pillar was to begin to develop a network of providers within Milwaukee's poorest neighborhoods, decentralize the Department of Social Services, and promote better access and cultural sensitivity. Our policies intended to help rebuild an institutional infrastructure in underclass neighborhoods which would provide jobs as well as supportive services.

But before we continue with our tale of the Youth Initiative, exploring the nature of reform, we need to take a brief detour. What we have seen so far are "candid camera" snapshots which show public social services as punitive and neglectful of minority communities. Some may dispute these pictures. But I think the evidence we've gathered indicates our photographs generally capture the current state of social services across the United States even as the national mood turns even more unsympathetic toward the poor.

How has a "helping" institution like public social services become so transmogrified? We have given a few hints in the first four chapters, but at this point our candid camera will not suffice as an explanation. We need more of a motion picture, a short newsreel of the history of social welfare reform, in order to understand why the current situation is so unsettling, where it is going, and what needs to be done to change it. This newsreel will feature many actors: lofty reformers and mean-spirited reactionaries, frightened politicians and greedy capitalists. But one of the principal players, it can now be revealed, is a resource-hungry, self-interested bureaucracy.

# PART II

## THE HISTORICAL CONTEXT OF THE REFORM OF SOCIAL SERVICE BUREAUCRACIES

# 5

# THE FRUSTRATION OF REFORM

The history of social service reform is a history of sacrificing the poor on the altar of bureaucracy. The role of bureaucracy in the social welfare institution has been largely an untold story. The interests of social welfare bureaucracies have often been hidden behind misdirected debates between "bleeding hearts" pleading for more resources and the "cold hearted" wanting to cut back. Since the Reagan era, the role of bureaucracy has been hidden even more, as those who wanted more resources for social services to "do good" faced a wave of punitive dictats from a conservative Washington. This swirl of ideological struggles has masked the fact that social service bureaucracies have their own interests separate from liberal or conservative agendas. The next two chapters explain how the self-interest of social welfare bureaucracies has repeatedly helped stifle fundamental reform.

Social welfare history as a whole is often written from one of three different points of view. The first, the "uneven progress" school (Wilensky and Lebeaux 1965), sees the history of social welfare as an upward march of humanity toward ever more enlightened policies. While there are occasional set-backs, this view argues, social welfare, including the social services, are growing more and more humane. A second perspective, identified with David Rothman (1971; 1980; 1981), also sees upward movement, but claims the good intentions of reformers have been often betrayed by the self-interest of those who run large institutions, like prisons. This is sometimes called the "we blew it" theory of social welfare (Cohen 1985, 19). A third perspective is one of hidden intentions, the less frequently told story of the social control functions of social welfare and their uses by elites (Galper 1975; Piven and Cloward 1971; Platt 1969).

But each of these well-known viewpoints, to one degree or another, underestimates the significance of the self-interest of welfare bureaucracies and their role in the misdirection of reform.[1] Indeed, the social welfare literature and the literature on bureaucracy are academic strangers. Bureaucracy is typically treated in the academic social work journals as private troubles or "red tape" (e.g., Patti and Resnick 1972; Rai 1983). Most historical reviews scarcely deal with bureaucratic self-interest, or if they do, they criticize one type of bureaucracy— prisons, poorhouses, etc. — and assume that other types of welfare bureaucracies are "doing good" (e.g., Rothman 1980 ). Reform in these accounts is treated as an ideological matter, a struggle of good versus evil, liberals versus conservatives, working class versus business interests, or doing good versus social control (Handler and Hasenfeld 1991; Rothman 1981; Meyers 1993).

Our historical stroll, on the other hand, will wander from this yellow brick road of social welfare history and occasionally peek into the dark, dense woods of organizational theory. It will examine how organizational reforms in social welfare bureaucracies and in industry were linked and how they controlled and divided the working classes. Later, as public bureaucracies expanded and institutionalized, social service reform was diverted in a punitive direction in a way that facilitated the capture of resources. This excursion is brief and looks at a different side of social welfare than most historical accounts. It does not purport to be a new theory nor a complete explanation of social welfare history. Rather, it attempts to fill in the blanks on many unanswered questions of how and why welfare bureaucracies have reformed as well as resisted changes that benefit the poor. It lays a foundation for understanding the present naure of the child welfare system, the meaning of real social service reform, and how to get it.

## THE EMERGENCE OF BUREAUCRACIES

In the 1800s, Katz (1986, 6–18) points out, most people lived near their work. In the North, losing a job meant moving. In fact, it was the growth of large-scale economic organizations—mills and crude factories—which began the unraveling of the northern colonial order. The creation of new factory jobs pulled workers from the small villages and countryside and from town to town. The new industries quickly overshadowed the agricultural economy in New England.

The factory attained this dominance in part because of its bureaucratic organization (Gordon, et al. 1982, 58). The factory presented a new phenomenon to a predominately agrarian workforce—a division of labor—which wrenched as much profit as possible from the labor process (Braverman 1974, 70–83; also cf. Foucault 1979, 142–43). The organization of work itself was remade, from the more holistic agricultural process, into the "rational" image of a machine (Morgan, 1986, 19–39).

While the the mills and factories may have been "rational" for their owners, conditions for their employees were terrible. Workers seldom stayed in one workplace for very long. As late as the early 1900s, a survey found, annual turnover in many industries was as much as 100% (Gordon, et al. 1982, 148). Worker dissatisfaction and unrest was attenuated by the existence of the frontier and the widespread availability of unskilled work. When conditions became intolerable, workers simply packed up and moved to another town to work in a new factory or on the farmlands of the west.

This increased movement of workers threatened the stable growth of industry. A way had to be found to contain the increasing number of vagrants, as well as to teach the work ethic to what were called "germ(s) of disorder" (Rothman 1971, 27; also cf. Katz 1986, 12). One effective method to teach labor discipline, as well as to deter working people from leaving their jobs, was a new institution: the poorhouse. Those who could not find jobs, the Jacksonian era forces of law and order decreed, would be placed in the poorhouse and forced to work for their keep.

So in the shadow of the factory there arose a parallel public institution, the poorhouse, a compassionless reminder to workers of the stark new order. Like schools, prisons, and mental asylums, the poorhouse was consciously designed to be "plain and factory-like" (Rothman 1971, 153). For vagrants and other victims of the new harsh conditions of industry, poorhouses were not a "safety net," but punishment meant to curb deviance and instill discipline.

Worker unrest and the sheer numbers of the impoverished ended capitalist dreams of an endless stream of docile workers and pliant immigrants. The end of the civil war and the depression of 1873 increased the number of vagrants and swamped the northern poorhouses. They became overcrowded and nearly impossible to manage (Katz 1986, 25). Administrative problems compounded by untrained superintendents, corruption, and a lack of classification of inmates exposed the new institutions as little more than warehouses for the poor (Rothman 1971, 29).

The depression of 1893 made matters even worse. Workers were agitating for the eight hour day and waging bitter strikes like the one led by Eugene Debs against Pullman (Lindsey 1942, 361). The "rationality" of the new social arrangements was wearing thin. As Katz (1986, 35) says, "despite the diffusion of poorhouses, the volume of outdoor relief continued to grow." The poorhouse had failed in its stated goal to reduce the number of those on relief. Reform was urgently needed.

## Scientific Reform = More Supervision

At the turn of the century, the spirit of rebellion against the abuses of industry and the poorhouse burned across the country, prompting the rise of "parallel movements for social reform and social welfare" (Wilensky and Lebeaux 1965, 89). Both the Progressive movement and Taylorism, or "scientific management, "were reforms which aimed to rationalize the failing new organizations. Above all, in both industry and government, "scientific" reforms would vastly expand the size of their respective bureaucracies.

In industry, as factories added workers to become more profitable, a "crisis of control" erupted. The force of arms by which earlier strikes had been suppressed was not sufficient to guarantee the labor peace necessary for profitable expansion (Edwards 1979, 48–71). Taylorist reform of rational economic organizations of the nineteenth century basically meant increasing the layers of supervision, called the "drive system."[3] The number of foremen was sharply increased and a hierarchical system of control was built, replacing the simple control of the factory owner (Edwards 1979, 52). Work was reorganized, particularly in large companies, around the assembly line. Plants grew rapidly in size and added management layers:

> The number of foremen in manufacturing increased from 90,000 in 1900 to 296,000 in 1920, an increase of more than 300 percent, whereas total manufacturing employment increased by only 96 percent.
>
> *(Gordon, et al. 1982, 135)*

In social welfare, reform also meant increasing the types of supervision for delinquents and criminals and the bureaucratization of private welfare agencies. Pre-Progressive era social services were often delivered as patronage. In the 1800s, rationalization of social welfare functions was retarded by local influences, particularly the power of urban political machines. For the Progressives, reform meant expanding governmental involvement in welfare and social services. The state was seen as "the friend of equality." Expanding government was "in harmony with the spirit of the age" (Rothman 1980, 60).

Public spending on social welfare increased by 168% between 1903 and 1928. Much of the increase, rather than being spent on direct benefits for the poor, was spent on expanding local welfare agencies and hiring social workers. By 1930 the number of social workers increased to 31,241 (24,592 of them women). The number of social work schools increased from 5 to 45 between 1915 and 1930 (Katz 1986, 209).

This expansion was primarily at the local level. Katz (1986, 209–10) bemoans the "bewildering administrative pattern" of Massachusetts, where "355 towns and counties each formed distinct units for poor relief" or Ohio where 88 counties had 1535 local government units who retained some responsibility for welfare. Across the United States, Progressive reform built a fragmented edifice of local social welfare bureaucracies.

But Progressive reform also meant adding on a new form of surveillance to Jacksonian era institutions like poorhouses, asylums, and prisons: probation and parole officers.[4] While most accounts of this era focus on the expansion of discretion brought about by probation and parole, the era also meant more poor people could be monitored than ever before (Rothman 1980, 75; Platt 1969, 99). Rather than take clients away from institutions, social welfare reform meant the expansion of institutions and the formation of new probation bureaucracies.

New York's history was typical of the times. In 1907 the New York courts committed 12,053 persons (adults and juveniles combined) to correctional institutions and placed another 1,672 on probation. Twenty years later they dispatched 17,373 persons to correctional institutions and put 23,154 on probation (Rothman 1980, 110–11).

Progressive reform greatly benefited both institutions and the growing maze of local social welfare and correctional agencies. Pay was increased, probation officers received civil service status, psychologists and psychiatrists were added to prisons, and social workers increased in number (Rothman 1980, 147). And what did the new personnel hired in the institutions do? Rothman (337) scathingly reports that apparently all that changed was the intake report went from one or two pages in 1900 to a fifteen page document in 1920.

Some segments of the poor, African Americans and other minorities, were almost completely ignored by the Progressive era. The 1890s saw the formation of black ghettoes in the north. But the mainline charity volunteer organizations neglected the newcomers (Axinn and Levin 1982, 135) and African Americans began to develop their own institutions (Spear 1967, 91–110). Just at a time when European immigrants were integrating into the urban political machine, black ghettoes were consolidating, not disintegrating (Wilson 1978, 80; Lieberson 1980). Many African Americans, Latinos, and other minorities found jobs in peripheral industries which were not effected by Progressive era labor regulation (Gordon, et al. 1982, 153; Axinn and Levin 1982, 121).

Probation and parole fundamentally marked the addition of a supplemental form of supervision over the poor and the growth of new bureaucracies, tied to local courts, to carry out the new supervisory tasks. Like scientific management in economic organizations, Progressive reform meant increasing the amount and levels of direct supervision as means for "efficiency." But how efficient were the scientific reforms of that time? And for whom?

## The More Things Change...

Most commentators have asserted the Progressive era failed in its promise to reform institutional practice and improve the quality of life for the poor. The Jacksonian emphasis on institutions, Patterson (1986, 23) states, was simply recast: "the progressive's remedies featured new labels on old bottles" (also cf. Platt 1969, 98).

Rothman's central criticism of the Progressive era was that institutions "turned innovations into add-ons, not replacements. " Reformers "believed that institutions....could coexist with, and even sponsor, non-institutional programs." Despite anti-institutional rhetoric of the Progressives, the number of institutions "rose dramatically" in what Katz (1986, 120) believes may be the largest growth of institutions in history. Rothman's *Conscience and Convenience* is an exposé of the failure of Progressive reform to curtail the growth of institutions or to alter the punitive and custodial practices of social welfare and correctional bureaucracies.

But from the perspective of the evolution of bureaucracies, the Progressive era was a startling success. The rational organizations of the earlier Jacksonian era were marginally efficient, but in the end had proved incapable of forcing immigrants to adjust to stark industrial conditions. Industrial barons embraced scientific methods and Progressives demanded reforms which streamlined the management of their agencies and strengthened their control over a restive working class. The core of nineteenth century reform was a vast increase in the amount and type of supervision over workers and the poor.

Rothman (1971, xiv–xv) is surely wrong in his assertion that "there was nothing inevitable about the asylum form" and in his doubts that institutions were "the logical response to scientific progress." On the contrary, rational organizations were the epitome of nineteenth century economic and public life. The Progressive era fundamentally represents the rationalization of organizations launched in the prior Jacksonian period. It was the new bureaucracies and their masters, not workers or the poor, who benefited most from nineteenth century reform. This pattern would continue as unrest hit unprecedented levels in the 1930s.

## THE NEW DEAL AND THE SEGMENTATION OF LABOR

Neither business nor government were prepared for the scope of human misery and anger during the Great Depression. Unemployment spiraled upward from 3 million in the spring of 1929, to 4 million in January 1930, to 5 million by fall, and up to 8 million by spring of 1931 (Piven and Cloward 1971, 49). For those still working in the mass production industries, conditions were becoming intolerable (Gordon, et al. 1982, 128). Spontaneous rebellions by workers and the failure of craft unions to organize the new industries prompted John L. Lewis to plan a militant new labor strategy (Alinsky 1949, 178). Both industry and social welfare would be overwhelmed by the turmoil of the thirties. Both would also take advantage of reform movements by segmenting the working class while streamlining and adding on to their bureaucracies.

The spectacular sit down strikes led by the Congress of Industrial Organizations (CIO) told management loud and clear that the "drive system"—relying on foremen to speed-up production in ever larger plants—was not working. The closed rational organization whose only goals were profits for management could no longer deny the aspirations of its dependent employees. The limits of scientific management had been reached.

The human relations school sought to rescue management from the impact of unionization. The "Hawthorne" effect, expounded by Harvard Business school scholars (Roethlisberger and Dickson 1947), inspired the notion that "the simple act of paying positive attention to people has a great deal to do with productivity" (Peters and Waterman 1982, 94; but cf. Jones, 1992). It was not inhuman conditions that caused worker unrest, this line of thinking assured managers, but group norms and "nonrational" sentiments (Perrow 1979, 94). Human relations consultants could be dispatched to assist management to streamline their organizations and coopt worker rebellion. One result might be a stable, more predictable workforce, an objective much in demand by large industrial concerns. The worker demand for unions, some speculated might in the end be used to management's advantage.

Similarly, the federal government was facing mass discontent. Amateurish local welfare bureaucracies were incapable of meeting the needs and containing the militance of the unemployed. As Katz says:

Like a small nineteenth century firm, the government lacked the means
to coordinate increasingly complex, national business.

*(Katz 1986, 207)*

Compounding the problem of local bureaucratic inadequacy, many of the
newly unemployed were voters who had given the presidency to Roosevelt and
Congress to the Democrats. FDR therefore was forced to act or risk defeat at
the polls (Piven and Cloward 1971, 66–72).

The Federal Emergency Relief Administration (FERA) was driven by one
major goal: to get as much aid to as many people as fast as possible. Five hun-
dered million dollars was immediately channeled through local relief agencies
(Axinn and Levin 1982, 178). While other New Deal projects carried out
discriminatory practices, African Americans and other minorities were welcomed on FERA payrolls based on need (Piven and Cloward 1971, 76).

While FERA provided badly needed assistance to the unemployed, it also
beefed up local relief agencies. They were forced to hire "more professional
personnel" and increased "their administrative equity and efficiency" (Katz,
221). FERA was a life saving transfusion for overwhelmed local welfare organizations. It provided $250 million to states on a matching basis, $1 of federal
money for $3 of state aid. Federal dollars were a carrot which immediately led
to expanded local spending on relief. Katz notes dryly:

Even though states had clamored for federal aid because they claimed
to be stretched to their financial limits, they found money to match the
new federal grants.

*(Katz 1986, 221)*

The role of social workers would be transformed as well. In Regulation
No. 3 of FERA, Harry Hopkins, who zestfully headed the agency, required that
eligibility for FERA relief should be determined only by public welfare investigators (Axinn and Levin 1982, 181–2). Trattner (1979, 231) reports that regulations stipulated that every local relief office "was to employ at least one experienced social worker." Social workers would find expanding employment
opportunities within rejuvenated state and local government relief programs.

Social work was reconstituted as a public function "absorbed with problems of relief-giving" (Axinn and Levin 1982, 192).[5]

FERA represented an immediate response by a frightened government, accepting federal responsiblity for welfare in the face of local failure. Federal policymakers would henceforth become the principal designers of the contours of the budding welfare state. But such measures in themselves did not quell the unrest among workers and the poor.

## Common but Separate Purposes

The main problem facing the large mass production industries was the loyalty of their employees. Unionization dispelled any notion that there could be only one set of goals within a firm, those set by management. A solution to curtail worker unrest was found by dividing labor into various competing segments.

This solution was not a careful plan or conspiracy, but the result of several underlying factors. First, there was the increasing division of industry into core and peripheral sectors (Gordon, et al. 1982, 190; 201). Large mass production firms were needed to efficiently produce steel, autos, and other industrial goods. It was in these firms that unions took root, where a large number of workers were concentrated in one factory. But smaller, specialized "job shop" types of industries continued to thrive both due to their innovative practices and the demand by core industries for a variety of goods. Smaller firms bore more of the risk and thus enhanced "the profitability of the corporations at the center." These peripheral industries were often family controlled and typically non-union and low wage (191).

Within the larger companies, the development of detailed job descriptions, routine procedures for promotion, and union-backed seniority rules were all aimed at cementing worker allegiance. "Jobs were finely divided, frequently situated within detailed job ladders and internal promotional systems" (Gordon, et al. 1982, 189). A worker who held a job in a core industry was expected to stay and even if laid off, to return.

Job security and job ladders were intended to break up the

solidarity that united a firm's workers...moreover the workers' long-term identification with the enterprise was necessary to establish the context in which the firm could elicit compliance and coopera-tion...seniority and tenure pay off.

*(Edwards 1979, 153)*

A second factor contributing to controlling labor was a major increase in the post war period in the number of foremen and other white collar staff (Edwards (1979, 135). Since job categories were also increasing, it became necessary to increase the number of supervisors. And the supervisors also needed supervising. Along with this escalating number of foremen, was the continued emphasis on human relations theory, particularly in the growth and rationalization of personnel departments. Rules had to be written, job evalua-tion criteria developed, and labor relations had to be systematized.

Finally and paradoxically, unions also helped to segment and pacify labor. The human relations consultants and personnel departments focused their pri-mary energy on coopting the militance of the company's workforce. Unions needed to be incorporated into management practice in a way to increase both predictability and the allegiance of workers to the firm. The trade union move-ment, for their part, swapped goals of "an injury to one is an injury to all" for grievance procedures and job security and increased benefits for workers within specific companies. They also failed to vigorously expand their organizing to the small job shops in the secondary labor market. These union tactics undercut any spontaneous militance of the rank and file (Gordon, et al. 1982, 179). Indeed, the union movement turned on communist and other militants within their ranks as early as the late 1930s (Gordon, et al. 1982, 182–84; Piven and Cloward 1980, 164–72). Those who sought control of the workplace as a pre-eminent goal were ousted in favor of well-paid union bureaucrats who supported hefty pay increas-es and security for workers who remained with their companies.[6]

This drive by management to institutionalize a loyal workforce had conse-quences for the entire working class. Those workers protected by union con-tracts received qualitatively better wage and benefit packages than non-unionized workers in peripheral industries. Internal job ladders and seniority provisions helped build a "common purpose" between labor and management in large firms like never before. While the tidal wave of plant closings of the 1970s and 1980s would ultimately mock this "common purpose," management had succeeded in segmenting their opposition and maintaining a firm grip on their companies. The above factors add up to what Edwards (1979, 132) calls "bureaucratic control …the most important change wrought by the modern corporation in the labor process."

But for those workers not in "good jobs" ("primary" or "independent primary" labor markets), management's division of the workforce undermined their economic security. This "secondary labor market" included generally non-unionized, low-paying and often part-time jobs which required few skills of workers and seldom any training. In these firms, workers change jobs frequently, have few benefits, are often out of work for long periods, and need to periodically rely on welfare.[7]

## A New Deal for Some and a Raw Deal for Others

Industry's incipient segmentation of labor was supported by similar changes in New Deal social welfare legislation. The existence of a segmented workforce became the fundamental basis for the legislation which built the U.S. "semi-welfare" state.

On the one hand, the New Deal greatly expanded benefits for the poor. During the 1930s 35% of the population received public aid or social insurance. Public funding for these programs, almost non-existent in 1929, amounted to $5 billion in 1939 or 27% of all local, state, and federal government expenditures (Patterson 1986, 76). Social welfare spending jumped from 0.1% of national income in 1923 to 7.1% by 1939 (Katz 1986, 246). These were powerful gains won by the disadvantaged classes.

But social welfare expenditures didn't benefit all the poor and unemployed equally. The prime New Deal legislation, the Social Security Act, "established a dual system for federally supported income maintenance" (Axinn and Levin 1982, 185). The industrial unemployed and the working class base of the

Democratic Party would gain much, while agricultural workers, minorities, and the very poor would gain little, if anything.

Employers cemented the loyalty of workers in large industrial firms with wage increases and benefits. Then the New Deal covered these same workers with social security and unemployment insurance. Included in the benefits of the New Deal would be civil service employees of social welfare and other public bureaucracies. Large numbers of the long term unemployed, migrant workers, fatherless families, African Americans, Latinos and those working part-time would be left with few or no benefits.

Franklin Delano Roosevelt opposed any formula which would expand "the dole" to benefit all the poor (Orloff 1988). By rejecting the funding of Social Security out of general revenues, as proposed by Harry Hopkins and others, FDR reasoned he could protect Social Security from the "vagaries of congressional politics" (Patterson 1986, 77). But this policy also had the effect of restricting benefits.[8]

Patterson sees the New Deal as fundamentally "institutionalizing the distinction between the deserving and undeserving...it was concerned more with restoring jobs and morale than with attacking poverty" (Patterson 1986, 76; cf. Katz 1986, 235). The "deserving" poor were defined as those who were temporarily thrown out of work in core industries or government. The "undeserving" poor were mostly minorities and women who worked part-time, slaved in peripheral industries in the secondary labor market, or cared for children. The New Deal mainly covered the industrial working class and civil servants, while handing out only meager benefits to others. Segmented labor markets, created by the reform of private businesses, in effect were institutionalized by the New Deal.

## CONCLUSION: EXPANDED BUREAUCRACIES, MINORITIES, AND INSTITUTIONALIZED DIVISIONS

An unjust economic order, challenged by upsurges at the turn of the century and again in the 1930s, maintained itself through incremental reforms which streamlined its bureaucracies and divided the working class. The segmentation of labor guaranteed a long term need for welfare institutions to manage a super-

fluous "underclass" (Spitzer 1975). A main beneficiary of both Progressive and
New Deal reforms was the growing edifice of local, state, and federal social welfare bureaucracies with a stablilized and relatively well-paid workforce.
Amateurish local bureaucracies, built up by Progressive reform and rescued
with New Deal federal grants, began to mature and grow (Janowitz 1976, 8). A
bureaucratic constituency had sprouted up which would make increasing
demands on its own behalf to federal, state, and local governments.

> The early welfare state thereby acquired two assets that proved invalu-
> able as time elapsed: an organized constituency and a bureaucratic
> momentum that could not easily be stopped.
>
> *(Patterson 1986, 77)*

Before the New Deal, Wilensky and Lebeaux (1985, 138) wrote, social
welfare had been merely a "residual" organization, or a mechanism to be used
"only when the normal structures of supply, the family, and the market, break
down." But from the 1930s on, social welfare became "institutional," performing "normal 'first line' functions of modern industrial society." The post war
period saw social welfare growing through its own logic:

> Since 1955 expenditures for social welfare have been less and less the
> result of Keynsian policy designed for economic expansion through
> federal measures. Instead, the logic of social welfare expenditures has
> become more and more a system of self-sustaining expansion in
> response to the social and political definitions of welfare requirements.
>
> *(Janowitz 1976, 46)*

Welfare bureaucracies continued to add staff and build "rational" hierarchical structures. But while social welfare bureaucracies expanded, the poor,
and particularly African Americans, did not fare very well. The new improved
social welfare bureaucracies carried out stringent policies, particularly in the
south, as local bureaucrats kept eligible African Americans off the welfare rolls,
adapting their policies and practices to local political conditions (Piven and
Cloward 1971, 136).

While the New Deal had curtailed discrimination and provided real relief for millions of minorities, its exclusion of agricultural workers from social security and unemployment coverage had left the majority of black laborers in the South and Latino migrant workers without benefits. Southern states also kept ADC benefit levels low and used the local autonomy of the new ADC grants-in-aid to continue to discriminate (Piven and Cloward 1971, 115; 130–45). When technological changes would sweep away the old agricultural system, discriminatory practices and the lack of unemployment insurance and social security helped convince African Americans they had no continuing stake in the South. They moved north in large numbers.

Arriving in the North, African Americans would be forced to start over with no accrued social security benefits or eligibility for unemployment compensation. Years of labor in the cotton fields had counted for nothing. For the many African Americans who found jobs in manufacturing, they would ominously begin on the bottom rung of the economic ladder, in the near-twilight years of the industrial state. Manufacturing jobs for African Americans would increase in the 1940s and then come to a virtual standstill in the next decade (Gordon, et al. 1982, 207). For those who could not find jobs, ADC benefits would only be available to fatherless families, accelerating, rather than retarding, family break-up (Stack 1974, 112–13).

The urban rebellions in the sixties, however, would shake up both business and welfare bureaucracies. While business altered its organizational forms to deal with a more turbulent environment, social welfare bureaucracies expanded but did not reform their centralized organizations. Rather than restructure to better meet the people's needs, welfare bureaucracies took advantage of discontent to benefit themselves. Social welfare bureaucracies had developed interests of their own. And those interests did not necessarily coincide with the needs of the poor.

# 6

# REFORM AND PUNISHMENT

In the 1960s, both business and social welfare again faced a crisis. Internationally, the United States was pursuing interventionist policies against a rebellious Third World. Domestically, resistance to war and civil rights protests had created the most uncertain situation since the 1930s.

African Americans had migrated North in large numbers after World War II, doubling their population in Northern cities between 1940 and 1960 (Gordon et al, 1982, 206–07). Faced with a lack of good jobs and often denied welfare benefits, African Americans, Latinos, and other poor people rebelled, just as workers had in the late 1800s and 1930s. In the 1960s, social welfare agencies would again be overwhelmed and caseloads increased dramatically.

While business began to vary its form of organization to better pursue profit under different conditions, social welfare was busy using War on Poverty resources to expand its monolithic structures. Since the 1970s social welfare has been busy adapting to a more punitive climate and resisting reform. Rather than downsize, decentralize, and experiment as did many businesses, social welfare bureaucracies found a hierarchical structure to be functional for maintaining themselves and carrying out more punitive tasks. Reform in social welfare the past twenty years has meant "more staff" for bureaucracies regardless of whether those staff were helping or punishing the poor.

## CONTINGENCY THEORY AND STRUCTURAL REFORM IN BUSINESS AND SOCIAL WELFARE

The segmenting of labor markets and a dynamic post-war environment presented business with new challenges in how to structure their operations. No longer would one type of structure or technology be sufficient for a varied and changing market place. This more complex environment, theorists discovered, "set varied tasks for different organizations" (Perrow 1979, 200). "Contingency theory" basically asked the question, *"What kind of organization does it take to deal with various economic and market conditions?"* (Lawrence and Lorsch 1969, 1; italics in original). The answer: The technology and structure of a firm is contingent on the type of market where it competes, among other factors.[1]

Business organizations had to become more sophisticated to deal with more changing markets, an uncertain political environment, and other turbulent conditions.[2] Thus organization in primary labor markets, i.e. those jobs calling for highly technical and professional skills—like scientific research or medicine—could be decentralized, democratic, and participatory. Such organizations were appropriate to ensure the commitment of a swelling workforce of professionals and to master a constantly changing marketplace and revolutionizing technology. But in the sweatshops and on the assembly lines in small job shops, where tasks were routine and fixed, organizations were likely to be hierarchical, faceless, and repressive. Such organization was well suited to squeeze every drop of profit from part-time and non-unionized workers. Business thus learned to vary its structure contingent on task and environment. Social welfare bureaucracies, however, stubbornly refused to learn this basic lesson.

As the 1960s began, welfare bureaucracies were experiencing slow but steady growth (Wilensky and Lebeaux 1965, 159). The Black migration to Northern cities, as Piven and Cloward (1971, 222-46) demonstrate, did not have an immediate effect on AFDC caseloads. Discriminatory policies and outright racism kept many black migrants out of the welfare system until the mid-sixties. Then all hell broke loose in ghettoes across the United States and caseloads rose exponentially. Piven and Cloward point out that AFDC caseloads rose by 53% between 1960 and 1964. Then between 1964 and 1969, in seventy-eight Northern urban counties, caseloads rose an astounding 80% (335). Clients would gain by loudly demanding access to benefits.

You may have already guessed that it wasn't only clients who benefited by the turbulence. Welfare bureaucracies also "seized the time" for their own advantage. For example, Milwaukee caseloads during 1964–1969 rose 102%, far greater than the national average. While more clients received greater benefits, budgets for social worker salaries during the same time rose 300%. Costs for overall administration jumped from $12 million in 1962 to $34 million in 1970 (Milwaukee County 1962–1988). Urban welfare bureaucracies were adding workers and managers as fast as possible to meet the rising demand.

Social welfare bureaucracies even appropriated money intended for community action agencies. Halpern (1991, 352) accuses local bureaucracies of "siphoning off" significant amounts of community action funds for "administrative costs" before they ever reached the community. Janowitz (1976, 126) points out the War on Poverty should be seen not only as aid to the poor, but also "in part a campaign to obtain municipal, state, and federal employment."

Welfare bureaucracies were rapidly expanding, but hardly innovating. In fact, they further bureaucratized with hierarchical structures patterned after the operations of a factory. Eligibility and processing benefit payments could be organized in assembly line-like fashion.

> In the late 1960s and continuing through the 1970s welfare departments in the U.S. were usually configured as a line operation: high volume standardized processing that flows through a preset sequence of steps…Benefit issuance became a classic governmental example of attempting to construct the kind of smooth flows that we more commonly associate with manufacturing assembly lines.
>
> *(Rosenthal 1989, 298)*

This method of organization was not suitable for serving a changing environment, like the dramatic changes in urban poverty of the time. But rather than radically restructure to serve a more dynamic population, as did many private businesses, welfare bureaucracies opted for tinkering with their managerial ideology. New accounting systems, more line supervisors, and better training substituted for more fundamental changes.[3]

While there was some experimentation with program innovations within welfare bureaucracies, in the main they entrenched and stayed hostile to their new and more demanding clients. Gideon Sjoberg suggested at the time that

> (t)he primary means of overcoming the problems that have been associated with the lower class have been more and more bureaucracy...social problems...are to be resolved through expansion of existing bureaucratic structures or the addition of new ones. This has been the main thrust of most legislation on both the national and state levels since the 1930s.
>
> *(Sjoberg et al. 1966, 332)*

The upsurge in the sixties could not be coopted like the upsurge in the 1930s. The Vietnam War, unlike World War II, failed to provide full employment. A modernizing economy had little use for the unskilled minority poor. The service bureaucracies, staffed largely by white civil servants, and structured like a nineteenth century factory, would prove to be too inflexible to head off a confrontation with this new and militant minority clientele. War on Poverty policymakers, as we've seen, plotted to bypass the recalcitrant service bureaucracies and fund a vast army of smaller, more flexible community-based organizations to deliver services. Thus, in a way, the two "contingent" approaches of market bureaucracies were replicated on the broader public agenda. Hierarchical bureaucratic structures would coexist with smaller, flexible community action agencies.

But this presents us with a problem. There was plenty of evidence that major urban social welfare institutions were not responsive to their new minority clientele.[4] Contingency theory would suggest that hierarchical bureaucracies are particularly unsuited to the tasks of providing education, safety, social services, and financial assistance to a changing and uncertain environment. Inefficient organizations are usually thought to fail and efficient ones persist (cf. Meyer and Zucker 1989, 51–53). Why then did the "inefficient, "cumbersome public bureaucracies expand while the smaller, more flexible community action agencies withered away?

## The Institutionalization of Public Bureaucracies

The reason basically lies in the ongoing process of the institutionalization of public bureaucracies. As public bureaucracies expanded, some sociologists discovered they were developing a life of their own. Philip Selznick (1949, 50) defined this process of institutionalization by describing the natural history of the Tennessee Valley Authority (TVA) as it grew, adapted to its environment, coopted sources of resistance, and displaced many of its original functions. Selznick found the TVA expanded and was strengthened at the expense of performing its official functions. The "grass roots" ideology of the TVA was exposed as a rationalization, camouflaging its principal goal of survival and expansion (60–62). The essence of institutional analysis was to expose the subversion of values by large organizations. "The major message is that the organization has sold out its goals in order to survive or grow" (Perrow 1979, 182).

Organization, Selznick argued (1957, 5), refers to an "expendable tool, a rational instrument to do a job." An institution "is more nearly a natural product of social needs and pressures—a responsive, adaptive organism." As an organization becomes more concerned with a complex environment, it adapts and becomes focused on necessary processes for its own survival. According to Selznick, such a persisting organization loses flexibility as it gains stability.[5]

In the 1930s, social welfare and other government organizations began to develop a life of their own, fighting for their own interests of survival and growth regardless of how their actions impacted clients. Marshall Meyer and Lynne Zucker (1989, 19) provocatively call bureaucracies like social welfare "permanently failing organizations," or organizations that persist despite low profits or poor performance (cf. Hannan and Freeman 1977). They point out that the classical notion that "efficient organizations succeed and inefficient ones fail" is not supported by research (Meyer and Zucker 1989, 74). Three factors explain how some bureaucracies are "permanently failing" while resisting reform.

First, civil servants ("dependent employees") quite logically fight to maintain their jobs. As social welfare and other public bureaucracies have grown, their interests played a major role in determining policy. The bureaucracies' workers were civil servants, protected by New Deal reforms, and basic components of urban Democratic Party machines. Dismantling these bureaucratic dinosaurs, even if an alternative organizational form might benefit clients more, was politically impossible (Piven 1973).

As workers and their unions gained political power, reforms aimed at worker performance, have been strongly resisted. The persistence of an organization despite low levels of performance is the definition of "permanently failing."

> In cases in which the dependent actor's motivation to preserve low-performing organizations is transformed into effective power to do so, permanent failure results.
>
> *(Meyer and Zucker 1989, 45)*

There are few good alternatives in today's tight labor market to the relatively well-paid jobs with benefits within public bureaucracies. Therefore workers and their unions have as their underlying perspective the maintenance of the organization unrelated to issues of what they do or whether their jobs help anyone but themselves.

Secondly, social welfare and other institutions have also persisted because they have successfully spread the "myth" that their bureaucracies are essential and "doing good" (Meyer and Rowan 1981, 305–08; also cf. Wilson 1989, 158–71; Drucker 1985, 179–80). One myth, as we've seen in Chapter Two, is that social workers help families. Social service bureaucrats present themselves as compassionate champions of the needy, regardless of the fact that social workers do little else than investigate poor families and remove their children. The "myth of doing good" is functional to maintain taxpayer support of the bureaucracy as well as internal morale of social workers. Meyer and Rowan (1981, 316) point out that "institutionalized organizations"[6] must not only conform to myths but must also "maintain the appearance that the myths actually work."

When criticism of inefficiency mounts, change can be promised as a means of assuring legitimacy. But this can be dangerous. Meyer and Rowan (1981, 316) point out that by defining an organization's "valid structure as lying in the future" the organization's current structure is made to seem "illegitimate."

Public bureaucracies have resisted change and maintained their hierarchical and non-responsive structure because reform threatens to undermine the myths that define the institution (cf. Perrow 1986, 267). It's simply too risky for bureaucrats to admit that their agency may not be "doing good." The erosion of that myth may lead someone to investigate them or even to propose cutting their budget.

Finally, those who hold political power have vested interests in maintaining institutionalized public bureaucracies. The myths of "doing good" benefit those who are advantaged by existing institutional arrangements. Such myths, Perrow (1986, 269) says, "are not politically neutral; they can be created and propagated by political and economic elites." Those who run public bureaucracies are the ones who have created "rationalized myths" of their own indispensability and importance. While politicians are constantly criticizing "bureaucrats" and "bureaucracy," they also approve millions of dollars of public funds to keep the bureaucracies running. Those appointed to run the agencies are usually politicians themselves or politicians' close friends. The system has worked—for politicians and other elites.

To say public bureaucracies have "institutionalized" and developed interests of their own means that all of these factors interact in putting the bureaucracy's needs ahead of other concerns, including reforms which might benefit the poor. Since the 1930s, social welfare has institutionalized as a a set of hierarchical bureaucracies, expanded, fought off threats to its growth, and resisted reform.

## Social Welfare Expands Its Social Services Component

The social welfare institution would not restrict its role to grudgingly providing welfare checks to growing caseloads. The new War on Poverty community agencies were advocating for poor people and sharply criticizing the inadequacy of social services provided by welfare bureaucracies. Would the new agencies become the principal providers of social services? Institutions, Selznick pointed out, do more than grow, they adapt, develop new components, adopt new tasks, and seek to undermine opposition. The expansion of social services in the 1960s is a prime example of the process of institutionalization: how the welfare bureaucracy adapted, met the threat from community agencies, and developed new social service functions.

The 1960s saw a renewed emphasis on the importance of social services, with substantially increased funding. Much of the new focus was on African American children, who had largely been ignored by social services prior to the 1950s (Pelton 1989, 20). Social welfare bureaucracies at first gobbled up the new funds and expanded social services in the only way they knew how: increasing the number of caseworkers. "Under the 1962 amendments" Gilbert (1977, 630) points out, "federal grants for social services went mainly to pay the salaries of caseworkers."

The politicians' rationale for increased funds was that social workers would be able to trim the rolls of the ineligible (Gilbert 1977, 626; Kamerman and Kahn 1989, 42). Social services became more "universal" and in the first year after eligibility standards were loosened, more than 30% of all service recipients were exempt from a means test. Following President Kennedy's advice, social services would be extended to cover those who "might" become dependent (Axinn and Levin 1982, 243; Katz 1986, 262). In 1967 Congress broadened the use of Title XX funds to include reimbursements to states for almost any service imaginable, including purchase of social services from private agencies (Gilbert 1977, 632).

Rather than "prevent" welfare dependency, these policies helped open the floodgates: from 1962 to 1966, one million additional welfare recipients were added to the rolls nationally (Gilbert 1977, 630). Federal spending on social services literally took off, rising from $194 million in 1963 to $740 million in 1971, then more than doubling in one year to $1.7 billion in 1972 (625).

The highest rate of growth occurred during Nixon's Republican presidency. Derthick's (1975) fascinating account of how social service spending unintendedly went out of control documents how social service dollars were mainly used to prop up local welfare bureaucracies. Derthick points out that the new social service dollars were intended to increase the amount or quality of services for the poor, but instead were seen by the states as an opportunity to pay social worker salaries and administrative costs with federal, not state or local funds. Political pressure led to the rewriting of administrative regulations allowing state and local welfare departments to purchase services from the states. In

effect this change allowed states and local welfare bureaucracies to use the new
federal dollars to pay salaries of caseworkers and cover costs of existing programs, subverting the original intention of the legislation. States saw federal
social service dollars as a horn of plenty, bailing out their own budget problems, rather than providing new services for clients. In Derthick's view the grab
for social service dollars was a prime example of state greed which led to an
inevitable Congressional reaction of capping federal social service dollars.[7]

As the sixties ended, welfare bureaucracies were receiving increased funds,
but the Office of Economic Opportunity and other federal agencies were still
funding an array of community-based programs and alternative services. Both
welfare bureaucracies and the new community agencies claimed to be delivering social services. The social welfare institution developed two strategies to
assert its dominance over federal funding for social services and guarantee survival: specialization and counterattack.

## Response by a Threatened Institution

As federal dollars for social services became more available, welfare bureaucracies adapted to take advantage of it. In 1967, Congress enacted a sweeping new
set of amendments to the Social Security Act which were a mix of punitive regulations and extensions of services. Following a recommendation from the New
York City commissioner of welfare, Congress administratively separated financial assistance from social services (Axinn and Levin 1982, 251–52).

The separation of social services and financial assistance in theory allowed
clients to receive services without fear of losing their AFDC grant. The
National Association of Social Workers and others supported the separation as
a way to dispel reactionary and racist claims that equated being on assistance
or being a minority with being in need of social services. In that way, the separation was progressive and helpful.

On the other hand, specialization had not only divided social welfare
departments, but also began to "divide the client." Social workers concentrated on specialized functions and often lost sight of the overall problems a family
might face: for example, authorizing food stamps might be one social worker's

responsibility, providing vouchers for daycare another's, and investigating claims of neglect or abuse a third. Specialized social workers tended not to inform clients about availability of services or pay sufficient attention to client rights (Sosin 1990, 620; Wilensky and Lebeaux 1965, 252).

As we've seen, the fragmentation of social work into specialties has been carried to the extreme in recent years and was a major target of our Milwaukee social service reform. But from the point of view of welfare bureaucracies, specialization placed the new social service departments in a better position for expansion.

> Proliferation of new structures—subunits and subsubunits within organizational hierarchies—advantages existing units and is therefore one of the principal causes of bureaucratic growth.
>
> *(Meyer and Zucker 1989, 71)*[8]

For social service bureaucracies, their separation from financial assistance allowed them to discover new tasks and compete with the small and less powerful community programs for funds.

Social welfare bureaucracies then counterattacked to end the competition from social service-providing community action agencies. The new community-based agencies, some experts asserted, were "inefficient" and lacked sound accounting principles. One prominent social welfare theorist attacked the new social service programs as unable: 1) to find stable bases of support; 2) to forge links with public bureaucracies; 3) to develop adequate management information systems; and 4) to establish effective staff-client relations (Hasenfeld 1974, 686).

And if the new community programs were inefficient, who should take their place? Why, the bureaucracies' new social service components would do just fine by expanding their role to include the service functions of the community action agencies. The large bureaucracies were poised to take advantage of Washington's disenchantment with the chaos of the sixties "maximum feasible participation" of the War on Poverty.[9]

## Social Service Bureaucracies in Search of a Mission

Welfare bureaucracies expanded social service functions as well as gained control over funds for the new community action programs. As many as 80% of all community action programs were eventually controlled by city hall, school boards, and representatives of other local bureaucracies (Halpern 1991, 352). As the seventies began, funds spent directly for the poor decreased while federal funds for social services, used mainly to pay social worker salaries, increased. Katz reports that welfare bureaucracies took an increasing amount of service dollars for "administration": 30% of all welfare dollars in Indianapolis, 49% in San Francisco, and an astounding 60% in Washington (Katz 1986, 262–63). Local welfare bureaucracies institutionalized on a steady diet of federal funds intended to assist the poor.

The 1970s saw unsuccessful attempts at the federal level to integrate the "fragmented and incoherent" social service system for families (Halpern 1991, 355). But federal dollars steadily withered away from the community action agencies and increasingly were spent on social service programs run by the large public bureaucracies or contracted to established providers (cf. Chapter four). Despite cynical rhetoric about adopting the role of some sort of "community organizer," the newly formed social service components stuck to what they could do best, social work. Federal expenditures paid largely for child care, services to the elderly, and foster care (Kamerman and Kahn 1989, 44), all services easily performed by social workers.

As we've seen in Chapter Two, the child abuse campaigns of the 1970s led to the dominance of child abuse investigations in social work practice. Rather than focus on social services which could help keep families together, public social work began to mean little more than investigations of child abuse and removal of children from their homes. Costs to pay for social workers to supervise out-of-home placements for abused and delinquent children began to gobble up most federal social service dollars.

The 1970s and 1980s would see welfare bureaucracies more powerful than ever but also struggling to adapt to times which were less favorable to welfare spending. Social work, in particular, had to define core tasks which could secure resources necessary to guarantee its survival. The issue of child abuse was tailor-made to help social service bureaucracies expand in more cost conscious times. By the 1980s, social welfare bureaucracies would join the Reagan bandwagon as a means of self preservation. Social welfare reform would mean opposition to budget cuts while at the same time faithfully implementing the mean-spirited policies of the Reagan revolution.

## THE REAGAN REVOLUTION AND BUSINESS REFORM

The 1980s belonged to Ronald Reagan, a decade of the "politics of the rich and poor." Those who had money made even more. Incomes for the top 1% of America's families increased an astonishing 74%. The "average" family in that top 1% lived in modest comfort with an income of over $300,000 per year (Phillips 1990, 14).

For the poor, budget cutting for entitlement programs was on the very top of the public agenda. Conservative theorists, who had the ear of the White House, speculated in print about "scrapping the entire federal welfare and income-support structure for working-aged persons, including AFDC, Medicaid, Food Stamps, Unemployment Insurance, Worker's Compensation, subsidized housing, disability insurance, and the rest" (Murray 1984, 227–28). The Reagan revolution was seen by liberals as the Great Society's Thermidor: a "new class war" on the poor, a "mean season" threatening to undermine the welfare state itself (Block, et al. 1987; Piven and Cloward 1982). In the 1980s the rich got richer while the poor faced an uneasy and uncertain future.

The 1980s opened with alarm over the faltering U.S. economy, particularly the "deindustrialization" of America (Bluestone and Harrison 1982, 3). The U.S. working class, who made social peace with the capitalists during the New Deal, were finding their gains lasted little more than a generation. As heavy industries closed or moved to take advantage of cheap labor, the secondary labor market expanded offering lower wages for workers and increased profits for new service industries. Phillips (1990, 21) noted that "the 'contingent work force'—part-timers and temporaries—had doubled between 1980 and 1987, expanding to include roughly one quarter of the total work force." Bluestone and Harrison (1982, 47) found the eighties began with people having "a deepening sense of insecurity, growing out of the collapse all around them of the traditional economic base of their communities. Their very jobs are being pulled out from under them."

The deindustrialization of America, however, was also part of another trend. Business theorists were reexamining fundamental principles of how market organizations were organized—and reaching some startling conclusions. Business took the lessons of the contingency school to heart and advanced notions of "uncertainly," "ambiguity," and "discontinuity" as it sought to become leaner and more competitive in an expanded world economy (Drucker 1968). New management principles were being developed to liberate a rejuvenated entrepreneurial spirit, down-size, and decentralize corporate America.

Peters and Waterman (1982) summarized the underpinnings of this revolution in their #1 best seller, *In Search of Excellence: Lessons from America's Best-run Companies.* They point out that over the past two decades the prestige of U.S. business had dramatically fallen. Now Japanese and German management were looked to as management leaders and U.S. business had grown flabby. The problem, simply stated, was too many U.S. businesses still clung to the "rational model" of Weber and Frederick Taylor. It was how business was organized that was doing the U.S. in, not Japanese or German competition. The chains of "rationality" had to be broken in order to get U.S. business moving again. Business organizations needed to be radically restructured if they were to survive.

In the past organizations were normally conceptualized with military metaphors, pictured as drab pyramids with those on top passing down orders to underlings scurrying to obey. However a new school of organizational theorists came up with a series of jolting, counter-intuitive images, comparing modern organizations to soccer matches, garbage cans, and holographs.[10] Clark writes the epitaph of the metaphor of organizations as machines.

Whatever alternative metaphors may emerge, the mechanical metaphor is under deadly attack. Its survival rests on rationality, sequence, and calculability. On all of these counts it is fatally flawed.

*(Clark 1985, 71)*[11]

The 1980s would bring radical restructuring to the top of the business agenda. Peters and Waterman found that "excellent companies" based their performance on principles which had little to do with the old rational models. Rather than having clear cut organizational charts and an emphasis on rational decision-making, successful companies sometimes resembled "organized anarchies." Corporations like Japan's Honda made decisions by flexible project teams and had no comprehensible overall chain of command. David Packard of Hewlitt-Packard is quoted as saying bluntly "I've often thought that after you get organized, you ought to throw the chart away" (Peters and Waterman 1982, 50). To make money, Peters and Waterman agreed, American companies had to toss out the old rule book.[12]

Significantly, to gurarantee profitablitiy, Peters and Waterman continued, complex organizations ought to be broken up into decentralized, independently acting components. Rather than CEOs managing huge divisions of a vast hierarchical monolith, they advocated "chunking... breaking things up to facilitate organizational fluidity and to encourage action" (126). It is organizational fluidity and a "bias for action" that best describes excellent companies. Long comprehensive planning processes were eschewed as being a drag on action. It was through action that companies learned best and were able to become "learning organizations," capable of competing in a complex and ever-changing market ( 1982, 110). As Karl Weick pointed out in an oft quoted dictum:

Be willing to leap before you look. If you look before you leap, you may not see anything....

*(Weick 1985, 132)*

Excellent companies learned and adjusted their goals through action, not through drawn out planning processes.[13]

But the point is not to extol the virtues of U.S. business. The more relevant question is how this new organizational theory has been applied to public bureaucracies, particularly the social services. While in the 1980s and 1990s social service bureaucracies were pressured to reform, reform has not meant structural changes of the type some market organizations experienced. Rather reform has been translated into a series of punitive measures toward the very poor and the underclass. Paradoxically, social service bureaucracies have taken adantage of Reagan's conservative rhetoric to stabilize as hierarchical monoliths, add new punitive functions, and resist change. How can we account for these developments?

## Welfare Bureaucracies Help Swing the Reagan Budget Ax

The message of "small is beautiful," swift radical change, and decentralization horrified managers of stodgy public bureaucracies and their unions. However, any potential for structural reform was drowned out in the eighties by the threat of a tidal wave of budget cuts.

Welfare bureaucracies mobilized to defend themselves and maintain their funding amidst a public climate which was hostile to human services. They successfully preserved themselves without making any substantial structural changes. Despite Reagan's image as an opponent of big government, public bureaucracies nationally experienced moderate growth. For example, in Milwaukee County during the years of the Reagan cuts, administrative costs for the Department of Social Services increased by one third, from $32 million in 1982 to more than $45 million in 1988 (Milwaukee County 1962-1988).

The Reagan era stands out in one distinctive way from other eras of reform. The absence of mass pressure in the 1980s transformed "reform" from measures which might benefit the poor to polices geared to step up punishment. There were no demonstrations in the street demanding services and extension of benefits, as there were during the Progressive era, the New Deal, or the War on Poverty. The nihilistic "slow rioting" (Curtis 1985, 8) of violence and crime fueled a liberal/conservative consensus for punitive proposals and demands for massive cutbacks of federal bureaucracies.

Welfare bureaucracies braced for a struggle and looked for ways to safe-guard their interests. The extreme right's proposals were unworkable. Charles Murray's (1984, 227) call for "scrapping the entire federal welfare and income-support structure" was quickly rejected. After all, what would happen to all those federal and local bureaucrats—and voters—whose jobs depended on the "undeserving poor?" Welfare managers began to look for ways their bureau-cracies could accommodate Reagan's anti-poor message.

They found them. Programs which provided benefits for the poor were cut, while the bureaucracy lived on to carry the ax for the Reaganites. The largest budget cuts which were actually carried out under Reagan eliminated or cut back real fiscal benefits, like food stamps and housing subsidies to the poor (Piven and Cloward 1982, 16–19). By reducing grants to the states for benefits for the poor, the net result was the states reduced cash benefits but continued to experience bureaucratic growth. Some programs, like subsidized housing, which benefited the poor (particularly the minority poor) alone, were almost completely eliminated (Slessarev 1988, 360).[14]

Meanwhile millions of Americans, and especially African Americans, Hispanics, and other urban minorities, toiled in low-wage jobs. Already by 1970, 60% of African American workers were employed in the secondary labor market (Gordon, et al. 1982, 210). Poor women had to choose between jobs with no health benefits, which hardly paid enough to support their families, and AFDC, which had health benefits but did not provide even a poverty level income (Edin 1991). As opportunities in "core" industries declined, African Americans became increasingly intolerant of low paying jobs (Gordon, et al. 198, 209; Wilson 1978, 109). AFDC was increasingly seen by African-American women as just "another substitute for low-wage and menial employ-ment" (Wilson 1978, 108). Both resentment among the poor and long term spells of welfare "dependency" increased (Murray and Laren 1986).

It was African American and other minority women whom policy makers had most in mind when they devised schemes like "workfare" in the 1970s, which sought to require work in exchange for welfare benefits. As William Julius Wilson points out, "new-style workfare" was in vogue with both liberal and conservative support in the Reagan years. This "new-style workfare" seems to have had little success in actually getting jobs for the poor (cf. Abraham 1983; Wilson 1987, 162; Piven and Cloward, 1993, 389), but has successfully saved jobs within welfare bureaucracies.

New bureaucrats were added to administer the work programs and monitor clients.

> Even if very few of the programs were directly administered by governmental agencies, greatly increased monitoring capacity would still be required to oversee substantial new expenditures and enforce the (frequently unpleasant) work requirements.
>
> *(Weir et al. 1988, 438–89)*

For example, in Wisconsin, a highly publicized "learnfare" program reduces the AFDC grants of mothers whose children do not attend school. The program was funded from a 5% across the board cut in AFDC benefits for all recipients. But learnfare evaluators discovered that far from reducing costs, 48 additional positions in Milwaukee and Madison alone had been created to administer the program and oversee the reductions in grants for families with truant children. The ratio of state learnfare bureaucrats, overseeing the cuts, was an astounding one bureaucrat to every fifteen sanctioned families (Quinn 1991). While learnfare reduced AFDC grants in 1991 by $1.2 million, it cost $9.9 million annually to administer (*Milwaukee Journal* 1992b). Local taxpayers experienced a fiscal net loss, AFDC mothers and their children received a cut in benefits and further degrading regulation of their lives, and the welfare bureaucracy expanded.

Wisconsin is often cited as a national model of welfare reform. Governor Tommy Thompson's much-ballyhooed proposal to "abolish welfare," echoing the Clinton administration, has gained much publicity. But following the analysis in these pages, the proposal is basically a grandstand play with the governor and the welfare bureaucracy having the most to gain. The governor and other politicians can take credit for "ending" welfare, while doing nothing more than increasing funding for the welfare bureaucracy under a new and more punitive "monitoring" or "workfare" label. Thus the core tasks of the welfare bureaucracy slide ever more dangerously toward punitive, not progressive routines.

Welfare bureaucrats have discovered that punitive policies can be good for their business of adding and safeguarding jobs. One example: investigating welfare fraud. In 1991 Milwaukee County recovered $267,000 in fraudulent welfare payments but spent $1.9 million on salaries for investigators and prosecution of violators. "Is this sufficient to handle all suspected fraud? No!" Milwaukee County Human Service Director Tom Brophy thundered to a legislative panel. More fraud investigators were needed. The absurdity of paying nearly $2 million to recover $267,000 was not mentioned in the newspaper article reporting Brophy's testimony *(Milwaukee Journal* 1992a). In fact to halt the investigations, no matter how unsuccessful they had proved to be, would eliminate federal dollars and force lay-offs. Of the $1.9 million spent by Milwaukee County on fraud investigations, over $1.4 million were federal funds.[15] Many punitive programs were adopted by welfare bureaucracies simply because federal money for those programs was available.

It would be a mistake to see the commitment of most welfare bureaucrats to punitive policies as differing fundamentally from their past support for expanding supportive programs. Some of the "human service" bureaucrats who applied for workfare money were the same officials who had taken federal funds in the past to extend benefits. Both supportive and punitive programs are normally looked at through the same amoral lens of "how can more resources be captured," not from a perspective of how programs might benefit the poor. The fundamental interest of local bureaucracies is survival, as Selznick long ago explained. Public bureaucracies

> are essentially neutral, aligned with neither class nor party, except as such alignments serve jurisdictional claims or determine the availability of necessary resources.
>
> *(Cloward and Piven 1972, 208)*

Rather than restructure, as the new organizational theories suggest, to benefit their "customers," welfare bureaucracies looked for ways to maintain themselves as ponderous hierarchies and to be useful to the new administration. Reagan's pious demands to trim the bureaucracy had to be treated respectfully, but in the final analysis, ruled out as impractical. After all, who was better suited to carry out the new punitive polices than the bureaucracy itself? As a new round of "welfare reform" begins with the Gingrich-led Congress, welfare bureaucracies have gained valuable experience in making themselves useful in an era of punishment.[16]

## The New Authoritarianism

This pattern of bureaucratic response to the Reagan era was a bit different than what many had expected. For example, Piven and Cloward (1987) predicted the Reagan cuts would be defeated by a new protest movement joined by the self-interest of the bureaucracy. In their first book, *Regulating the Poor* (1971, 8), Piven and Cloward had conceptualized social welfare as a social control institution which systematically cut benefits whenever it was expedient and restored them as a response to protest. This cyclical pattern of "cuts in welfare followed by protest followed by the restoration of cuts" was historically traced from the origins of social welfare in the "mass disturbances that erupted during the long transition from feudalism to capitalism beginning in the sixteenth century" to the U.S. welfare rights protests of the 1960s.

But the welfare institution became transformed in their later work and seemed to reappear as a "progressive" force, if only out of self-interest. Beginning with the New Deal, a bureaucracy had formed which would oppose cuts to human services which might threaten bureaucratic jobs.

> The changes in American society that gave rise to this development lead us to the conclusion that the cyclical pattern of providing subsistence resources by the state has been replaced by a variety of permanent income-maintenance entitlements....*Regulating the Poor* represents a better characterization of the past than a prediction of the future.
>
> *(Piven and Cloward 1982, xi)*

A "safety net" had been created and social welfare bureaucracies had been "democratized" by their very jobs of giving benefits to the poor (1982,

119–21). Piven and Cloward concluded Reagan's assault on the welfare state must fail since protest would explode (139) and the bureaucracy itself would resist its own demise (143–44). Presumably, for Piven and Cloward, the social control functions of public welfare had at least been attenuated by permanent entitlement programs.

But while all entitlements were not slashed, financial support for the poor is still basically miserly, seldom lifting welfare recipients out of poverty. As Piven and Cloward (1987, 85) themselves note: "being a recipient of means-tested programs… is a rotten existence." Permanently maintaining a huge surplus population on a less than poverty level income is far from humanitarian and comes rather close to anyone's definition of "social control."

A mass movement to protest the cuts failed to materialize. Therefore public pressure played little role in the political drama during Reagan-Bush Congressional budget hearings. Public bureaucracies successfully resisted cuts by allying their raw political power to the new conservatives, with their mass right wing constituency. Rather than build broad opposition to Reagan on the basis of support for "jobs or income" and delivering quality human services, public bureaucracies adopted much of the Reagan "anti-poor" rhetoric by incorporating punitive polices, like workfare, into bureaucratic routines. The Clinton rhetoric about "ending welfare" played into the hands of those who wanted to cut back or eliminate support for the poor and fueled a new round of attacks on the poor. Thus Piven and Cloward's (1993, 343) cycle continues with more rituals of punishment.

Weir et al. (1988) point out that a "new authoritarianism" uniting liberals and conservatives has emerged. Conservatives see workfare and similar policies as a means to force welfare mothers off the dole and into the labor market at any wage. Some liberals also support these reactionary programs by appealing to themes of "economic independence and mutual obligation" by the poor (439). While some workfare programs provide generous benefits like child care, they also purport to decrease taxes of the middle class at the expense of the poor. The broad consensus for workfare programs emphasizes the bipartisan tilt of present policy toward punitiveness.

Police, prisons, and other criminal justice bureaucracies have also experienced accelerated growth in the eighties and nineties as they adapt to an anti-poor climate. As Gary Orfield laments,

> Even in minority led cities, where more support for social service ben-
> eficiaries might be expected, it often seems as if the only strong
> demand in times of severe cutbacks is for a larger police force.
>
> *(Orfield 1991, 517)*[17]

While defense spending is being cut back, the "peace dividend" has been
lapped up by new prisons, vast expenditures on the drug war, and a bonanza of
funds for law enforcement. This "new authoritarianism" seems to enjoy broad
based support among the U.S. electorate, which contains comparatively few of
the lower classes (Piven and Cloward 1988). To fight this new war at home,
public bureaucracies are stressing punitive functions and joining the police as
frontline warriors against the poor.

As Janowitz wrote in 1976:

> The problem is whether authoritarian solutions can be avoided—for
> even a limited increase in authoritarian sanctions would destroy the
> moral basis and the goals of the welfare state.
>
> *(Janowitz 1976, 5)*

Since that time, "authoritarian sanctions" have become a central mission of
social welfare and other public bureaucracies.

## CONCLUSION: SOCIAL SERVICE BUREAUCRACIES IN NEED OF REFORM

This is the broader, bureaucratic context of the punitive state of social services
described in chapters two through four. The Milwaukee County Department
of Social Services is a typical example of how social services have adapted to a
punitive climate and resisted reform. Like "workfare," a preoccupation with
investigating the poor for child abuse snugly fits into the ethos of the age. Some
conservatives stress adoptions and are critical of those who would encourage

welfare bureaucracies to remove more children from their homes (Murray 1994, 416). However, this view is in the minority among the New Right. Knowing where their bread is buttered, welfare bureaucracies have milked the issue of child abuse as a rationale for expansion.

Rather than preserving families, the social service bureaucracy has chosen to preserve itself. It has survived by defining its "core tasks" as child removal and foster care rather than providing services to the poor. The structure of the bureaucracy has been fragmented in such a manner as to facilitate social work routines dominated by paperwork and carrying out court orders. Integrated or decentralized organizational structures, as suggested by the new organizational theories, have been staunchly opposed by top bureaucrats. Services have not been purchased from agencies located in poor neighborhoods, where they could be closer to their clients and more effectively delivered. Rather, lucrative contracts have largely gone to established private agencies located outside central cities whose self interests lie with maintaining the present system. Clients and residents of underclass neighborhoods have had few accessible services and no input into decisions which affect them.

The principles of the new organizational theories—a "bias for action," "small is beautiful," and "staying close to the consumer"—were all but ignored by public bureaucracies in the Reagan years. Social welfare bureaucrats grabbed what dollars they could as they maintained their bureaucracies as inflexible hierarchies. These structures were not functional for preserving families but were well suited to carry out specialized court related tasks to punish the "undeserving poor."

Reforming social service bureaucracies is more than replacing a top bureaucrat or electing a new regime. We've seen that these bureaucracies are not "expendable rational tools" of whoever is in charge, but institutionalized organisms with a life of their own. If reform in the past has meant little more than adding resources to hungry bureaucracies—regardless of whether the resources help or punish the poor—what are the characteristics of real reform? How much can be accomplished in this era of punishment, especially if protest in the streets fails to materialize? It's time to return to Milwaukee and finish the tale of the Youth Initiative.

# PART III

## THE DIRECTION AND MISDIRECTION OF REFORM

# 7

# WHAT IS REAL REFORM?

## Six Hundred Seventy-Five Easy Answers

We started out with so much hope. We began our administration of the Department of Health and Human Services with an unmistakable "mandate for change." The old county executive, who had been in charge for the last twelve years, had stifled any creative urges, especially within social services. Public policy had amounted to little more than blaming the state legislature for not delivering enough money to pay for rising costs.

David Schulz, the new county executive, had ridden the winds of change to an upset election. As past Parks Director, Schulz had been the consummate showman. The 350 pound Schulz had been photographed in bright colored jams going down a water slide in one of his many successful publicity campaigns for the park system. He capitalized on his image as an innovative thinker and problem solver to an electorate that was tired of the old regime and their tired old non-solutions.

Schulz, in a controversial move, hired my boss, Howard Fuller, to "make a difference" to Milwaukee County's young people. We were told to get beyond the scapegoating of the past and figure out innovative ways to improve the delivery of services for youth. Since the Milwaukee School Board had also just appointed a bright and creative superintendent and city voters had just elected a shrewd new mayor, Fuller and I asserted to all who would listen that a "window of opportunity" existed to bring fundamental change.

But the window started to slide shut almost before it opened. Schulz was not exactly crazy about our Youth Initiative, especially when he figured out it wasn't a "water slide": that is, reform isn't always a press event. As the Schulz administration made one blunder after another, the social service bureaucracy, who had opposed Schulz's election, realized they only had to wait four years and Schulz would be gone and Fuller with him. The tactics of the management team we inherited were to go slow, slower, and slowest.

Our incipient reforms were going nowhere. In October of 1988 the Youth Initiative had declared "a state of emergency" existed in Child Protective Services (CPS). Six months later I barged into Fuller's office and challenged him to tell me that things were any better. "If there was an emergency last fall," I asked passionately, "can you tell me there's not an emergency today?" Fuller hurriedly ordered a six week "emergency plan" to fix some of the most glaring problems and demanded the bureaucrats come up with some long term solutions. But everything we tried to do encountered one insurmountable obstacle after another. Fuller ordered change and nothing happened. He removed the head of CPS, but her replacement was equally overwhelmed. The snickers started up among staff.

The old, easy answers ominously began to resurface. Social service managers asserted the real problem was resources. They said we just didn't have enough staff to do the things we were supposed to do, much less change anything. I admit I was bamboozled over what to do next. Then, as nothing appeared to be getting any better no matter what we did, I asked myself the heretical question: "Do we really need more workers?" On the face of it the question was absurd. Child abuse referrals were skyrocketing and everyone told me we just didn't have enough intake workers to investigate each referral. But, still, I decided to see for myself.

Early one day I strolled over to offices housing Child Protective workers. Walking through the area, I physically counted the noses of intake workers available that day for assignment. Out of forty-one allocated intake worker positions, I could locate only fifteen noses: fifteen of forty-one social workers who were present and could respond to a referral. The next day there were even fewer noses—thirteen. No wonder they were overworked! If nearly all of the forty-one had been present, intake caseloads would easily have been within Child Welfare League standards. Where were the other workers?

I found out. Some workers were out on sick leave for physical or psychological reasons. A few were on vacation. Three positions were occupied by full-time union staffers who did no social work. Several social workers were in court and would be there all day. The largest number of vacant positions were intake workers who had transferred. Civil service rules and the union contract allowed them to leave while their intake position remained unfilled. (Imagine a teacher leaving the classroom for another job, and no substitute showing up for six months!) Unfilled positions benefited top managers since they saved money, which helped keep the agency within County spending limits. Working conditions at Child Protective were so terrible that few new staff stayed past their six month probation period. No one in CPS worked intensively with families to keep them together. It was all court, court, court; paperwork, paperwork, paperwork. No wonder few workers wanted to stay. Would you?

The most serious problems, it became clear to me, were not caused by a shortage of staff. We couldn't even get the ones we had on the job. More staff under the same conditions would do little to alleviate stress, but would likely burn out the new staff and the revolving door would continue. Worse, to do more investigations with no services would be a bizarre way of "helping" families.

But the bureaucrats brilliantly offered up their own solution. They told the county executive all we needed was 675 new social work positions to fix everything that was wrong. Yes, you read right—six hundred-seventy five new positions! In case you had any doubts, the bureaucrats also neglected to suggest a single change that might be needed in how the system could be run. With much fanfare, Schulz, posing as the champion of social services, included a request for 675 more social workers in his proposed 1990 budget.

Our much ballyhooed "emergency plan" to reform Child Protective Services faded away as Fuller dutifully campaigned for more staff. After political reality set in, the County Board reduced the 675 requested positions to 13 new budgeted slots (which we weren't allowed to fill until mid-year). Our claim that the Youth Initiative would "fundamentally reorient" social services began to sound more and more like business as usual. "Reform," I concluded, certainly meant different things to different people.

What does it mean to "fundamentally reorient" social services for youth? We've seen how reform has historically meant the "easy answers" of adding more resources and adapting to the prevailing ideology of the times. This chapter will discuss the two basic elements of "real" bureaucractic reform: altering core tasks of line staff and changing the relationship between bureaucracies and client neighborhoods. I'll use lessons from restructuring modern business as a guide to how social service bureaucracies could be reformed in a way to benefit poor families.

But let me warn the reader before I begin. The "solutions" presented here are not glitzy reforms which will easily win support from adoring liberals or cost-conscious conservatives. Nor are they drastic measures which look good on paper but will never be accomplished. The changes I advocate do not rely on a massive influx of new resources from Washington, though additional resources are necessary if we are to provide more than token support for poor families. To be sure, the reforms detailed here are not an overall solution to the problems of poverty and the underclass.

What I propose are prosaic and concrete measures that reformers at the local level can adopt today. These measures are meant to do no more than incrementally tilt social service bureaucracies away from their current punitive orientation. The set of reforms I advocate would build within public social service agencies a new unit structure for social workers. These new units would begin to shift the daily routines of social workers from child removal to family preservation. These same reforms would also begin to organizationally link departments of social services to client neighborhoods. While this may sound simple, anyone who has ever tried to reform the structure of a bureaucracy knows how hard any change is to accomplish.

## ALTERING CORE TASKS

"Government agencies change all the time," James Q. Wilson (1989, 225) points out, "but the most common changes are add-ons...Real innovations are those that alter core tasks." A "fundamental reorientation" for social services means first to change what social workers do: to get them away from being stuck in the courts and pulling children from their homes and back to a focus on social work with troubled families. Real reform in welfare bureaucracies means changing what line staff do with their clients, not just having more social workers doing more of the same old thing.[1]

Note that it is core tasks that are the tangible targets of change, not goals. Social welfare and other public bureaucracies always have had diffuse and contradictory goals, reflecting various stakeholders (Wilson 1989, 26). Debating broad new "mission statements," as some advocate (e.g. Halpern 1991, 362), is part of the broader ideological debate, but by itself cannot produce change. Both punitive and supportive goals coexist in the welfare institution's political environment. Hardened liberal and conservative camps and their separate agendas are unlikely to dissolve soon and bureaucrats must take both camps into account when preparing budgets for legislative approval. Furious debates on mission statements usually don't end up meaning a "hill of beans" for what social workers really do. While not shrinking from the debate on the lofty goals of the social services, our reform agenda subversively aimed quite a bit lower: at reorganizing what social workers do everyday.[2]

Practically speaking, our strategy for in-house reforms was to set up integrated units, where workers would perform all child welfare and probation functions, including new "family preservation" services. Most workers would be generalists, not fixed on performing a single task, like investigation or foster care. All intake, ongoing, foster care and specialty services were to be included in each unit of twelve to fifteen people. These new units would also have special linkages to their clients' financial assistance workers. A social worker would stay with a family from intake until discharge, minimizing disruptive transfers. Social workers were more easily able to look at a troubled family as a whole, not just as a "case" of abuse, a "case" of someone who needs monitoring in drug treatment, or a "case" in court where children are to be put in foster care. At the broadest level, our reforms aimed to change the way social workers think about clients.

Our proposed changes met resistance from every level, so we started with two units to pilot the concept. The new units were intended to be teams, not miniature hierarchies. The Miller Brewing Company provided team building training based in part on getting social workers to see troubled families as "consumers," not just as "clients" (Osborne and Gaebler 1992, 166–194). The notion that child protective clients could be seen as consumers of services began to chip away at the standard social work construction of clients as uncaring abusive parents with the social workers as policemen or policewomen, but without a gun.[3]

The concept of a team approach was also designed to combat the isolation and defensiveness social workers feel in relations with clients. Lipsky (1980, 208) points out that when social workers have group rather than individual caseloads—like our new units—accountablity to both one another and to clients is enhanced. Team members consult with one another, share responsibility for decisions, and ideally are more open to client input. Social work routines can therefore be more receptive to family needs. Our reforms attempted to instill a culture of supportive services in a civil service bureaucracy which has long been conditioned to see child investigation and removal as their prime duty.

But old ways died hard. For example, a minor firestorm was set off in one of the pilot units when a family walked into our neighborhood outstation and asked the pilot unit for help. This is most unusual, since social workers today are almost always sent out only to investigate official complaints, called "referrals," by relatives, teachers, or neighbors. Their appeal should have been welcomed as a sign the unit was being seen by the community as a source of support, not just as "child snatchers." But the supervisor refused to assign a worker to the case since there was no child abuse "referral." The "walk-in" was turned away, using the bureaucratic excuse that DSS social workers are already over-burdened with mandatory referrals. This family's problems simply lacked relevance to a system which only functions when a "referral" prompts an "investigation." The new units were designed to serve voluntary, not just "non-voluntary" clients, but changing the culture of social work takes time.

On the more mundane level, the team-based system had built-in incentives for social workers to work with families, not focus on narrow bureaucratic problems or transfer them when they become troublesome. The old system actually encouraged workers to "dump" difficult cases by transferring them to another unit, making them someone else's problem. In the new system, there was no place to "dump" a problem family, since the family remains within the unit no matter what happens. If worker A was not the family's worker, than co-worker B would be. Co-worker B would not take kindly to having a problem family "dumped" by worker A with whom he or she shared an office. Thus the structural incentive for social workers was to get the family functioning and keep it out of the system entirely.

## The Importance of Organizational Structure

The key element in altering core tasks is changing the structure of work itself. Recall from Chapter Three how the fragmented structure of social services is more functional for the courts than for families. The maze of specialized tasks facilitates looking at the client as no more than the sum of bureaucratically relevant criteria and not as a real person who is part of a real family. This means social workers today are mainly concerned with whether or not to remove children and how to supervise court orders (cf. Galper 1975, 92). To tilt the emphasis in social services away from punishment and back toward services, this fragmented bureaucratic edifice must be obliterated.

Creating new unit structures was meant to be a change that would be difficult to undo. A policy can be quickly thrown away by a new administrator. But to change the organizational structure of social services takes a major effort. The power of routine is on the side of the existing structure. Our organizational changes were meant to be what we would leave behind and our guarantee that "business as usual" could not easily reemerge when we left. There is strong support from the organizational literature for this position. Perrow points out that other solutions to bureaucratic problems have not been successful.

> If we cannot solve our problems through good human relations or through good leadership, what are we then left with? The literature suggests that changing the structures of organizations might be the most effective and certainly the quickest and cheapest method.
>
> *(Perrow 1978, 322)*

Kanter (1983) points out that ineffective organizations are marked by a "segmentalist approach" which assumes that problems can be solved when they are carved into pieces and the pieces assigned to specialists who work in isolation. She opposes such dinosaur-like thinking with an "integrative approach" where people "aggregate subproblems into larger problems, so as to re-create a unity that provides more insight into required action." Integrative thinking, she found, was more prevalent in organizations which did away with segmented structures (28–29). Social service bureaucracies are the quintessential example of the segmentalist approach.

Collegial models, like the one we proposed in Milwaukee, have been supported by experts throughout the years, but seldom adopted (e.g., Wilensky and Lebeaux 1965, 316; Sosin 1990, 620; Morgan 1986, 101). In the sixties, Sjoberg pointed out:

> The collegial organization...stresses, for example...the need for generalists rather than specialists. The generalist, unencumbered by highly formalized rules, can view clients in holistic terms and thus examine weaknesses relative to their strengths.
>
> *(Sjoberg et al. 1966, 333)*

Adopting Kanter's "integrative" approach, we designed our pilot units to be small flexible organizations with everyone trained to do every other job. This "redundancy" is diametrically opposed to the specialization which dominates contemporary social services. The specialized bureaucracy sees redundancy or duplication as a prime sin and strives to eliminate it (Wilson 1989, 274). But redundant functions can have important benefits, especially by making "the system more effective because when one component of the system fails, the entire system does not fail" (Streeter 1992, 98).

If clients were predictable and their problems could be listed and treated routinely, the current fragmented social service bureaucracy might be more efficient in "processing" more cases. A segmented bureaucracy is best suited to apply guidelines on when to remove children and when to drag them into court. However, if the unit is more concerned with meeting the complex needs of a troubled family—with removal being only one option—a more flexible organizational form is required.

The norm in social services is confronting unique client problems, with worker absences and transfers, and making decisions in the face of uncertainty (Meyers 1993). The business literature stresses this situation requires decentralized organization based on redundant functions, not specialized parts. For example, many private firms have placed their entire production process in teams of 14–18 workers. Such teams often "can develop a remarkable ability to find novel and increasingly progressive solutions to complex problems" (Morgan 1986, 103–04). An innovating organization, Kanter (1983, 179) showed, "begins to substitute a control system based on debate among peers for one based on top-down authority."

But will organizational changes alone "fix" what's wrong with the social services? No. In Selznick's (1957) terms, institutionalization in social services has been accompanied by an infusion of values (16–17) where social workers have stressed "child protection," that is, removal and foster care, over "family preservation" and kinship networks. The Youth Initiative hoped to "institutionalize" changes which would reduce fragmentation and legalization, providing a new structural framework for values which stressed supportive services. Those supportive services depended on the introduction of family preservation practices within each unit.

## Family Preservation Services as Structural Change

I visited the Behavioral Science Institute's Homebuilders program in the Bronx in the winter of 1989 and quickly became a supporter of their family preservation philosophy and techniques. Homebuilders, a nationwide agency specializing in intensive in-home services, is the leading advocate of "family preservation" practices. Briefly, family preservation incorporates

> a family-centered approach to assessment and treatment; use of the home as the primary delivery and treatment setting; cultivation of an intense and egalitarian professional-client communication; a deliberate limitation in the duration of the intervention; and finally, an

expressly broad, flexible, and generalist response to the multiple problems presented by the families served.

*(Nelson 1991, 217)*

What is unique about family preservation is that social workers go out into the homes of families in extreme distress and assess them for whatever problems families believe they have, not just those which prompted the attention of the bureaucracy. Staff works intensively over no more than six weeks to get the family back on its feet. It provides "soft" services like conflict mediation, counseling, and brief family therapy, as well as "hard" services like emergency payment of rent or purchases of appliances or clothes. The family preservation worker links the family to other ongoing support systems and does not prolong the often dependent social worker/client relationship. The philosophic approach is empowerment, based on social learning theory (Bandura 1977), of getting clients to identify their own needs and helping them to develop the capacity to solve those and similar problems. Finally, family preservation is inexpensive, costing only six weeks of staff time rather than expensive out-of-home placement costs (at times $40,000 or more per year).

Family preservation does not mean leaving children in danger. Where there is "imminent risk" to the welfare of a child, family preservation obviously calls for the child's removal. But the practice of family preservation is more like the ideal practice of social work before that profession became captured by child abuse investigations and enmeshed in the courts (Edna McConnell Clark Foundation 1990; Nelson, et al. 1990). Family preservation directs social workers to do what they can to preserve most families as the best means to "save" the child.

We did not conceive of family preservation as an "add-on" service to already overburdened social workers. Routines of working with families who could be "preserved" were intended to replace routines of taking that same family to court. In other words, instead of spending time sitting in court or doing paperwork, some social workers would spend that time working with troubled families.

We held a conference in 1990 to introduce family preservation to local policy makers. We received a $1 million dollar five-year grant from the Philip Morris Companies to develop innovative family preservation services in collaboration with the Milwaukee Public Schools. We contracted with an African American and an Hispanic agency to become trained in family preservation practices and deliver services to our clients. We disbanded one poorly functioning "family-service" unit within the Department of Social Services and reconstituted it as a Homebuilders-style family preservation unit.

I insisted each new pilot unit have family preservation staff within it, a point which was actively resisted by the bureaucrats and became the arena of a furious struggle. This change was perceived by top social service managers as a major threat to business as usual. Changes are almost always strongly resisted, Wilson (1989, 223) stresses, when they "alter tasks." Resistance sharpens as the "generality or depth" of a change increases (Patti 1974, 370). The bureaucrats said family preservation staff in the units was the kind of change that would be nice if we had enough staff, but had to wait until then. Right. If you believe that "grand day" would ever have come, I have a bloated bureaucracy or two I'd like to sell you.

This struggle was the only time in the nearly three years I spent at the department where I threatened to resign if a change was not made. The following field note gives a good flavor of the stress of reform.

> Boy, was this a depressing day. Fuller told (Department of Social Services Director) Brophy that Brophy should decide whether to do family preservation within the pilots. Brophy said he would not okay it. To not do family preservation...means to undermine the pilots. The pilots were always intended to be self-contained and an innovative experiment. Family preservation was the tool these units needed to work with families, not just process them for court....

> The main question is, what now? I think a battle has to be fought on the family preservation issue within the pilots. One first step has to be to lay it out clearly to Fuller: his decision means defeat....I need to see it from his perspective, but I need to make my case for action—that

Fuller can force change if he only has the will. I don't think I'll succeed, but I have to try.

*Field Notes, September 30, 1990*

Well I was wrong. When faced with my ultimatum, Fuller relented and "convinced" Brophy to okay family preservation workers within the pilots. The bureaucracy's recalcitrance underscored the significance of the battle.

It must be stressed that the most important reform was not family preservation, per se. Most social service departments have separate "family preservation" units to which child abuse investigators refer cases. Rather, the introduction of family preservation as the centerpiece of integrated child welfare units sets a structural foundation for altering the core tasks of social workers. Family preservation within each unit was the key element in our reform precisely because it organized the unit around services, not investigation or foster care. It provided some services to a family in a system where punitive routines had dominated.

The bureaucrats had good reason to resist so strongly. This reform threatened to undermine the basic premises of contemporary social services. Nelson puts it best when he says that family preservation

> is a basic challenge to the categorical character of human service funding and delivery. Family preservation works, in some measure, because its workers assume responsibility for the broad range of problems that may threaten family capacity, and because they have the training and resources to respond to multiple and often changing needs...In their most extreme formulation, the implications of family preservation practices probably point to a thoroughly reorganized service system.
>
> *(Nelson 1991, 217)*

The introduction of family preservation staff and philosophy into the pilot units is subversive to the punitive nature of today's social service bureaucracies. Milwaukee bureaucrats resisted our proposed changes so strongly for two reasons: 1) some were opposed to deemphasizing the present core tasks of child removal or they believed that most troubled families could not be "preserved," and 2) they knew that centering units on services would fundamentally change familiar routines.

In many ways, the heated debate over the effectiveness of family preservation is irrelevant (Wald 1988 ; Yuan and Rivest 1990; Bath and Haapla 1994). The fact is that family preservation adds services to a nearly service-less system. Many families may respond positively to family preservation workers because they have never received any services from the system at all. Having family preservation services in their arsenal allowed the new pilot units to be seen by clients as doing something besides child-snatching. It has helped instill a culture of service back into the social services and gain a measure of confidence from clients.

It's important to remember that family preservation does not mean saving every family, or refusing to remove children who are in danger. There are still many parents who are a threat to their children's welfare. Rather, the incorporation of family preservation into unit routines is the key factor in tilting social workers' core tasks back toward supportive services. Our reforms sought to restore the balance to a child welfare system that has become one-sidedly dominated by investigation and foster care.

Family preservation, however, even within each unit, is necessary but not sufficient. To complete our vision of reform, the new supportive child welfare units had to become more accountable to strengthened client neighborhoods.

## EMPOWERING POOR NEIGHBORHOODS

Social work has had a long history of neighborhood-based service (Halpern 1991). In the decades since the sixties the imperatives of bureaucratization and specialization and its focus on child abuse and the courts drove public social services away from decentralization. Real reform means not only altering core tasks of social workers, but also changing the sour and exploitative relationship between social service bureaucracies and neighborhoods where their clients are clustered (Schorr 1988).

Neighborhood-based reform has two aspects. First, it means social service bureaucracies need to be made more sensitive to the real needs of clients and poor neighboroods. Community organization and decentralization needs to be once more embraced by social work. Second, the bureaucracy itself cannot be the final arbiter of community needs. It cannot continue to dole out resources in a manner which ignores the need to rebuild devastated communities. As we saw in Chapter Four, social service bureaucracies have actually contributed to the deterioration of poor communities.

Our basic strategy was reminiscent of the strategy of the War on Poverty to overcome bureaucratic barriers, increase access, and develop a sense of community.[4] The central focus of our reforms was to strengthen the social service institutions within poor neighborhoods (Wilson 1987). Our Youth Initiative empowered client neighborhoods by: 1) decentralizing the basic operation of the bureaucracy, making it more neighborhood-based and accountable, and 2) investing more purchase of service dollars into neighborhood-based agencies by creating area councils to develop neighborhood service delivery plans.

## Decentralized Pilot Units

Our two pilot units had geographically organized caseloads; that is, only cases from our two targeted zip codes would be referred to the unit. Each unit was outstationed in buildings located in the neighborhoods they served and housed alongside financial assistance workers. Though probation officers were intended to be part of the units from the start, that change was vetoed by top managers. Other agencies, including job training and public health services, were also located at the site, helping to make our units part of a "one-stop-shop," multi-service concept. The practice of these units was similar to the "patch" approach in the United Kingdom (Adams and Krauth 1994). Two neighborhood coordinators were hired whose job was to organize neighborhood councils of residents and community-based providers to which the pilot units would be accountable.

Civil service and union regulations made it difficult to fill the units with dedicated staff. Most social workers were skeptical of the Youth Initiative, but there was a group of mainly African American workers willing to risk the ire of the old management team and try experimental services. We tried to discourage workers who were not in sympathy with our community orientation from bidding into the units. This led to some touchy situations.

For example, one veteran social worker, after listening to us repeatedly praising the virtues of serving the community, told us bluntly, "I don't work for the community. I work for the county." That summed up the attitudes of many workers who saw the potential of being "outstationed" as essentially a softer, less carefully supervised job. Despite our most discouraging efforts, this worker signed up for the pilots, but fortunately retired soon after. We succeeded in getting other less committed social workers not to transfer in. About half of the workers in our pilot units were new hires and our south side pilot had both Spanish- and Hmong-speaking staff.[5]

We encouraged other public agencies to similarly reorganize their caseloads based on zip code location of their clients. The city health department and a few others followed our lead. We met regularly with the Milwaukee Public Schools to develop relationships at all levels. A unique collaboration with several schools, funded by a grant from the Philip Morris Companies, produced better and more coordinated services between our department and several schools. Unquestionably, the pilot staff had better and more extensive relationships with community agencies and area schools than did other units.

It was hoped that outstationed social workers, freed from the isolated and cynical bureaucratic chatter in a large office building, might be more open to hear pained neighborhood voices.

> Decentralized units would be far more likely to develop routines consistent with responsive and efficient client treatment than authorities removed from the scene.
>
> *(Lipsky 1980, 207)*

In my field notes, I told myself our reforms would make the department "more vulnerable" to pressure from clients and community organizations. While there was little pressure from the community at that time, decentralized units could be the first to respond to protest and community sentiments. Along with the neighborhood coordinators, the pilots were symbols of a new community-based approach which was intended to put the department in a position where it could better respond to community needs. The new units, organized around services for families and not "child-snatching," would strengthen the social welfare institution within the community. *The Youth Initiative Institutional Impact Evaluation* summed up:

> In a physical sense at the very least they (the pilots) can be seen as a sign of DSS meeting the community half-way and on its own territory.
>
> *(Devitt 1992, 23)*

But even the pilots, by themselves, weren't enough. To change the relationship between our department and poor neighborhoods we needed community participation. More importantly, that participation needed to lead to real accountability and a redirection of money into those neighborhoods.

## Neighborhood Councils and Their Service Delivery Plans

One of our first Youth Initiative actions was to create neighborhood councils, which were planning bodies made up of residents and providers located in the targeted zip codes. The councils turned out to be actually dominated by community-based providers with some resident, but unfortunately with no client, involvement (Devitt 1992, 19–20). We designed the councils to be broadly-based neighborhood planning bodies. An early memo laid out our perspective:

> 1. What are the coordinating councils' functions?
>
> We still think they are fundamentally planning bodies, not sixties style community action agencies. We see them to be similar to New York City's old Community Planning Boards. The immediate functions of the councils are: 1) Collect the inventory of services of each institution, provider, and agency in the target areas; 2) Utilizing the inventory and the needs assessment, develop a plan for a neighborhood based service delivery system.
>
> *Undated 1989 Memo*

Two councils were set up in our targeted zip codes and we hired neighborhood coordinators to staff them. Funding for two coordinators was the only new request for positions for the Youth Initiative we ever made in the Department of Social Services (DSS) budget. The councils gave input to DSS policies and practices that concerned people in their zip codes. One bureaucrat, sympathetic to our reforms, told evaluators:

> From my perspective, probably the clearest thing that I see with the Youth Initiative was...the outgrowth of the councils...because certainly the relationship between the Department...and the community was almost nonexistent prior to that....I do think the councils are critical because now at least people have access to what kind of programs ought to come into their area, how they ought to be funded.
>
> *(Devitt 1992, 17–18)*

Through monthly council meetings, pilot social workers could get a feel for the broader community and listen to neighborhood concerns. Reviews of proposals which affected residents of the zip code, which before had been routinely done by in-house bureaucrats, now were conducted by bureaucrats and neighborhood persons recommended by the councils. One council member said proudly:

> It's beautiful because people come back, like a panel that was reviewing proposals, and they get to see from the inside, to be there...to actually make a decision in terms of which program [is]...the best...and to feel that they have the power of decision-making...like, "Boy I actually can do something about it." When you're always on the outside, you think that is the way it is and that's the way it's going to be and you have no way to change things. When you are inside it, then you start seeing it differently. And that's what's happening right now with our councils.
>
> *(Devitt 1992, 18)*

The most important task of the councils was the development of a neighborhood service delivery plan. Research we commissioned into the two targeted neighborhoods produced a detailed report on neighborhood needs (Moore and Edari 1990b). That research was discussed by the fledgling councils and with great effort transformed into concrete proposals for service delivery changes and new programs for the two zip codes. I prodded the councils in December 1989 to begin meeting on the 1991 budget. The councils were a bit perturbed that I insisted on time-consuming meetings near the holidays to distill proposals for a budget that was more than a year away. At the time they didn't have a clue about how our budget process worked, with proposals for the next year's budget due in the Director's office in February. The budget, more than any other document, is a description of the agency (Downs 1967, 249) and to change the agency requires changing the budget.

Recalling my radical past, I decided to produce an agitational and informational pamphlet to explain the social service budget process and why the councils had to structure their activities around it. I flooded the councils with speakers and information on the budget. The first service delivery plans produced two important proposals. Both councils demanded DSS set up the neighborhood pilot units, which were then bureaucratically stalled. Second, each council developed proposals for programs they felt would best benefit their neighborhood. These programs—one an African American run community-based drug treatment program and the other a family preservation program for Latinos—would be run by agencies physically located in the neighborhood.

As the process unfolded, I didn't have a plan for how to get the money to fund the programs. Still, momentum was being created which hopefully would produce something. Investing in the two zip codes was perhaps Fuller's main objective in his stint as Human Services Director. Rescue came from an unlikely source: the "war on drugs." Fuller "found" $1.6 million in new "war on drugs" money which he designated to be used to fund the neighborhood service delivery plans. You should have seen the look on the faces of stunned social service managers when they found out what Fuller was going to do with the "war on drugs" money. The good old boys had already divvied the $1.6 million "pot" up and were ready to dole it over to their favorite white providers. Designating more than a million dollars to fund programs proposed by residents of poor minority communities was to their minds, outrageous. To us, it was overdue.

It was one of those special days when I went to meetings of the councils to tell them that their service delivery plans had been accepted and funding would be recommended as part of the 1991 budget. I've lost my field notes for those days, but I can still remember the disbelief and then thrill of accomplishment that set in when the councils realized they had actually gotten our bureaucracy to do something their neighborhood needed! A Youth Initiative summary reported

> The Youth Initiative was most successful in building on strengths within two targeted neighborhoods in zip codes 53204 & 53206. Coordinating councils were formed as neighborhood planning bodies and staffed by DSS-hired personnel. Assisted by research into the strengths and needs of these neighborhoods, service delivery plans were developed by the councils and funded with $1.6 million in 1991. DHHS purchased programs in the two targeted neighborhoods jumped more than ten times from less than $300,000 per year in 1988 to more than $3 million in 1991. Purchase contracts with minority agencies increased by 100% since 1988.
>
> *Youth Initiative Summary Report 1988–1990*

The councils subsequently received a $20,000 award from the Ford Foundation for innovation in human services. The Youth Initiative began a process of reinvesting into the poorest neighborhoods in Milwaukee and strengthening those communities' institutional infrastructures, as William Julius Wilson's (1987) work implies. Through structured involvement in the department's budget process, poor neighborhoods could attain a degree of empowerment.

## CONCLUSION: IDEALS AND REALITY

Real reform in the social services means changing core tasks of social workers and investing in client neighborhoods. It means altering the structure of work to integrate family preservation services within child welfare units staffed by generalists. It means tilting the actual routines of social workers away from specialized court related tasks to concerns for the needs of families. Reform also means child welfare units should have close ties to client neighborhoods. Accountability should be horizontal to the community and not just vertical within the bureaucracy. Reform means money has to be spent within poor neighborhoods and some of that money has to be diverted from those traditional providers who control most purchase of service dollars.

But stop! At this point I have to reign in the readers' enthusiasm. While the Youth Initiative may sound impressive, unfortunately most of our reforms were stifled by the bureaucracy. The pilot units started up in the fall of 1990, but probation officers were never assigned to them. Other specialty functions, such as court studies, adoptions, and authorizing medical cards, were never fully integrated into the units, limiting the pilots' usefulness as a test case for reform. The manager of the pilot units was an old-line bureaucrat who opposed any non-hierarchical reforms. Restructuring the rest of the child welfare system was opposed strongly by the union representing social workers and many managers. The first phase of unit integration was ordered in February of 1992, three years after it was proposed, and it stagnated at a preliminary level. The new reorganized divisions became a loose amalgam of intake, ongoing, and foster care units, with no within-unit family preservation staff, and no efforts to develop a more supportive culture. While reform had its supporters, most workers believed they were pawns in another useless reorganization that in the end would change nothing. They were basically right.

On the neighborhood side, while significant new resources from the war on drugs had been invested in the two zip codes, none of the existing $50 million of purchase dollars were diverted from powerful established providers to neighborhood-based agencies. The neighborhood councils have struggled to remain independent of the bureaucracy. While there have been some encouraging results, the pilot units have been unable to show significantly improved outcomes for clients.

I left the department at the end of 1990 to direct a gang and drug research study, my job eliminated in a cost-cutting move. Fuller left in the spring of 1991 to become Superintendent of Milwaukee Public Schools. Milwaukee County's ship of reform barely left port before it was called back for an overhaul. New county elections in 1992 meant a return to business as usual. The last of our reform team left the Department of Social Services by the end of 1993. The good old boys whom we had tried to depose returned victoriously, and completely, to power. In 1993, the American Civil Liberties Union sued the Department of Social Services for failure to provide services for children (Baird et al. 1995).

While our experience was rich in potential accomplishments, the Youth Initiative ended in failure. Milwaukee's public remained more concerned with punishing abusive parents than restructuring social services to be more supportive. No mass protest movements from poor communities arose which could provide pressure for change. The punitive national mood continued to push bureaucrats to emphasize investigating the poor and taking their children away. It would be a stretch to say that we succeeded in "making a difference" for children in Milwaukee County.

But the story is not over yet. While it is important to understand how reform failed in Milwaukee, I believe it would be a mistake to use our defeat as an excuse for inaction. Were the reforms we sought unattainable? I don't think so. Did they seem so "far out" to you? Much of our failure resulted from a changed political climate that undermined support for reforms. We also made mistakes and didn't seize chances for change when they presented themselves. I still believe the Youth Initiative's design can be studied as a rough—and attainable—blueprint for real reform.

To finish our tale, it is necessary to sum up the lessons of the Youth Initiative, examine the "symbolic" nature of what is usually called "reform," and ferret out some encouragement to those who want to organize for real change.

# 8

# SYMBOLIC REFORM VERSUS REAL SUPPORT FOR SOCIAL SERVICES

## THE STORY THAT HASN'T ENDED

At times I've felt like a traitor. I left the Department of Health and Human Services at the end of December 1990. I worked on my dissertation for a few months and then started a job as project director of a National Institute on Drug Abuse study of gangs and drugs. Fuller left in the spring of 1991 to become superintendent of the Milwaukee Public Schools. The reforms we initiated were left to others to carry out, although I tried to do consulting work and stay involved as best I could. But the reality is that I moved on, and those who are still there are stuck with what I helped start.

One day after work I met with a group of social workers and managers who had supported our reforms. As we all sat in a restaurant, I asked them what had changed most in the year after I left? How had the disintegration of our reform team most affected what they had to face day-to-day?

Frank, a long-time employee, sat back in his chair. He was "unwinding" from the day's work, nervously smoking a cigarette and sipping a glass of Beck's beer. He thought hard about what I asked, and then leaned forward and almost whispered: "What's missing most is the vision. There is no vision of what can happen today. What we are doing in the department is no longer tied to a 'big picture' of change. We are all trapped in the day-to-day madness. There's little feedback or critical questioning. Things have gone back to 'business as usual.'

The culture here is to hold on to what you have. There's no dream anymore." The others nodded sadly in agreement.

I was surprised. I had expected to hear that since we had left, the power to make changes was in the hands of others. I thought I would get more complaints of how the "good old boy" network was attempting to undo the Youth Initiative. But rather the talk focused on ideas, supportive criticism, and linking what workers and managers do day-to-day to a notion of where it was all heading. I silently scribbled the comments down and mumbled an empty response.

When I got home I thought more about Frank's comments. In 1988 we had launched this venture to try to "make a difference" to young people. Nearly every member of our reform team had seen their marriages break up as the stresses of the struggle wore on us and our families. We had thrown our lives into a fight for reforms we weren't even sure were right or could work. Now several years later it still was not clear we had made much of a difference. Some of my friends argued we made matters worse by raising expectations, then dashing them. The "good old boys" were snuggled back into power, chuckling over their good fortune. They must have been as happy as pigs in shit that we "reformers" had come and left so quickly. They must have won. They were still there and we weren't.

But then I thought of my dissertation. I was writing it as much for me to understand what had happened, as to get my Ph.D. Maybe that wasn't enough. Maybe a book summing up our experience would be useful to others. Maybe my organizational analysis of history could help others see a "bigger picture." Maybe my casting out a sensible vision of reform could encourage other reformers. Maybe, just maybe, these pages might influence the social services more than anything we had accomplished in Milwaukee.

I decided to try.

◆ ◆ ◆

The anti-poor mood of the nineties is nothing new. This book contends that for more than two decades child welfare bureaucracies have been forsaking our children in order to maintain themselves.

We can predict that in the coming more conservative years the public social services will do whatever it takes to survive. For example, welfare bureaucrats will certainly be first in line to request federal funds for administering orphanages. We also can predict that these same welfare bureaucrats will argue their budgets should not be cut because of "increasing" child abuse among the "undeserving" poor. Finally, and with great certainty, we can predict that social service bureaucrats will insist that more efficiently investigating the underclass and removing their children will require additional resources. Sadly, the 1990s do not represent a new chapter in the history of the social services, but merely an add-on to an all too familiar, dark chapter.

Pressures for welfare "reform" today often come from conservatives who claim to favor less government and lower taxes. Some conservatives do not believe government should be unduly interfering into the lives of poor families. They believe "family values" means letting the poor help themselves by reducing public subsidies, and even privatizing the child welfare system. Other conservatives, however, advocate the liberal use of taxpayers' dollars to better scrutinize and supervise the poor. It is to these "big government" conservatives that many welfare bureaucrats have sold their souls, hoping to save their jobs.

These twin pressure from the right to punish or reduce support for the poor cannot be successfully opposed by simply calling for more resources to be dumped into an unreformed child welfare system. That liberal strategy, the favorite of bureaucrats everywhere, has lost... for now. Historically that strategy has gained very little for the poor and very much for public bureaucracies. I believe deep cuts in social service budgets can only be averted if either: 1) we support stepped-up investigation of the poor and increased funds for placing their children in foster care or orphanages, or 2) child welfare bureaucracies are reformed to become truly supportive of troubled families.

It is clear that I reject the first option. This book was written to show that social workers already are too busy in court and doing paperwork to provide meaningful services for families. I believe, with Lizbeth Schorr (1988), that the American people, including many cost-conscious conservatives, are willing to support programs that help strengthen families to carry on traditional responsiblities. But we cannot gain public support by championing the dumping of resources into bureaucratic black holes that devour resources but never get around to helping the poor. I believe only by detailing a crystal-clear picture of genuinely supportive bureaucratic reforms do we have a chance to win the American people away from the politics of punishment.

Trying to take root in an arid and hostile climate, our Milwaukee family and neighborhood-centered reforms had little chance to flourish. But little doesn't mean none. Social service bureaucracies are complex systems, with both punitive and benevolent goals and both mean-spirited and well-intentioned bureaucrats. This book argues that, despite difficult times, reform must take advantage of divergent goals and differences among bureaucrats. We must try to restructure local child welfare bureaucracies as examples of how a reformed system would function.

There are three general lessons that I learned both from my practical experience and from researching and writing this book. First, and simply, it is necessary to struggle for bureaucratic reform today, and not give up. This means that reformers must resist cynicism that change is impossible and not advocate defeatist solutions. Second, reformers have to keep focused on changing core tasks and the relationship of their bureaucracy to poor neighborhoods. Given how hard change is, and the conflicting pressures of the political environment, it is easy for managers to placate critics with reforms that are more "symbolic" than real. Finally, reformers need to seize any available opportunity for change rather than to depend on comprehensive, planned reform. Reform, I discovered, is usually more a matter of daring leaps than careful steps.

## LESSON ONE: REFORM THE SYSTEM—DON'T GIVE UP!

The first lesson is a categorical imperative: it is an absolute necessity to struggle to reform the structure of public bureaucracies now. They are too important in the lives of the poor; too harmful when they are supposed to help; they've had too many resources dumped into them to allow them to the carry out their missions unchecked. The alternatives are either to give up on reform and allow the present situation to continue or to abandon the system of public social services altogether. In Fuller's office our reform team would regularly get frustrated with the pace of change and someone would say, "The only answer is to blow it up." It was always funny when one of us said it. Today I think that view is defeatist and dangerous.

The organizational literature takes strong exception to defeatism, both theoretically (March and Olsen 1976; Perrow 1986; Pressman and Wildavsky 1973; Weick 1976) and programmatically (Osborne and Gaebler 1992; Peters and Waterman 1982). There is no room to review it here, but this literature provides numerous examples of successful changes in both private and public bureaucreacies. Regardless, cynicism about the possibility of reform remains the dominant current in public welfare. One defeatist line of argument, from a friend of social service reform, must be specifically addressed.

Leroy Pelton (1989) has argued a strong, but dangerous case for reform. Pelton agrees with most observers that the child protective system has a "dual role," that is, 1) child protection and removal and 2) family preservation. He advocates that the "investigative/ coercive roles" should be shifted to law enforcement with a new child welfare agency created and "freed to pursue its helping role, with the goal of preserving families, unencumbered by investigatory functions and child removal decisions" (156). Pelton recommends shifting the investigation of abuse and neglect to police (157) and moving the foster care system directly under the courts (159). In essence, Pelton wishes to separate punitive and supportive functions and create a child welfare system dedicated only to supportive goals. His argument is consistent with some of those who wish to privatize the child welfare system. Pelton's argument is flawed on two grounds.

First of all, Pelton underestimates the power of the current social service bureaucracy to resist the removal of "child protection," one of its prime functions. Bureaucracies may redefine their functions, but they will fight to the death any attempts to transfer any of their core tasks to other agencies (Wilson 1989, 184). Social service bureaucracies would resist with all their power transferring their child protection functions, which would result in lay-offs and reduction in resources. Pelton's recommendation is unrealistic or would result in the gross underfunding of services in a privatized system. Private agencies would be pressured to duplicate existing child welfare functions for even less money, once again forsaking our children.

Second, if successful, Pelton's reforms would strengthen, not weaken, child removal and other punitive policies. Pelton admits that shifting removal and supervision functions to law enforcement would mean a transfer of resources from the social service system to law enforcement (162). It would encourage law enforcement agencies to argue for more resources to remove more children, unfettered by social work restraints of the "best interests of the child" or "permanency planning." The new child welfare agency would be forced to compete with law enforcement for scarce resources.

To counteract this danger, Pelton argues for narrowing the statutory definition of child abuse to curtail the number of cases entering the new system (157). But all we know about organizational expansion suggests the opposite would result: once child removal functions would be transferred to law enforcement bureaucracies, pressure to broaden child abuse definitions and further criminalize the conduct of poor people would be enormous. The new "child protection police" would naturally seek stability and expansion of their bureaucracy. Pelton's new child welfare agency, since it would be voluntary and would provide family services, would likely be inclined to serve a more middle-class constituency, tendencies Wilensky and Lebeaux (1965, 171) noted prior to the 1960s "discovery of child abuse." Transferring investigation and child removal functions to the police would inevitably abandon the poorest of the poor to stepped up criminal investigation. Public family services would become mainly the province of those who could afford them. This result would be anathema to Pelton, who has argued passionately that children have been essentially removed from their homes "for reasons of poverty" (cf. Cohen 1985, 264).

Pelton argues that attempts to shift welfare resources to family preservation have historically met with failure. Therefore, he said, we should stop trying to reform "dual role" social service bureaucracies. This book examines those same historical frustrations of reform, but draws the opposite conclusion. We have no choice but to resist cynicism and struggle to reform social service bureaucracies. To give up, as Pelton's work implies, courts disaster for poor families.

## Lesson Two: Beware of Symbolic Reforms

If we have no choice but reform, how do we know that "reform" will acutally help the poor? Michael Lipsky has captured this dilemma. He asks whether reformers:

> Should...struggle from within to change the conditions under which citizens are processed by their agencies? This path seems the hardest to maintain and is subject to the danger that illusions of difference will be taken for the reality of significant reform.
>
> *(Lipsky 1980, xiv)*

I always worried the "reforms" we initiated might be consequential only to us. Demands for reform, this book has shown, have historically been coopted by bureaucracies and used to feed their self-interests. The second lesson I've learned is that it is important to guard against the "easy out" of symbolic, rather than real, reforms.

"Reforming," one commentator points out, "seems to be a typical government activity." Studies show most reforms "produce hardly any change, at least in the light of the conventional expectations" (Czarniawska-Joerges 1989, 532). In the last chapter we saw that real reform means altering core tasks and changing the relationship between the bureaucracy and poor neighborhoods. On the other hand, the significance of most bureaucratic reforms does not lie in what they accomplish for clients, but in their symbolism for the public that "change" is taking place. Has the press exposed a problem? Then all that is needed is for the press to report that a "reform" is underway and everything will be all right...at least for a time.

Reform, Meyer and Rowan (1981, 315) explain, "has ritual significance: it maintains appearances and validates an organization." Reform is typically more concerned with the public perception of the agency than with changing line workers' routines.[1] Since reform has objectives other than actually changing what line workers do, we need to explore further those "symbolic reforms" which often substitute for real change. Our experience in Milwaukee illustrates four ideal types of "symbolic reform" which reformers must especially be on guard against.

## Symbolic Reform Number One—Reform as "Adding On"

The demand for more resources is a holy sacrament of public bureaucracy, the quintessential symbol of reform. How one stands on support for more resources for public bureaucracies has long symbolized who are "progressives" and who are "reactionaries," who has a "heart" and who doesn't. There are three reasons why, as Lipsky said (1980, 199), "we should be extremely skeptical of proposals for additional resources."

First, as Lipsky points out, more resources do not solve the problem of the quality of work. New resources often are diverted to new programs, not used to improve conditions of workers performing core agency tasks (33–36). Formal caseloads may be reduced, but such reductions normally only trim "inactive" cases from a worker's caseload and the number of active cases remains the same (36). Increases in staff often reduce caseloads marginally, and "often fail to show an effect, since the feeling of harassment remains when case loads are marginally reduced, say from 50 to 45 cases" (205). Finally, new resources are often temporary and therefore not to be relied on. Lipsky throws up his hands on more staff as a solution:

> Street-level bureaucrats work in situations where the resource problem in most cases is not solvable… the problem of the quality of service delivery is not likely to yield easily to any imaginable resource increments.
>
> *(Lipsky 1980, 37–38).*

Second, adding more resources may not solve the problem simply because the problems of high caseloads are often not as bad as they seem. One example is the story which began Chapter Seven. Did our Department really need 675 new caseworkers? Another good example is found in a *New York Times* article (Dugger 1992) complaining that the Dinkins administration cut the number of child protective investigators from 1080 to only 826, despite 50,000 New York City abuse and neglect referrals in 1992. The article implicitly criticized the transfer of some "badly needed" investigative workers to family preservation activities. One beleaguered intake worker complained to journalists his caseload had risen to 43!

But let's do a little arithmetic. If in 1992 New York City had 50,000 referrals, 826 caseworkers would investigate about 60 referrals per year, or 5 per month (50,000 referrals/ 826 caseworkers/12 months). Only about half of all referrals are substantiated, so each worker should be substantiating no more than three actual child abuse cases per month. That's hardly an overload. What's needed here? More workers, or a thoroughly reorganized system? What do you think happened in New York? The Dinkins administration, keeping faith with the symbolic nature of reform, responded to the press criticism by—you guessed it—hiring 300 new caseworkers.[2]

Finally, more resources may be added only to increase the punitive functions of social workers. As in New York City, hiring more social workers often means more investigation of the poor rather than increasing supportive services. For another example, let's look at the foster care system.

In the last few years foster care rolls have again risen (Wulczyn 1991; Wulczyn and Goerge 1992) prompting a beating of the drums for more social workers to handle the overload. Foster care workers in Milwaukee were often cited in reports to the County Board as the most overburdened of all social workers, with average caseloads in excess of 100. Along with Attorney Deborah Schwartz, I looked at what I could do as a consultant after I left the department in 1991.

After foster care cases were categorized by social workers and a reviewed by a panel of experts, we found that most children did not need to be in foster care at all. The social workers and our expert panel agreed that a third of all children in foster care could be immediately reunited with their families, if family preservation services were available; one third were currently staying with relatives and were likely to need few services, one sixth were categorized as having no chance of reunification and should be placed for adoption, and one sixth had been recently placed in foster care and there was insufficient information on service needs.[3]

The study concluded:

To simply increase the number of foster care workers under the present system will not decrease the foster care population. It will increase the number of foster care workers waiting in court.
(Hagedorn and Schwartz 1992).

The real issue is what the new foster care workers should do: supervise children in foster care, or work to reunify them with their families or arrange an adoption. The only way to have an immediate and positive effect on troubled families would be to target additional staff to reunification services, adoptions, and support for placement with relatives. It is services which need to be increased, not supervision and investigation.

Demanding more resources for public bureaucracies is a convenient symbol that one is "concerned" about social problems. Getting new resources becomes the symbol that something is being done, regardless of whether the poor ever benefit from added staff. It is the easiest of the "easy-outs" of reform. Those legislators who want to express their concern for social services should insist on targeting increases in funding only to those changes which provide real services or invest in poor communities.[4]

## Symbolic Reform Number Two—Reform as a Diversion

A second type of symbolic reform is reform which diverts attention from the need for structural change. Often reform administrations begin the difficult job of altering core tasks, but soon give up, finding the job too hard. Here are two examples.

As our "emergency plan" to reform Child Protective Services ground on, it became clear there was a stalemate. Seeing he was in a no-win situation, Human Services Director Fuller quietly switched his attentions to an emotionally charged proposal to fund a "safe house" for abused children. Fuller had ridden one night with a child protective worker and discovered that workers sometimes did not have any place to bring children who were removed from their home, if relatives or foster parents couldn't be found immediately. A highly publicized hearing led to a site being found which was resisted by NIMBY ("Not In My Back Yard") residents. The safe house was finally funded. However, the by-product of the fight was that reformers, managers, and the public alike lost sight of the need for much more difficult and far-reaching child protective reforms.

While the safe house serves at most a couple of hundred children per year, Milwaukee's child abuse system processes 10,000 cases annually. Our first attempt to reform Child Protective Services died a quiet death, drowned out by the applause for the "victory" of setting up a temporary home for abused children.

Another kind of diversion is the periodic reorganizations of bureaucracies that seem to consume new administrators. Peters and Waterman (1982, 317) write of "a generic willingness to reorganize and reshuffle the boxes" as an attribute of an excellent organization. I obviously think it is a good idea to shake up the system now and then. However, reorganizations often shuffle boxes and give the illusion of reform while leaving the basic structure of work untouched.

For example, as our reform agenda bogged down, Fuller hired consultants to plan a major overhaul of the entire Health and Human Services Department, including social services. One latent intention of the reorganization was to outmaneuver the old management team, who were blocking reform. Other reforms were put on the back burner as Fuller put "reorganization" at the top of his agenda. His "Reorg" passed, but it resulted in little change. Who really benefited? I described the scene in my field notes:

> A purpose of the Reorg was to ice the old management team, to allow a new team to be built to carry out the changes we need. I predicted strong resistance and likely defeat. But that didn't happen. Why? First, the Reorg strengthened the good old boys network, it didn't weaken it. It stayed in place and even gained. The whole thing turned into a dog and pony show for the County Board who saw it only as a way to save $11.7 million, which was the second reason for its success...it didn't change what workers do or what happens to clients.
>
> *Field Notes, November 30, 1990*

While reorganization is necessary for structural change, reformers must ask whether restructuring means any change for the day-to-day routines and core tasks of line workers. If not, reorganization is no more than a diversion, symbolic and not real reform.

## Symbolic Reform Number Three— Reform as Phony Participation

Reforms can also provide the symbols of participation, but carefully exclude the new participants from power. Money may sometimes be distributed to the poor, but power is seldom shared.

For example, our neighborhood councils developed neighborhood service delivery plans which captured $1.6 million dollars in investment for these two very poor zip codes. But that initial investment consisted of dollars diverted by Fuller from new "war on drugs" grants, and was not part of the $50 million dollars of purchase of service contracts annually handed out by the department. The councils' plans were advisory with no binding authority. For Fuller, whose political base was the African American community, delivering contracts to minority agencies was a priority. He listened to their concerns. But after he left and a new, white director was apppointed, the councils still gave "input" but had little real influence.

During the War on Poverty, this issue was extremely contentious. While Moynihan (1969) and other conservatives criticized citizen participation as "maximum feasible misunderstanding," grass-roots organizations criticized "maximum feasible manipulation" (North City Area-Wide Council 1972) and liberals explored the implications of "community control" (Altshuler 1970). One way participation was conceptualized in the sixties was as a ladder, with numerous rungs beginning with "manipulation" on the bottom, keeping poor people informed and consulting with them in the middle, and "citizen control," or actual decision-making power by poor people on the very top. The key component of the ladder was power (see the illustration on p. 151, from Arnstein 1969, 216–17).

# EIGHT RUNGS ON A LADDER
# OF CITIZEN PARTICIPATION

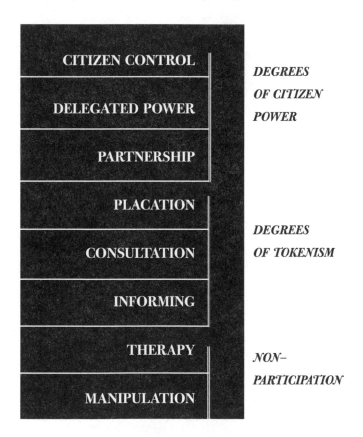

Reprinted with permission of the Journal of the American Institute of
Planners, 35 (July 1969).

"Citizen control" means "have-not citizens obtain the majority of decision-making seats, or full managerial power." The real objective of "manipulation" is not to enable people to participate in planning or conducting programs, but to enable powerholders to "educate" or "cure'" the participants. The intermediate levels are seen by the author as "tokenism" where "citizens may indeed hear and be heard," but " lack the power to insure that their views will be heeded by the powerful" (Arnstein 1969, 217).

If we use this ladder as a way to look at the neighborhood councils, it is clear that the councils were at best "partners" who were placated, but their counsel carried little or no weight. No bureaucracy will willingly give real power to poor people who are outside the bureaucratic structure. The real question was how high on the "ladder of participation" our neighborhood councils could climb.

Our initial plans were to institutionalize the councils as official planning bodies for their zip codes, moving them a rung or two higher, but that idea was rejected. The councils ended up with little bureaucratic standing. While social service bureaucrats have regularly attended council meetings, their participation "rather than being seen as the basis of policy, has become another program element" (Galper 1975, 43). The neighborhood councils continued to develop service delivery plans, but there were no mechanisms to guarantee those with power had to give more than token attention. The councils became little more than a symbol of the "good intentions" of the Milwaukee County Department of Social Services toward minority communities.[5]

## Symbolic Reform Number Four—
## Reform Without Evaluation

A final kind of symbolic reform is the standard practice of initiating programs without formal and independent evaluations. In the Youth Initiative, millions of dollars flowed to agencies in the two targeted zip codes, but no formal evaluations were tied to those new dollars. What is usually called "evaluation" by bureaucracies is nothing but program monitoring, which provides symbolic legitimation but no critical data.

The reason most evaluation is symbolic is that evaluation, properly done, can be subversive, for it can provide unsettling information. Meyer and Rowan soberly point out:

> Evaluation and inspection are public assertions of societal control which violate the assumption that everyone is acting with competence and in good faith. Violating this assumption lowers morale and confidence. Thus evaluation and inspection undermine the ceremonial aspects of organization.
>
> *(Meyer and Rowan 1981, 318)*

The result is that evaluations in social services, as in most public bureaucracies, typically monitor a program's inputs and do not evaluate outputs (Osborne and Gaebler 1992, 138). To evaluate reform, we had to deal with sensitive issues. Chapter Four showed how traditional agencies were unevaluated and had low performance. Perhaps out of a misguided sense of fairness as well as a desire to maximize program dollars, rigorous evaluation of the new neighborhood-based programming was not required.[6]

Did the increase in purchase of service contracts within our two zip codes have a positive impact on clients and not just prop up neighborhood agency bureaucrats? It was an important objective of the Youth Initiative to build the institutional infrastructure in the two target neighborhoods. In that sense, funding any programs based in the two zip codes would do. But while increasing the budget of neighborhood agencies was one goal, providing better service to clients was a more basic goal

While some are strong advocates for neighborhood-based organization (e.g., McKnight 1987), others question how representative these agencies are and how influential. For example, a review of studies on neighborhood organizations reports that nationally "two thirds of the residents in black neighborhoods could not name even one important local group" (Cnaan 1991, 622). Sosin (1990) reports that local providers often copy out of date technologies and seldom change. Further, Hill (1981) reports welfare programs often do not reach poor clients. Just because neighborhood agencies are funded does not mean that services have improved.

Lipsky counts himself as a supporter of "radical decentralization," but he stresses that he would add performance as the measure of change.

> The analysis of street-level bureaucracy presented here has been supportive of that strand of neighborhood control advocacy which focuses on the creation of standards by which to judge improved bureaucratic performance.
>
> *(Lipsky 1972, 180)*

A failure of our reforms was our inability to develop those standards, except in the case of family preservation, where measures of families being kept out of system, improved family functioning, cost-benefits, and other performance measures are becoming standard practices (Wells and Biegel 1991a; Yuan and Rivest 1990). Initiating new programs is a standard feature of reform. But when performance and outputs are not properly and critically measured, those programs can leave clients no better off than before (Wilson 1989, 373). New programs are often a symbol of reform, rather than steps to real change.

## LESSON THREE: GET IT WHILE YOU CAN

This book might be more persuasive to would-be reformers if it was an unmitigated success story. In reality, many of our reforms were small and fragile, and by the time you read this, have already been undone by the "good old boys." This book is an unambiguous attempt to use our Milwaukee experience to influence social service reform in other cities.

That doesn't mean this book is a call for reformers to carbon copy the Youth Initiative, and just do it better. The third major lesson I've learned is that reform isn't so much a planned, rational activity, as it is a determined effort to seize opportunities as they present themselves. As Marris and Rein commented on the War on Poverty:

In practice, programmes evolved less from any process of planning than as a response to opportunity, or defense against attack.

*(Marris and Rein 1967, 111)*

Our notions of reform are altogether too rational. Innovation in human services can be the result of the "policy planning" model, meaning careful planning to implement comprehensive reforms, scrupulously trying to avoid mistakes. Or innovation can be the result of the "groping along" model, which "deemphasizes the initial policy idea in favor of rapid action, modified by experience" (Golden 1990, 220). An examination of seventeen successful innovations in human services found that in all cases success in innovation was more related to the groping than the planning model.[7] As in business, successful human service reformers have a "bias for action" (Peters and Waterman 1982). This notion is similar to Karl Weick's advice to managers:

Accuracy is less important than animation. Any old map or plan will do if it gets you moving so that you learn more about what is actually in the environment. A map is not the territory; a plan is not the organization.

*(Weick 1985, 133)*

Weick's dictum should be slightly modified. I think "getting moving" needs to be aimed at altering core tasks and changing the relationship between bureaucracies and client neighborhoods. Otherwise change can turn out to be more symbolic than real. But our specific reforms certainly are not the only way social service bureaucracies could be changed. At one point I toyed with an organizational plan which would merge our social workers with social workers at public schools in new cooperative teams. Reforming two bureaucracies at once, I finally realized, was way too much to consider seriously. The point is that action is preferable to inaction, and the plan may not be as important as the act. My field notes show the evolution of my thinking:

There were sure a lot of false starts. It's important not to be retrospec-
tively rational about this change stuff. While I saw the importance of
the pilots, I also saw the importance of the schools and we could have
gone in more than one direction. And I don't think it would have mat-
tered much, as long as the direction changed core tasks and involved
the neighborhoods in a new way.

The point is that none of us were sure of the path, but we didn't jump
out on one of them and beat it like a dead horse. We got diverted, side-
tracked, locked into becoming managers of routine...we should have
gone with what makes progress, as long as it was confronting essential,
core tasks...The lesson is that if the opportunity is there, jump, fool,
jump! Don't wait for a better day that might never come.

*Field Notes, November 30, 1990*

I'm hesitant to write too much about the tactics of reform, because we
weren't really that successful. Some things are clear, however. I can see that my
enthusiasm for change led to a mistaken strategy of engaging the bureaucracy
on all fronts. Early on I trumpeted in my field notes:

Our strategy is like guerrilla warfare. We seek to engage the enemy on
as many fronts as we humanly can open. These fronts are relatively
small battles, but for the bureaucracy to refuse to carry out these small
tasks is contradictory to the very essence of a bureaucracy....But to
engage the bureaucracy head-on in an open confrontation on reform
would mean we'd lose.

*Field Notes, January 29, 1989*

The consequence of this strategy was that we were overwhelmed. Later I
reflected on my mistake:

I'm on my way to a meeting and another hectic day. The basic problem that we're having here is that we're overwhelmed with the com-

plexity of the tasks ahead of us, how much we've bitten off, and our inability to get the structure, the bureaucracy itself, to react, to do those tasks for us. We end up doing everything ourselves, which is exhausting us. I like the bureaucracy's strategy better than ours—to sit back and let us do it and watch us collapse.

*Field Notes March 10, 1989*

The lesson of how we went about our reform merits a more complete analysis than I am able to give here. It would be painful to analyze in these pages our strategy and tactics, since as this is being written the players on both sides are still active in Milwaukee. Some have been friends and my analysis is better shared privately. But one thing is clear: what success we had was always the result of acting, even when we weren't sure of exactly what all the outcomes would be.

I have come to be critical of detailed plans like those we developed in our "Youth Initiative Final Report." Our experience shows that even fundamental goals are often discovered through action and may differ from those in the initial plan. As March comments:

It seems to me that a description that assumes goals come first and action comes later is frequently radically wrong. Human choice behavior is at least as much a process for discovering goals as for acting on them

*(March and Olsen 1976, 72)*

Looking back at the Youth Initiative, I only learned what a "fundamental reorientation of services for youth" meant by trying to make change happen and then reflecting on what we had done. What was decisive was never our plan , which was radically changed in the course of its implementation. Rather, in almost all cases, what won the day was throwing all our energies into getting key "chunks" of our general plan up and running and not giving up when faced with setbacks (Peters and Waterman 1982, 126). Planning reform is necessary, but seizing opportunities when they arise is what gets the job done.[8]

## CONCLUSION: REFORM LOCAL BUREAUCRACIES

One important message of this book is that reform is possible. Our failure in Milwaukee should not dissuade others to follow in the same general direction. Quite likely, you can do it better.

We got off to a good start. Our small reform group had some general ideas of what it meant to alter core tasks or redirect resources, the daring to follow through, and support and participation by some—but not all—key constituencies. Our reform wasn't dependent on a charismatic leader, although having a "transformational" style leader like Howard Fuller often helped (Bargal and Schmid 1989). The Youth Initiative involved street-level bureaucrats, citizens, and providers in both formal and informal processes to advance some good ideas of reform.

One of our major weaknesses was that while we had support from both the community and many social workers and administrators, we never figured out how to involve youth or clients. The Youth Initiative was more of a "bureaucratic insurgency" than a "mass movement" (Zald and Berger 1978). Our reforms were mainly fought out behind office walls as struggles between various managers. This does not mean our efforts were insignificant, but probably helped explain why our successes were limited.

It does raise the question of how to analyze the local bureaucrats who run the present system. Across the country some are liberals and some conservatives, some are friends and some enemies of reform. But I think a case by case analysis misses the point. The response of social service managers of all persuasions across the country to the punitive Reagan era was fundamentally "rational," based on the self-interests of the agencies they ran. I'm sure many, if not most, social service bureaucrats, were personally opposed to mean-spirited Washington policies.

What I've tried to show was that unobtrusively, and not so much consciously, over time, the funding and assumptions of child welfare bureaucracies became based on investigations of poor families and child removal. "Services" became more myth and less deed, or something established private agencies had to do, given the scarcity of resources. Social service managers dutifully restructured their agencies to carry out the new core tasks more efficiently, link with the courts, and fight for resources to keep their agencies afloat.

A friend once asked if I thought those who ran Milwaukee's social service system were "amoral"? What do you think? My argument is that those who hold bureaucratic power have to sometimes stand on principle and go against the tide. That hasn't happened too often in the social services. This book is a call for administrators, social workers, and bureaucrats of every stripe to take a few small steps toward real reform.

Reform, I believe, has to reject a pure "tool" view of organizations, with evil elites directing events in preconceived directions. Reform also must reject a simplistic "puppet" view of bureaucrats as deterministically captive to larger economic or political forces. Both of these views condemn those of us concerned with change to do nothing or to wait on outside events. It also neglects the important differences between bureaucrats, many of whom are supporters of reform. A limited "agency" is possible, I believe, if reformers are willing to sieze opportunities when they arise, and not get bogged down in drawn-out planning processes. Real gains on a local level can be made even while our country seems settled on a generally punitive course.

Reform today, as we've seen in chapters three and seven, should focus on local efforts to change the structure of work. I suggest a few more people should aspire to be the designer of the ship of reform and maybe a few less aspire to be the captain. Meanwhile the nation-wide ideological battle to resist the punitive direction of the social services must also continue. I hope these pages have contributed to both ends.

Remember the story which began chapter one, where Mike McGee despaired of change and took to the streets? This book does not argue that organizing the poor and demonstrations are wrong, but rather that there also is an important role for those of us who want to reform the system from within. Indeed, I believe the two approaches are complementary. This book hopes to incite others to carry on the torch of reform which we lighted, but did not carry very far. It aspires to give life to a vision of how real services can be structurally embedded in welfare bureaucracies, displacing punitive routines. It tries to give practical advice on how public bureaucracies can help rebuild, not exploit underclass communities. To repeat, it seeks to make genuine reform of street-level bureaucracies look possible.

This book aims to transform Milwaukee's Youth Initiative into something that may yet "make a difference" to clients of social service bureaucracies.

# APPENDIX 1

# INVOLVED OBSERVERS
# AND ACADEMIC RESEARCH

This appendix is a narrative of how this book was researched and written. In essence, it's an examination of the strengths and limitations of the dual role I played as an "involved observer," both reformer and researcher (Clark 1965, xvi). I hope to show that reformers can do good research and that researchers can be good reformers.

This appendix is organized to discuss the problems which confronted each stage of the research: 1) the problem of taking sides as I began the research; 2) the problem of bias as I gathered data; 3) the problem of analysis or how I understood the data; and finally 4) the problem of audience, to whom was I was writing? This appendix is written for those who are concerned with these problems.

So what is this role of "involved observer?" How did a book emerge out of a reform struggle anyway?

## GETTING STARTED: THE PROBLEM OF TAKING SIDES

In some ways, the research that led to this book came about by accident. After dropping out of college in the sixties, I was an activist during the seventies and returned to college in the eighties, when I was thirty five years old. I got my bachelors in Community Education in 1985 and my masters in Sociology in 1987. A more academic version of this book was accepted as my Ph.D. dissertation in the spring of 1993.

While I ran a gang diversion program in the early eighties, I had taken classes at night to help me better understand the gang phenomenon. Although I ran a successful program, I turned to research in frustration over not being able to influence public policy. The result was *People and Folks* (1988), a moderately successful academic book, which conceptualized youth gangs as mainly a problem of the underclass.

Howard Fuller then intervened in my life and asked me to be part of his human service reform team. I had already decided to enter the Urban Studies doctoral program at the University of Wisconsin-Milwaukee. I had intended to write my Ph.D. dissertation on gangs, a natural topic to follow up my book. But it soon became clear to my dissertation advisor, Joan Moore, that all my energies were being focused on the Youth Initiative. She gently pointed out the obvious.

But seeing my reform activity as a research study raised a rather big problem. I didn't enter the "field" to do academic research, I was already "in the field" committed to playing an active role in reform. The research methods literature says very little about the participant observer who is primarily an active participant in the social situation he or she is also studying. For example, Schwartz and Schwartz (1969, 96-100) explore two possible roles. They contrast the "passive participant," a fly-on-the-wall who interacts with the observed "as little as possible," with the "active participant" where the researcher "interacts" with the observed in day-to-day activities. The "active participant," they caution, must be very careful to not get so involved as to distort the data (cf. Miller 1969).

But note that even the "active" observer is assumed to be a professional academic who enters a "research situation" and sees it as data to be gathered and analyzed. The participant observer is taught to minimize the observer's effect on the observed. *"Observers must conduct themselves in such a way that the events that occur during their observation do not significantly differ from those which occur in their absence"* (Bogdan and Taylor 1975, 45; emphasis in italics in original). William Foote Whyte (1943, 336) sums this point up best. Looking back on his taking sides in a local dispute during his research, he lamented: "Here I violated a cardinal rule of participant observation. I sought actively to influence events."

This gets at the nub of the problem under consideration. My role in the Department of Health and Human Services primarily was to "actively influence events." Are the roles of "change agent" and "social science researcher" mutually exclusive?

## Involved Observers

While most of the methods literature agrees fervently that the two roles should not be combined, there are some who think otherwise. Kenneth Clark in his classic *Dark Ghetto* (1965) contrasts a role of "involved observer" with both ethnography and classic participant observation. His comments are worth repeating at some length:

> This role is particularly difficult to maintain when one is not only a participant in the community but when one brings to the attempt to use this method, with that degree of clarity and objectivity essential for social science accuracy, a personal history of association with and concern for many of the people in the very community one seeks to study...The role of "involved observer"...demands participation not only in rituals and customs but in the social competition with the hierarchy in dealing with the problems of the people he is seeking to understand...the "involved observer" runs the risk of joining in the competition for status and power and cannot escape the turbulence and conflict inherent in the struggle."
>
> *(Clark, 1964, xvi)*

In *Dark Ghetto,* Clark was a good example of a researcher committed to social action who also rigorously described and analyzed the situation. The principal goal of such researchers is precisely to "actively influence events," but to do so in a manner which is reflected on, integrated into a broader theoretical perspective, and published to influence events some more.

The activist role has been controversial within the academy. Sociology in the United States has been sharply criticized, often from a Marxist perspective, for its arm-chair tendencies (Schwendinger and Schwendinger 1974; Benson

1981). The sociologists of the "Chicago School" did blend empirical research and social reform in initiating the Chicago Area Project (Glaser 1976). However, there have been few followers of that part of the Chicago tradition. In the 1950s C. Wright Mills broke from mainstream Parsonian traditions of sociology. He declared social scientists must play a role which will "risk trouble… It requires that we deliberately present controversial theories and facts, and actively encourage controversy" (Mills 1959, 191).[1] Mills wrote insightfully that "increasingly, research is used, and social scientists are used, for bureaucratic and ideological purposes" (177).

In the 1960s many social scientists actively joined the "social competition with the hierarchy," encouraged controversy, and agitated for social change. Some, like Kenneth Clark, skillfully performed both research and social action roles. Richard Cloward and Frances Fox Piven also combined impressive scholarship with on-going advice for the leadership of the welfare rights movement. They published "a strategy to end poverty" (1966) which challenged national income maintenance policy and they helped mobilize AFDC recipients to confront local bureaucratic practices. Other social scientists worked in a variety of capacities in promoting 1960s reform agendas.

Daniel Moynihan (1969) was one of the main critics of activism by social scientists. He blamed much of the failure of the War on Poverty on the involvement of academics who contributed to the "maximum feasible misunderstanding" of the War's true goals. Moynihan represented those within the Washington bureaucracy who were appalled by "community action" and its demands for change. Moynihan distinguished social scientists in government— "a teeming and irresponsible group" (191)—from social science itself, whose proper role "lies not in the formulation of social policy, but in the measurement of its results" (193; also cf. Nathan 1988). Moynihan wanted sociologists to stop using social science to agitate for change and get back in their proper place—as evaluators of social programs.

Others saw different problems in the participation of social scientists in the Great Society. Alvin Gouldner (1968) criticized war on poverty academics for naively making a "blind alliance" with Washington, failing to understand the federal bureaucracy as a one interested party among many. Gouldner called for more involvement and passion in research, but warned against social scientists being used by a federal bureaucracy eager to expand at the expense of local institutions. "It is to values, not to factions, that sociologists must give their most basic commitment" (116). Get involved with social change, Gouldner advised sociologists, but understand the self interests of local and federal bureaucracies.

Since the sixties, the role of "involved observer" has fallen into relative disuse.[2] Moynihan's and Nathan's prescription to confine social science to evaluation or become consultants is now mainstream sociology. Few social scientists urge involvement of their colleagues in reform, as intellectual discourse has been captured by the academy. The role of "public intellectual" as urged by Mills and others has been all but lost (cf. Jacoby 1987).

But the times they are a'changing. William F. Whyte, who in his early work had worried about involvement of researchers in action, later changed his mind.

As I gained experience in a wider range of research situations, I found myself gradually abandoning the idea that there must be a strict separation between scientific research and action projects. Through the rest of my career, I have been exploring how research can be integrated with action in ways that will advance science and enhance human progress at the same time."

*(Whyte 1984, 20)*

Whyte (1991) advocates "participant action research" (PAR), which is similar to the "collaborative" method of gang research I learned from Joan Moore (Moore 1977). PAR even has its own mailing list on the internet and a growing group of adherents. Feminists and some others have increasingly adopted collaborative and participatory techniques as a standard methodological tool (Cancian 1992; Reason 1994).

Whyte (1984, 341) even discusses an "involved observer" type situation "in which the writer bases the research report on a role played earlier simply as a participant." Whyte (1991, 8) has the last word:

...it is important, both for the advancement of science and for the improvement of human welfare, to devise strategies in which research and action are closely linked.

## Practical Problems

Even if "involved observation" can be a legitimate role, I found it is not so easy to implement. It is simply difficult and exhausting to both act and reflect in the same time period. An uninvolved researcher, who sees observations as principally data, is spending his or her energy on collecting that data, not "working" or "reforming" as well.

When I was at the Department of Health and Human Services, my days were filled with the drama of new projects and the never-ending struggle with the bureaucrats and the bureaucratic mentality. I was just too tired much of the time to carefully make field notes and thoughtfully sift through various observations. To be "reflectively conscious" (Sjoberg and Nett 1968) of each day's activities for an "involved observer" is extremely difficult, no matter how important the observations.

I found it hard to spend the necessary time crafting my field notes and molding them into a coherent form. For example, I found the notes I took asking thirty-three intake workers what they thought was wrong were useful diagnosis. My purpose was to figure out as quickly as possible what was going haywire with the system. On the other hand, the notes were lacking in the rich detail of observation that would have come if I had observed the workers for several days performing their jobs. The press of "reform" often didn't leave enough time to do more than write down some short hand notes and write a memo proposing some solution.

I also kept a journal and supplemented it with tape recordings of my thoughts after meetings. But my tape recordings lacked the depth of the written word, and couldn't be crafted at all until they were transcribed. All the same, taping my thoughts in the car immediately after meetings or on the way to or from work preserved a valuable day-to-day record. Unfortunately some of my "brilliant" comments were lost forever because I forgot to regularly check the batteries in the tape recorder. I told myself it was because I was tired all the time, but I have to admit it was more of an avoidable error. All the same, my recorder and my journal would sometimes go months without entries because of my absorption in the crises of reform.

But how objective can "involved observation" be? Isn't such research inevitably biased?

## GATHERING THE DATA: THE PROBLEM OF BIAS

On my last day on the job, I stopped in the office of one of Fuller's deputies to say good-bye. I told him I would be spending the next several months working on my dissertation. While it was no secret I was writing about the Youth Initiative, it suddenly dawned on this long-time bureaucrat that I might write something about him. Alarmed, he asked me if I was going to portray him as "one of the bureaucrats," and I assured him my dissertation wouldn't dwell on personalities. In fact, the only names used in this book are those of public figures and close friends.

This manager in fact was one of the chief bureaucrats who I thought tried to subvert reform at every step. I suspected he hated me, and he always tried to make me feel that I didn't understand the "big picture." He followed up his earlier question by asking seriously, " how can your dissertation have an overall perspective? How can your research be unbiased?" He and I were seldom on the same side of any issue and I decided to get in one last shot. I told him with a wry smile the dissertation would be my account. He'd have to write his own book to get his side of the story out. He laughed uneasily as I left.

I'm sure that bureaucrat has long since forgotten this incident. But he did make me think more about the issue. Isn't research by sole observers inevitably narrow? How can the "involved observation" of passionate reformers like myself yield unbiased research? These are in fact the two main forms of bias in participant observation: the bias of limited location and the bias of personal distortion. I tried to minimize both of these in the course of my research.

First, participant observation is always handicapped by the problem of "limited location" (Zelditch 1969, 13). The researcher cannot be everywhere and is limited to only what he or she sees. Ethnography and other forms of observation are based on a single researcher's impressions, which are then scientifically analyzed. One way to minimize the bias of limited location is the use of more than one method of observation and more than one observer.

Whyte suggests that some participant observers can be a bit arrogant, belittling the use of surveys, the study of local history, and other methods. It is better, Whyte found, to use all methods at your disposal, rather than rely only on personal observation. "Reliance upon a single research method is bound to impede the progress of science" (Whyte 1984, 149). But multiple measures are difficult and time consuming. They often give headaches to participant observers, with anomalous facts threatening to demolish the unique status of the researcher as the sole interpreter of reality. "To avoid the difficult task of interpreting contradictions," Webb and Weick (1979, 652) say bluntly, field researchers often "avoid multiple measures."

I tried to apply this insight. This study is not purely a participant observation, although I routinely cite my field notes. To better understand the present, I studied the history of social welfare, social services, and the Milwaukee Department of Social Services. The historical experience of reform became a crucial part of my argument, as you saw in chapters five and six. I also make use of official and unofficial records. I have five or six large boxes of documents and jam-packed computer files which I struggled through to prepare this work. Having memos on events in our administration from various managers did refresh my memory as well as remind me that my version of what happened was often a bit different than others'.

The Youth Initiative also commissioned research and evaluation, and those reports form a key part of this work. Interviews with social workers were carried out by contracted evaluators. I'm sure those interviews would have been quite different if I had conducted them. Would the line worker in Chapter One have told me that the Youth Initiative hadn't meant a "hill of beans" to her job? Maybe, but I can't be sure. We also contracted for research with clients and with residents in the two target neighborhoods, taking baseline measures to see if our reforms would have any impact on real people. Specific innovations were evaluated, as was the overall "institutional impact" of the Youth Initiative. Finally, I did output evaluations on the effectiveness of some programs and I cite some of those results. The use of multiple measures and multiple observers provides a much more rounded account of the experience of social service reform in Milwaukee than I could reconstruct only from what I observed.

All that is well and good, but what about my observations themselves? How do you, the reader, know my interpretations of reality aren't biased? What about the bias of personal distortion? To that charge I plead guilty. What I told Fuller's deputy in a way is true. This is my account of the Youth Initiative; his would undoubtedly be different. The observer is always a variable to be considered in research (Sjoberg and Nett 1968). I think it is wise for readers take into account my status as reformer when reading this book.

But is my account "objective"? There are two answers to this question, one from the classic school and one from "post-positivist" research.

According to Zelditch (1969, 13), some information is always not accessible because of how the observer is defined by the observed. Any researcher will be shielded from some information the observed wish to hide. Thus my role as reformer gave me access to some information, and not to others. Clearly I was not privy to the counsels of the bureaucrats as they grappled with the "threat" of the Fuller administration. On the other hand, I was a party to the inner workings of the Youth Initiative. All its decisions, options, and frustrations are a permanent part of my life and I feel confident reporting on them. An uninvolved observer might have been present when both camps planned their maneuvering, but would probably not have been fully trusted by either. I wouldn't have always talked freely in front of such a person about our tactics for fear word of them might get back to the bureaucrats.[3]

John P. Dean and William F. Whyte (1969) point out that there are reliable methods to reduce distortion, but in the end the researcher must take the "social situation" of research into account. There is no fundamental reason why researchers who are defined as reformers cannot report their findings as "objectively" as observers who try to be flies-on-the-wall. "The physician," Gouldner (1968, 113) comments, "after all is not necessarily less objective because he has made a partisan commitment to his patient and against the germ." Both involved and uninvolved roles influence how the observed act and have their advantages and disadvantages.

## Post-Positivist Research

Traditional field research methods teach that observers introduce "error" into research which can be partly compensated for by an honest reporting of the field situation (Hyman 1954). Post-positivist, or emergent research has a different slant on this issue. It is simply not possible to remove observer influence, they argue, so we should just stop trying. In *Naturalistic Inquiries,* a book that has had enormous influence on my research, Yvonna Lincoln and Egon Guba point out:

> Interactions between investigator and respondents cannot be eliminated from the research equation even if one wishes to do so...But one can regard their presence either as an intrusion leading to error or as an opportunity to be exploited.
>
> *(Lincoln and Guba 1985, 101)*

Recent developments in quantum mechanics and the natural sciences have further eroded the notion of neutral observation. Heisenberg's "uncertainty principle" demonstrates that it is impossible to both see a moving electron and measure its velocity at the same time (Lincoln and Guba 1985, 7–8). The fact that all observation is "disturbing" to one degree or another, say the post-positivists, compels us to do away with misleading notions of the absolute "objectivity" of any research.

Post-positivist theory advocates that research itself should be reconstructed within a "new paradigm" which makes use of modern physics' understanding of a world which doesn't always follow the laws of Newtonian mechanics. Sociology was developed in an era where the positive laws of science, like those of God, were thought to be knowable and absolute. We don't live in that simple world anymore, the new theorists proclaim, and our notion of social science needs to change as well (Lincoln 1985a).

It is not possible to go into this matter in more detail here. I refer interested readers especially to Lincoln's and Guba's works. The brilliance of *Naturalistic Inquiry* is the authors' application of the principles of quantum mechanics to social science research. The following table gives a brief overview of how "naturalistic inquiry" differs from the traditional school.

## Contrasting Positivist and Naturalistic Axioms

| AXIOMS ABOUT | POSITIVIST PARADIGM | NATURALISTIC PARADIGM |
|---|---|---|
| **The nature of reality** | Reality is single, tangible, and fragmentable. | Realities are multiple, constructed, and holistic. |
| **The relationship of the knower to the known** | Knower and known are independent, a dualism. | Knower and known are interactive, inseparable |
| **The possibility of generalization** | Time–and context–free generalization (nomothetic statements) are possible. | Only time and context bound working hypotheses (idiographic state ments) are possible. |
| **The possibility of causal linkages** | There are real causes, temporally precedent to or simultaneous with their effects. | All entities are in a state of mutual shaping, so that it is impossible to distinguish causes from effects. |
| **The role of values** | Inquiry is value-free | Inquiry is value-bound. |

Yvonna S Lincoln and Egon G. Guba, *Naturalistic Inquiry*
(Beverly Hills: Sage., *1985*), *p. 37;* © Sage Publications, 1985.
Reprinted by permission of Sage Publications, Inc.

Many researchers have successfully applied the idea that the observer can not be truly independent of the observed. *The Death of White Sociology* (Ladner 1973) contains several penetrating articles on various activist roles by minority researchers. Some contemporary feminists also criticize traditional sociological research as too often being nothing more than "a combined phonograph and recording system" (Oakley 1981, 37). Harding says:

> The best feminist analysis...insists that the inquirer her/himself be placed in the same critical plane as the overt subject matter, thereby recovering the entire research process for scrutiny in the results of research... the beliefs and behaviors of the researcher are part of the empirical evidence for (or against) the claims advanced in the results of research.
>
> *(Harding 1987, 9).*

In other words, "everything counts" as data, including the observer's motives, actions, and frame of mind (Schwartzman 1993, 48). The point is that post-positivist research suggests "involved observation" can be a unique "opportunity" to produce social science knowledge and should not be rejected just because the observer is partisan to reform.

## The Bias of the Paycheck

There is one final kind of bias which I need to discuss before we go on: the "over-rapport" of researchers... with the official who signs their paycheck. Traditionally, over-rapport relates to "going native," a form of personal distortion where observers uncritically adopt the attitudes of those being observed (Miller 1969). But perhaps more often a researcher, hired as a consultant or doing academic field work, consciously or unconsciously adopts the perspective of those who commissioned the study or allowed them access. Evaluators or researchers who do not tell institutional managers what they want to hear are seldom hired a second time or allowed access again. The seduction of the paycheck represents a particularly grave threat to the objectivity of social science research.

Mills (1959, 180) fretted about the tendency of sociology to "become merely a refinement of techniques for administrative and manipulative uses."

Researchers, evaluators, and consultants are often hired for ceremonial, not critical roles (Meyer and Rowan 1981). What is really desired from such research is technical or pragmatic advice, or a pat on the back, not a thorough reexamination. While such advice can be functional, it begs the broader question.

> ...much of what passes as scholarly "research" tends to avoid issues that might be critical of responsible officials and management, and instead caters to facilitating the efficient and smooth operation of established systems.
>
> *(Platt 1969, 181)*

In my case, the problem was a bit more complicated. My paycheck was dependent on my allegiance to Howard Fuller, who hired me to conceptualize reform. My main danger was not being coopted by the bureaucrats—no one who knows me thought that could happen. The main danger for my research was that the interests of what I saw as reform and the Fuller administration's policies might not always coincide. What would I do then?

This is what Gouldner (1968, 116) means when he says, "It is to values, not factions, that sociologists must give their most basic commitment." There's been much written on the cooptation of reform, beginning with Michels' (1915) notion of the inevitably of cooptation, his famous "iron law of oligarchy," updated by Piven and Cloward (1980). Social scientists should remember that objectivity means in part "admitting the factuality even of things that violate his own hopes and values" (Gouldner 1968, 114).[4] When Sjoberg and Nett (1968, 25) say that one principle of science is that "knowledge is superior to ignorance," they mean an "involved observer" like myself must have the courage to confront troubling facts even about the reform struggle itself. While being partisan, the social scientist must also be able to step "outside" of the role of reformer and be critical, even of reform itself. A social scientist, whether involved or uninvolved, must always be in some ways marginal to the group being studied (Park 1969).

My field notes are filled with frustration, not just with the bureaucrats, but with my friend Howard Fuller as well. Many of my field notes are extremely personal and inappropriate for publication. While I intellectually understood the need to enthusiastically support Fuller's complete agenda, it was emotionally painful to also maintain my own critical, separate standpoint. That pain is part of what differentiates the "involved observer" from uninvolved observers or simple reformers.


## UNDERSTANDING THE DATA: THE PROBLEM OF ANALYSIS

I left the Department of Health and Human Services at the end of 1990, after more than two and a half years of devoting myself to reform. Not really sure of how to make sense out of the data, I simultaneously plunged into reading historical studies, contemporary social service critiques, and organizational theory. I found it curious so little had been written about bureaucracy in the social services. At the same time I was faced with my field notes, paper and computer records and memos, evaluations and research reports, and an eight inch thick notebook of transcripts of evaluators' interviews with 28 social workers and supervisors. Thanks to my publisher Paul Elitzik, and friend in Chicago, Debbie Schwartz, my field notes had been transcribed and put on disk. I used Gofer from Microlytics™, a simple and cheap qualitative software package which would allow me to code my field notes and computer saved records and bring them up for analysis.

Alas, the interviews with the 28 social workers, which I had not yet read,[5] were only in paper form. A secretary at UWM's Urban Research Center had written over the disks thinking they were no longer useful. This meant I had to analyze those interviews the old fashioned way, with note cards and lots of tedious work. I hadn't begun coding my field notes yet, since I wasn't really sure what I was looking for. I believed the worker interviews were exactly what I needed to "frame" my dissertation.

I used grounded theory's "open coding" techniques (Strauss 1987, 28–33), of reading the interviews and coding as I went along, trying to create "core categories" (36) on which to base my analysis. At the same time I was coding, I was trying to apply the perspectives advanced by various social welfare and organizational theories. Two of the several dozen codes I developed were <family>, which signified anything in the interview that described social work with families, and <punishment> by which I meant investigating and removing children from their homes and other court oriented behaviors. I wrote the codes in the margins of the text and cited the interview number and page next to the codes on a separate sheet.

In one of the questions, social workers were asked to describe their daily routine, that is, what they did on a specific day. I had hopes that this question would produce more than "presentational data," or answers cushioned by social workers' concern for how they might appear to outsiders. Combined with my earlier personal observation of the routines of social workers, I thought the narration of an actual day's work might yield "operational data" of what actually goes on (Van Maanen 1979a, 54–43).[6]

About half way through reading and open coding the interviews, I noticed the code <family> had almost no entries, and the code <punishment> was getting used again and again. I thought I might be on to something, but I decided it was prudent to first finish coding all the interviews. I wrote a theoretical "memo" (Strauss 1987, 18) speculating on the importance of this discovery, if true, and kept on reading and coding.

After I finished my first reading of the entire interviews, I went back and looked at the answers to just the question on the workers' daily routine. To my surprise, only one of twenty-eight workers saw fit to say anything at all about service to families as part of what they did everyday. All the rest described routines of paperwork, time spent waiting in court, and other activities unrelated to service for families. I hadn't expected such answers and I began to think this discovery might have importance. Merton (1968, 158–59) says the process of "serendipity" includes discoveries which are unanticipated, surprising, and strategic which certainly seemed to describe the situation.

The readings I had been doing in organizational theory, the history of social welfare, and critiques of social services began to pay off. The entrapment of social workers in the courts, I thought, might be seen as the outcome of an historical process, one which may be related to how social service bureaucracies were interacting with the more punitive Reagan-Bush administrations. These ideas were pretty unformed, and I had several other theoretical insights at about the same time, some of which proved useful and others not. The numerous <punishment> codes, though, suggested to me that I should look into the issue more.

I eventually adopted the "emergent" organizational school as a provisional "orienting theory" (Whyte 1984, 228-233) to help me understand the nature of modern social work. This eventually led to a much more detailed historical analysis of social welfare bureaucracies, explaining how both "helping" and "punishing" the poor have been used as rationales for increased resources which end up benefiting the bureaucracy more than either the poor or taxpayers.

I began to reduce the number of codes and tagged the code <punishment> to appropriate places in my own field notes and the documents I was reading. I found more evidence that it was no accident that child abuse investigations and foster care, rather than family preservation, dominated social work. I applied Lincoln and Guba's five criteria of trustworthiness of the data (1985, 301–16) in an informal manner to ascertain whether the domination of social work by punitive routines was more than a product of my own mind or biases.

I found the idea was ""credible": the domination of court and punitive routines showed up in the worker interviews conducted both by outside evaluators and my own field notes. Articles in the social service journals also addressed this issue. My "peer debriefing" with colleagues about what I was discovering as I went along had also helped persuade me I was on a right track. "Negative case analysis" prompted me to look for examples of social workers who were not caught up in the courts. While I found some exemplary workers who had overcome the tendency to be enslaved by the courts and who tried to keep families together, they seemed to be more the exceptions which proved the rule. I found official documents and memos preoccupied with relations with the courts, demonstrating the idea had "referential adequacy". Finally, my dissertation was read by several of my co-workers from the Department of Health and Human Services—Lincoln and Guba's "member checks"—to make sure my overall findings were understandable to those who had similar experiences. I asked Howard Fuller to be a member of my dissertation committee to take advantage of his viewpoint. These checks persuaded me my analysis was, well, trustworthy. But before I could start to write, I had to deal with one more problem.

My research is an example of what Merton calls "post factum" theorizing, or developing a research hypothesis only after the research is concluded. Merton (1968, 147) chides such research as being "spurious....Post Factum explanations remain at the level of plausibility." Merton was criticizing the separation of theory and empirical research (153), or the eclectic tendencies of some researchers to depart from their hypotheses and fashion new interpretations that merely "fit the facts" (148).

First of all, I didn't have a lot of trouble with the notion that if the facts didn't fit the theory, it's the theory that must change. I'm a firm believer in the inductive method, agreeing enthusiastically with Henry Mintzberg ( 1979, 584) : "It is discovery that attracts me to this business, not the checking out of what we think we already know." Lincoln and Guba point out studies can be arranged in two types, those

> in which the investigator 'knows what he or she doesn't know' and therefore can project means of finding it out, and situations in which the investigator 'does not know what he or she doesn't know,' in which case a much more open-ended approach is required.
>
> *(Lincoln and Guba 1985, 209)*

Strauss's grounded theory as well as "naturalistic" inquiries directly confront the post factum problem by dialectically testing theoretical propositions with the data in an ongoing process of discovery. Theory is not preconceived, it is "emergent"; it emerges from the process of data collection, coding, developing core categories, theoretical sampling, and integrating theory with the data (Strauss 1987, 22–39; also cf. Lincoln and Guba 1985, 332–56). I entered the "field" with very few hypotheses or preconceived notions about what I would find. My theoretical treatment of bureaucratic behavior in the social services did not precede the analysis, it emerged from it.[7]

## WRITING IT UP: THE PROBLEM OF AUDIENCE

Writing for me has always had two functions: first, the act of writing helps me better understand what I'm writing about. Emily Dickenson said somewhere she didn't know what she thought until she'd written it.[8] But more important, it's always been vital for me to write in a manner that impacts a broader public than academia.

Some parts of these chapters have been rewritten at least fifty times. Writing doesn't come easy to me, it's hard work. Each time I rewrite a chapter or a section, I try to read it from the perspective of a specific person whom I expect to read the book. As C.Wright Mills (1959, 218) says, "To write is to raise a claim for the attention of readers." I learn more about what I am saying as I rewrite and try to make sure the book makes sense to each type of prospective reader. But who are those readers?

I do want to reach an academic audience: sociologists and social welfare professionals who think and write about these issues and whose opinions are heard by the powerful. I hope the book can also be valuable in teaching students about social services, bureaucratic reform, and social change. I also want to reach those working in local and federal bureaucracies—policy makers, managers, and line staff—as well as parents and taxpayers who are concerned with the future of social services. Another audience are former activists of my generation, many now working in public bureaucracies, who may still "feel the fire" and have stayed concerned about social change.

This audience is broader than the audience for the typical sociology book. Dissertations often have an audience of five, and only that many if the entire dissertation committee actually reads the manuscript. Many books and articles in academic journals don't fare much better. Sociologists are notoriously bad writers, partially because they are normally writing only for themselves.

> To put it sharply: the habitat, manners, and idiom of intellectuals have been transformed within the past fifty years. Younger intellectuals no longer need or want a larger public; they are almost exclusively professors… As intellectuals became academics, they had no need to write in a public prose; they did not, and finally they could not.
>
> *(Jacoby 1987, 6–7)*

This book is rhetorical, in the sense that it seeks to persuade "publics" of an idea, and encourage action.

> Sociological writing, like most of social science, is rhetorical in that it presents an argument; it is an effort to persuade....How persuasion is accomplished is a legitimate inquiry.
>
> *(Gusfield 1991, 62)*

To me good sociological writing is a book or article which can reach broader publics, while at the same time seriously engaging academic issues.

> The challenge for sociological prose, then, is to convey ideas and information with enough clarity to be understood outside the narrow precincts of the field and yet with enough precision to allow for careful inspection and evaluation within it.
>
> *(Erikson 1990, 27)*

The problem for academics is that while many "deconstruct" the latest theories with vigor, they often do it in a manner only the initiated can understand. Kai Erickson (1990, 25) accuses sociological writing of a style which is "ponderous, convoluted, hulking, bovine, full of a contrived profundity." I always suspected that those who write in an obscure manner may not know themselves what they are writing about.

> Perhaps quantum physics can only be understood in the context of a mathematical language, but our work is not so technical or esoteric that it cannot be explained in prose to an educated lay audience. (Or, if it cannot, there is probably something wrong with the work.)
>
> *(Fischer 1990, 58)*

Sociologists, as Becker (1986) says, need to improve their writing so they can be understood by most educated people.

## That Reminds Me of a Story

One neglected sociological form for reaching a broader public is the story. Stories come in many types. There are the often ribald tales that we tell of our work places at a bar after 5 p.m.; bible stories or fairy tales we tell our children at bedtime; and the anecdotes we remember about important things that happened in our lives which we tell our friends, relatives, and young people.

Narrative tales can be used in sociology too. Stories cannot replace data, but they often stick in our mind when the data is forgotten.

> Simply said, we are more influenced by stories (vignettes that are whole and make sense in themselves) than by data (which are, by definition, utterly abstract).
>
> *(Peters and Waterman 1982, 61).*

In this work, I began the non-historical chapters with a story from my own experience in the Youth Initiative, which makes the main point of the chapter which follows. This gave me two ways to try to make my point and convince you, the reader, of the validity of my argument.

> Because observers make selections among many available interpretations and seek out a "plot" that will make their observations hang together, storytelling is an important part of the art. Field researchers...must find ways of convincing their audiences that their depiction is real and true. It is the narrative that makes the account convincing, not the facts
>
> *(Milofsky 1990, 37–38)*

Emergent organizational theory downplays our notions of rationality, and that includes a reconsideration of how men and women learn. I've loved this "story," repeated by Peters and Waterman:

> a man wanted to know about mind, not in nature, but in his private large computer. He asked it, 'Do you compute that you will ever think

like a human being?' The machine then set to work to analyze its own computational habits, Finally, the machine printed its answer on a piece of paper, as such machines do. The man ran to get the answer and found, neatly typed, the words: THAT REMINDS ME OF A STORY. A story is a little knot or complex of that species of connectedness which we call relevance. Surely the computer was right. This is indeed how people think.

*(Bateson 1980, 14, quoted in*
*Peters and Waterman 1982, 62)*

Stories as a persuasive form have been used in medical journals (Hunter 1986, 619) and in the organizational literature (Van Maanen 1988). I've used stories of my own activities to try to bring to life the experience of reform and better persuade you, the reader, to accept my analyis and act on it. I've also used the stories to humanize me. Many ethnographers quote their own field notes as a way to prove how right or insightful they were all along. I just wasn't right all the time. The story format allows me to be seen as a real person trying to figure out what to do, rather than as an academic know-it-all.

## CONCLUSION: INCITING CHANGE

This book is a combination of many genres, and has ended up as a unique form. It is at once a participant observation of a special type, an involved observation. It is one of a growing number of field work studies in organizations (Schwartzman 1993). It is in part an exposé of the dysfunctions of social service bureaucracies within the institutional school of organizational theory (Perrow 1979, 177). Some of it is a case study using multiple sources of data, analyzing the real practices and structures of the Milwaukee County Department of Social Services (Yin 1990, 23; Milofsky 1990). It fits into a small category John Van Maanen calls "critical tales," or "fieldwork studies... strategically situated to shed light on large social, political, symbolic, or economic issues" (Van Maanen 1988, 127). It is an "organizational saga" (Clark 1972, 178) which deepens a group's understanding of their accomplishments by retelling or rewriting them. Finally, it's a brief history of social service reform and a review of the social welfare and organizational literatures.

Above all, this book is an attempt to use the experience of the Youth Initiative to encourage reform in the social services.

> The art and architecture of change, then, also involves designing reports about the past to elicit the present actions required for the future—to extract the elements necessary for current action, to continue to construct and reconstruct participants' understanding of events so that the next phase of activity is possible."
>
> *(Kanter 1983, 288)*

To promote change, I have thrown at the reader the field notes of an "involved observer," stories, reviews of the literature, history, exposé, and analysis one after the other. I've used all the arrows in my quiver to try to "encourage controversy" and point the way for others. The goal of this book is to make reform of street-level bureaucracies seem possible. But it also seeks to encourage more "involved observation" research, written in a readable manner. I hope I can reach at least a few people who are truly concerned with our children.

# APPENDIX 2
# AFRICAN AMERICANS IN MILWAUKEE: 1963 AND 1987

A year into our administration, Department of Health and Human Services (DHHS) Director Howard Fuller asked me to compare the situation of African Americans in Milwaukee in 1963 to today, for a Martin Luther King Day speech he was to give. At first I looked at the employment figures and the impact of the precipitous loss of manufacturing jobs in the eighties. Between 1979 to 1986 over 50,000 factory jobs were lost in Milwaukee or 23% of our city's manufacturing employment (White, et al. 1988). The plant closings and lay-offs had a major impact among African Americans. In 1980, prior to the downturn, 40% of all African American workers were concentrated in manufacturing—by 1989, less than 25% held such factory jobs (Moore and Edari 1990b). Entry level manufacturing jobs had all but disappeared.

Martin Luther King never imagined that due to an economic transforma tion of urban America, many poor African Americans would not be able to work their way out of poverty as did white ethnics before them (Steinberg 1981). But neither did Dr. King imagine a latent consequence of these economic changes: as good jobs became scarce, families which were previously intact began to break up. AFDC has become a principal means of long term support for poor African American families.

In 1963, when Dr. King had his dream, less than one in six of Milwaukee's African Americans were supported by AFDC. However by 1987, nearly half of all Milwaukee African Americans and two thirds of all Black children received AFDC benefits. In 1963, all transfer payments supported less than one quarter (23.8%) of Milwaukee's African Americans. But by 1987, more than two thirds of all African Americans (69.3%) were receiving one type of transfer payment or another representing about one half of all Milwaukee African American income. AFDC benefits jumped from $4.8 million or 5% of all black income in

1963 to $151 million or 21 % of all Black income in 1987. One basic change since 1963, I summed up for Fuller's speech, is the increased level of involvement of African Americans with welfare bureaucracies.

# The Extent of Social Welfare Influence
# Among Milwaukee African Americans: 1963 and 1987

|  | 1963 | 1987 |
|---|---|---|
| Milwaukee County | | |
| Total Population | 1,036,041 | 958,714 |
| Milwaukee County | | |
| African American Population | 63,024 | 165,000 est. |
| Total Children under 19 | 403,315 | 180,000 est. |
| African American Children under 19 | 29,839 | 70,000 est. |
| Total AFDC clients | 16,539 | 105,775 |
| AFDC as a percentage | | |
| of total Population | 1.6% | 11.0% |
| Total AFDC African American clients | 9425 | 71,411 |
| AFDC as a percentage | | |
| of African American Population | 15.0% | 43.3% |
| Total est. African American Income* | $97,120,800 | $716,636,100 |
| Total AFDC payments | | |
| to African American clients | $4,857,076 | $151,204,720 |
| AFDC payments as a percentage | | |
| of African American Income | 5.0% | 21.1% |
| Transfer payments as a percentage | | |
| of African American Income | NA | 47.6% |

\* Total African American income was arrived at by multiplying average household income by the number of African American households (Analysis 1988).

Transfer payments include welfare, unemployment compensation, social security, veterans benefits, and a few other categories of government assistance. Milwaukee data is consistent with national trends analyzed by Piven and Cloward (1982, 15) who point out "almost half of the aggregate income of the bottom fifth of the population is derived from social welfare benefits. The poorest people in the country are now as much dependent on the government for subsistence as they are on the labor market."

For the argument there is a correlation between the loss of good jobs and the attractiveness of welfare, see Block et al. (1987). For a cautionary note on the relationship of employment and family make-up, see Osterman (1991). Wilson (1987) and Lieberson (1980) among others make the point that Black family break-up occurred because of economic and social conditions in the North, not from the legacy of slavery in the South. On length of stay on AFDC, see the debate based on the analysis of the PSID data at the University of Michigan on welfare "spells." While some scholars (Duncan 1984) suggest AFDC is a temporary response to unavoidable problems, Murray, in an overlooked study (free of the ideological rancor of *Losing Ground* ) shows that when age is controlled in studies of welfare duration, the PSID data disclose over one third of all U.S. women who first received AFDC when they were under 25 stayed on AFDC for over ten years (Murray and Laren 1986, 40). Milwaukee data generally support Murray's findings: over a quarter of all Milwaukee AFDC recipients have a current "spell" of AFDC of more than nine years.

# Four Stages of Organizational Theory

## Stages of Reform in Business and the Social Services

| 1850–1930 | 1960s |
|---|---|
| Rise of Rational Organizations: the factory and the poorhouse. Protest provokes both scientific and progressive reforms which increase supervision of workers and the poor. | Business sees need to alter structure contingent on environment and task. Social welfare expands, taking advantage of protest. Social services separate from income maintenance but maintain hierarchical organization. |
| **1930s** | **1970-?** |
| Upsurge during the Great Depression brings increased supervision of both workers and clients and their division into manageable segments. Social welfare begins to institutionalize in the New Deal. | Business down-sizes and decentralizes, emphasizing a "bias for action." Welfare and social services maintain hierarchical structures and use them to adapt to a more mean-spirited era and become more punitive. |

This diagram is based on Peters' and Waterman's four stages of organizational theory (1982, 93).

# NOTES

## Chapter 1

1. This is an unduplicated count. Since some youth in the records may have reached 18 and their records are still open, 60% may slightly overestimate the percentage of youth involved in the social welfare system.

2. In 1989, as a beginning part of a four year evaluation of the Youth Initiative a team of researchers, hired by the UWM Urban Research Center, conducted a series of confidential interviews with social workers and administrators of the Department of Social Services. Twenty-eight social workers and supervisors from Child Protective Services and the Children's Court juvenile probation departments were randomly selected from listings of personnel grouped by race and sex (Zakhar 1989). Mary Devitt also conducted a series of interviews with key participants in the Youth Initiative in 1992 to assess the perspectives of different stakeholders.

3. Similarly, Moynihan details the life cycle of a typical poverty agency:

> First, a period of organizing with much publicity and great expectations everywhere. Second, the beginning of operations, with the onset of conflict between the agency and local government institutions, with even greater publicity. Third, a period of counterattack from local government, not infrequently accompanied by conflict and difficulties, including accounting troubles within the agency itself. Fourth, victory for the established institutions, or at best, stalemate, accompanied by bitterness and charges of betrayal.
>
> *(Moynihan 1969, 131)*

4. The war on poverty did turn out to be a major fund-raising venture for urban bureaucracies. Federal spending on social programs rose an average of 7.9% during the Kennedy-Johnson years and 9.7% during the Nixon-Ford years (Danziger, et al. 1986, 52). Those increases, however, were overwhelmingly not spent on the new OEO agencies. By 1974, OEO was dead and its programs littered around the federal bureaucracy

or folded into local government (Patterson 1986, 148). See chapters five and six.

# Chapter 2

1. Who do social workers cooperate best with in their jobs? A staff survey conducted by the Youth Initiative found that 68% of all child welfare staff thought coordination with the Milwaukee Police Department was "good" or "excellent" and only 1% thought coordination with police was "poor." This contrasts with 43% who thought coordination was "poor" with financial assistance workers (FAWs), who often are extremely knowledgable about clients' lives. Eighteen percent thougth cooperation with FAWs was good (Hagedorn 1990). What does this tell us about social work priorities?

2. Minuchin (1991, 7) illustrates: "I once suggested the possibility of training protective service case workers in family assessment to the head of a field office. He was curious, but as soon as he realized that "family assessment" would include assessment of the strengths and potentials of a family, including the exploration of resources in the extended family, he was very much against the idea. Such training might give his workers the idea that they were therapists, he explained, and that would slow their caseload processing."

3. The ETI report finds that the computer system may not be a reliable indicator of all activity of social workers, but just those entered into the computer. Regardless, between 1987 and 1989 the report documented 34,885 "service events" for 15,926 families, with 23,093 court centered and unrelated to any "service." Even some services, like "family reunification" are court related since even change of placement of a child back to the natural family requires permission of the court. "Family reunification" may not indicate any services were offered, but rather only indicates the court allowed the children to return to their parent(s).

4. This simultaneous growth in child protective services and referrals is a national pattern. For example, in New Jersey the state-run child welfare agency's employees increased from under 500 in 1965 to more then 2000 in 1975. Increased referrals for child abuse sparked caseloads to rise from 19,249 children in 1968 to 44,688 children in 1974 (Pelton 1989, 25). In the early 1980s, state and federal spending on child abuse doubled over five years (Kamerman and Kahn 1989, 51). While implementation of "permanency planning" in the Adoption Assistance and Child Welfare Act of 1980 reduced foster care caseloads temporarily, by the end of the eighties caseloads began to climb again (Fein and Maluccio 1992, 337–38).

5. Lipsky's central point, that public policy essentially consists of the actions of street level bureaucrats, needs to be seen in this context. Public social workers don't really have discretion to provide services, since their jobs have become limited to investigating poor families, supervisig a placement in foster care, and above all, reporting to the court. Their actual discretion is limited by this new, more punitive, occupational role. As Lipsky himself points out:

> This is not to say that street-level workers are unrestrained by rules, regulations, and directives from above, or by the norms and practices of their occupational groups. On the contrary, the major dimensions of public policy...are shaped by policy elites and political and administrative officials.
>
> *(Lipsky 1980, 14).*

For a different view of Lipsky's concept of discretion see  Meyer and Zucker (1989, 141).

## Chapter 3

1. Edwards (1979) describes how fragmentation is an essential component of "bureaucratic control:" "Polaroid's system of control is built on a finely graded division and stratification of workers. The divisions run both hierarchically (creating higher and lower positions) and laterally. They tend to breakup the homogeneity of the firm's workforce, creating many seemingly separate strata, lines of work, and focuses for job identity" (133). The relatively high pay and good benefits of a large company provided positive incentives "which greatly heightened the workers' sense of the mobility within the firm that lay in front of them" (143). This description could easily be applied to a department of social services.

2. Mary Devitt, in her institutional impact evaluation, was surprised that so many of the original Youth Initiative participants remembered Wilson's and Schorr's books by name and recounted the impact of reading selections from their works in the Youth Initiative Committee.

## Chapter 4

1. As part of a $50,000 per year evaluation contract for the Youth Initiative, we conducted research on a probability sample of 300 heads of household in 10 census tracts in the heart of zip codes 53204 and 06. Community residents were trained to conduct

an interview using a structured questionnaire. Respondents were paid $10 for a less than one hour interview.

2. I had also learned that many of our child protective workers informally divide referrals into "bad addresses" and "good addresses" corresponding to the central city and outlying areas respectively. Most referrals, they insist, come from "bad addresses."

3. There are also many arguments for the superiority of community-based programs. For example Goldstein (1991) points out that funding neighborhood-based programs ought to be preferred since recidivist rates are similar to residential programs. Community-based programs appear to be more effective than institutional programs for emphasis on the acquisition of inter-personal, vocational, and educational skills, family bonding; and rejection of anti-social tendencies (154). Our argument, however, was based primarily on the location, not the type of services.

4. This is what Gordon et al. (1982, 9) mean by the "social structure of accumulation…the specific institutional environment within which the capitalist accumulation process takes place." Unfortunately, like other Marxist and neo-Marxist scholars, the authors pay very little attention to the role of public institutions (which over the past fifty years have always been bureaucracies) in enforcing specific class arrangements. Also see Gouldner (1970, 77).

5. In contrast, zip code 53204 is dotted with community agencies, banks, merchants, and grocery stores. This southside neighborhood is an area of first settlement for Latino and Asian immigrants and nearly half of respondents in our survey reported they do not speak English well (Moore and Edari 1990b). But the area does not have the characteristics of social disorganization of the predominantly African American 53206 neighborhoods. Local agencies, however, may not effectively reach out to the poorest and more troubled residents (Hagedorn 1988; Hill 1981). The Latino underclass experience may be different than African Americans' (Moore and Pinderhughes 1993).

6. A lively institutional presence can also promote neighborhood-level social control, rather than merely relying on police and other formal systems. Social control operates best when community-level networks are voluntarily tied to external bureaucracies and other resources (Figueira-McDonough 1991). Suttles (1968) long ago had pointed out that as ties to external forces increased, local controls tightened, that is a community became more "provincial" (223–24). The expansion of secondary, non-punitive organizations within very poor communities, controlled by the communities themselves and not by large bureaucracies (Figueira-McDonough 1991, 74), can be an

important means of stemming the negative behaviors of the underclass. Such organizations were almost totally absent in predominantly African American zip code 53206.

# Chapter 5

1. But see Piven and Cloward's (1993) review of "State-Centered Interpretations" of the welfare state in their updated version of *Regulating the Poor*. Also see Weir, Orloff, and Skocpol's (1988) *The Politics of Social Policy in the United States*.

2. For a more complete account of similarities and differences in business and social welfare reform, see my doctoral dissertation published in 1993. See Appendix 3 for a graphic presentation of four periods of welfare and industrial reform.

3. "The Taylorites' ideological assertion, like the Progressives, was that both workers and employers would benefit from increased production. Thus both had a stake in seeing that "science" and "scientific methods" were used to determine the one best way that each task would be done" (Edwards 1979, 99; Rothman 1980, 60–61). As a rule, it was the smaller companies who embraced Taylorism, while the larger companies increased the number of foremen (Edwards 1979, 101). Taylorism, however, did "break the hold" of social Darwinist theories and forced management to begin to think of new ways to control workers through cooperation (Perrow 1979, 65). Both the progessive movement and Taylorism were based on classification systems, dedication to scientific methods, and identity of interests between the state and workers or clients.

4. Foucault (1979, 217) calls this period the beginning of an era of surveillance.

5. Private social work agencies, which still had a monopoly on the delivery of social services, were less than enthusiastic about New Deal reforms. Casework, which bases its approach on the failings of individuals to adjust to the environment, had little relevance during the depression, when people were clearly in need through no fault of their own (Axinn and Levin 1982, 191–92). Private agencies began a new orientation toward a middle class constituency (Wilensky and Lebeaux 1965, 171) and largely sat on the sidelines during the momentous days of the birth of the welfare state (Axinn and Levin 1982, 193).

6. The decisive crushing of militant challengers within the United Auto Workers took place in West Allis, Wisconsin, adjacent to the city of Milwaukee. There, Allis-Chalmers, the media, and the international union combined to break the strike and end left-wing opposition to Walter Reuther. In a frenzy of red-baiting, a September 23,

1946, front page *Milwaukee Sentinel* cartoon showed a picture of the head of Joseph Stalin on a spider's body grabbing Wisconsin (Dannenberg, et al. 1970).

7. The small size of these companies, their capacity to close or move when confronted by labor trouble, and the existence of a large reserve pool of unskilled labor has made unionization difficult (Edwards 1979, 167–70). It has created a "buffer" that allows large corporations to leave their core workforce in place, while forcing smaller companies to be exposed to the highest risk (Morgan 1986, 285).

8. The New Deal specifically rejected mandating assistance to all poor children, instead mandating aid only on the condition of the absence of the father (Piven and Cloward 1971, 115). Congress also omitted health insurance as part of the overall package (Orloff 1988, 75) and did little in the way of funding public housing, half-way policies which sadly distinguish the United States from other industrialized nations.

# Chapter 6

1. Both classical management theory and the human relations school were "closed systems" theories; i.e., they were based on the assumption that the firm was a closed system and could handle its own affairs (Peters and Waterman 1982, 100). Thus the reforms of "scientific management" and winning the loyalty of workers were policies which an individual firm could use regardless of what was happening in the outside world. A changing environment, however, and the existence of different types of labor markets, called for different types of firms and different types of management strategies. Market organizations might be better understood as "open systems…shaped and molded by forces outside itself" (Peters and Waterman 1982, 99).

2. Emery and Trist (1965), in an often-cited formulation, specify four types of "causal texture of organizational environments" 1. placid, randomized; 2. placid, clustered; 3. disturbed-reactive; and 4. turbulent fields. Basically, Emery and Trist argue that hierarchical organizations are suited for more placid environments while more disturbed environments require more complex, matrix-style organizations . Another variant of this approach is population ecology, which asks, "why are there so many types of organizations?" This school examines how external and internal constraints shape organizations and why some organizations persist and others die (Pfeffer 1982, 181–92; Hannan and Freeman 1977). However, see Zucker and Rosenstein (1981) for an ethno-methodological critique of contingency theory. They find "little evidence of sectoral differentiation" and suggest a "reformulation" of organizational taxonomies should be undertaken.

3. According to Rino Patti (1975, 25), this "new scientific management" stressed technical efficiency rather than human concerns. Patti compares the changes in social welfare management as a throwback to Taylorism's nineteenth century preoccupation with precise job descriptions and evaluations of performance.

4. See the epilogue of Marris and Rein (1967) for a rounded critique of the War on Poverty. Ironically, Marris and Rein believe the two most lasting success of the War on Poverty both center on its impact on public bureaucracies: 1) the creation of legal advocacy services, giving the poor legal help in their battle against the public bureaucracies, and 2) its paving the way for black leaders to get jobs in the bureaucracies (267–70). This is also Halpern's (1991, 354) conclusion.

5. Other examples from this school are Gouldner's (1954) study of a gypsum plant, Zald and Denton's (1963) study of the YMCA, and Walmsley's (1969) study of the Selective Service System. For a more complete review see Perrow (1979, 177–83) and Morgan (1986, 39–76).

6. "Institutionalized" organizations differ from business or "technical" organizations which are judged more often by their outputs, or the market. Business must produce a quality product or risk failing, while public bureaucracies need only to sustain their myths in the public eye. Lipsky (1980, 54–55) points out that welfare and other street-level bureaucracies persist regardless of the quality of the services they offer and with little measurement of the performance of their workers.

7. Derthick pointed out (1975, 76) "The loophole was closed when the exploitation of it became absurd. The states killed the goose by asking too much." The $2.5 billion social service spending cap imposed by Congress in 1972 remains today.

8. Weber long ago had pointed out that "it may be said that 'normally'—though not without exception—the vigor to expand is directly related to the degree of bureaucratization" (Gerth and Mills 1946, 210). Also see Downs 1967, 16–18 for explanations of why bureaucratic units seek to expand.

9. In a 1965 introduction of *Industrial Society and Social Welfare,* Wilensky and Lebeaux carefully differentiate support for social welfare spending from supporting the new community action programs which were budding at the time. The new approach, they claim is "romantic" and unrealistic. "Decentralization," Wilensky and Lebeaux (1965, xliv–xlvi) warn, "like patent medicine, is not really good for what ails you." Rather than funding new service delivery agents, Wilensky and Lebeaux advocate funding "ombudsmen" and other cosmetic reforms to make the service bureaucracies

appear more rational and responsive.

Social work, Wilensky and Lebeaux caution in the closing pages of their book, has been "underdeveloped." What is needed are new roles for the social welfare professional, including that of "community organizer," and for the welfare institution to "expand and define its area of competence" (Wilensky and Lebeaux 1965, 333–34). For the social welfare institution to survive it had to adapt. In short, social welfare bureaucracies had to expand beyond the functions of determining eligibility for assistance and sending out benefits. They had to speak in the language of community action, claim to be able to deliver services more "efficiently" than neighborhood agencies, and sieze control of the new federal funds. For the new social service departments, it was either act or risk the slow death of declining resources.

10. Karl Weick, passing on a comment from James March, compared organizations to an unconventional soccer match:

> There are goals scattered haphazardly around the circular field, people can enter and leave the game whenever they want; they can say 'that's my goal' whenever they want to, as many times as they want to, and for as many goals as they want to; the entire game takes place on a sloped field and the game is played as if it makes sense.
>
> *(Weick 1976, 1)*

James March and Michael Cohen (1972) topped Weick with a brilliantly crafted, if somewhat bizarre image. Rather than see organizations as vehicles for solving well-defined problems, March et al. saw organizations as "garbage cans":

> A choice opportunity…into which various kinds of problems and solutions are dumped by participants as they are generated…From this point of view, an organization is a collection of choices looking for problems, issues and feelings looking for decision situations in which they might be aired, solutions looking for issues to which they might be the answer, and decision makers looking for work.
>
> *(Cohen, et al. 1972, 2)*

Finally, Morgan (1986, 95–103) suggests organizations are similar to holographs. Each part of a holograph contains information from which the whole can be reconstructed. Holographic organization emphasizes redundancy, capacity for self-organization, and is decentralized with most of the firm's functions being reproduced in each of its parts, often by multi-task work teams. This kind of organization is also modeled after the functioning of the brain, which exhibits a high degree of interdependence among its parts, has a pattern of rich connectivity between neurons, is creative, and adjusts by itself to new situations (95–96).

11. In an insightful review of the history of organizational theory, Clark (1985) recounts the attempts of "neo-orthodox" theorists to save rationality. Clark's view is that the human relations and contingent schools should be seen in the context of trying to reform the old rational paradigm in Kuhn's (1970) sense. For example, "informal organization," which Weber neglected and the human relations school championed, was seen by Clark as "a real factor to be taken into account, but it was noise in the system" (52). The rational paradigm was in hot water and numerous concepts were launched to save it: like Simon's concept of "bounded rationality"(57), which pointed out that rationality was limited by the incapacity to have all the necessary information (Simon 1956). Clark and his fellow contributors see such ideas as merely last ditch efforts to hold on to the old "positivist" paradigm (Lincoln 1985a, 32; see also Morgan 1986, 107). Lincoln and Clark believe the "emergent" school is a "post-positivist" paradigm ready to replace the old positivist one. The characteristics of the new paradigm are a shift: 1) from a simple probabilistic world to one that is complex and diverse; 2) from a hierarchically ordered world to one ordered by hetarchy; 3) from mechanical to holographic imaging; 4) from a world of determinism to indeterminism; 5) from direct causality to mutual causality; 6) from change by assembly to change by morphogenesis; and 7) from outlooks and research which claimed objectivity to a posture that is perspectival (68–75). The new paradigm goes beyond organizational theory and is intended to be germane for the sciences generally (see Lincoln 1985b; Schwartz and Ogilvy 1979).

12. Peters and Waterman came up with eight "attributes" of excellent companies derived from the new theory (1982, 89): 1) A bias for action; 2) Staying close to the customer; 3) Autonomy and entrepreneurship; i.e., breaking large companies into small independent thinking units; 4) Productivity through people; 5) Hands on, value driven style; 6) Stick to the knitting; i.e. keeping in touch with core technology; 7) Simple form, lean staff; and 8) Simultaneous loose-tight properties; i.e., dedication to the company and tolerance for all employees who accept identified corporate values. Do these "attributes" describe public bureaucracies?

13. Examples of the new thinking abound in the corporate world. To take just one example, in 1991 the "battleship," IBM, was forced to radically decentralize to become a "family of loosely affiliated subsidiaries." The strategy was aimed in part "at rekindling initiative and entrepreneurship among IBM employees and executives" and also was a

last ditch move to save itself. Wall Street responded enthusiastically to the "overdue" changes and IBM's stock jumped up $2.75 to close at $97.875 (Markoff 1991). Peters and Waterman argue that excellent companies have "a small is beautiful, small is effective philosophy" (1982, 111).

In the secondary labor market, where contingency theory asserts tasks are routine and organization hierarchical, companies like McDonald's have it both ways. While employees cook hamburgers and french fries to precise instructions—"Cooks must turn, never flip, hamburgers"—McDonald's has excelled with comparatively little organizational structure on the top. Ray Kroc's philosophy on size of management was always "less is more" (Peters and Waterman 1982, 255–58).

14. Slessarev (1988) contrasts the successful subsidized housing cuts to the unsuccessful attempts to cut Medicaid. Subsidized housing benefited mainly African Americans and Latinos who were concentrated in public housing (379). Medicaid, however, benefited doctors and hospitals as well as the poor (373). Medicaid is the largest program in some states' entire budget. Even Republican governors broke rank and opposed Reagan's Medicaid cuts (375).

15. Fraud investigations also reinforce popular beliefs that welfare recipients are dishonest and welfare benefits promote dependency. In an interesting analysis, Edin shows that informal or extra-legal income is necessary to survival for AFDC recipients in Illinois (Edin 1991; see also Ellwood 1988).

16. For a more general approach to the question of resource dependency and public organizations, see Pfeffer (1982, 178–207) and Pffeffer and Salancik (1978).

17. Orfield' s plea for more resources for social services unfortunately poses the problem as competition for resources between "punitive" and "service" bureaucracies. He fails to consider that social services, along with other public bureaucracies have also been emphasizing punitive policies as a means to play to popular sentiment and to maintain resources. It's no wonder Orfield is surprised that: "Even the clients of the services frequently denounce the professionals and blame them for part of their problems" (Orfield 1991, 517).

# Chapter 7

1. For education and police, two other prominant street-level bureaucracies, altering core tasks is also at the center of reform. Police need a structure of work that promotes mediation of disputes and community relations, not just arrests. Teachers need classroom routines which enable them to educate students who come from poor minority families as well as those who come from a more educated background.

2. This perspective is a basic one in the organizational literatures. March and Olsen say, "Action is driven by routines. Individuals attend to decisions when, and because, that is what they are expected to do....Time is not so much allocated by decisions as by socialization into and acceptance of roles and by the connection to routine procedures" (March and Olsen 1976, 49). Lipsky (1980, 204) adds, "The most powerful agent in professional socialization is the work setting." And once again from James Q. Wilson (1989, 48): "Peer expectations not only affect how hard people work at their jobs, they can affect what they decide the job is." Heydebrand (1983, 307) calls changes in routines "technocratic" or "true structural change."

3. The nature of many of our reforms resembled those described by Osborne and Gaebler (1992, 19–20) in *Reinventing Government:* "Most entrepreneurial governments promote competition between service providers. They empower citizens by pushing control out of the bureaucracy, into the community. They measure the performance of their agencies, focusing not on inputs but on outcomes. They are driven by their goals—their missions—not by their rules and regulations. They redefine their clients as customers and offer them choices—between schools, between training programs, between housing options. They prevent problems before they emerge, rather than simply offering service afterward. They put their energies into earning money, not simply spending it. They decentralize authority, embracing participatory management. They prefer market mechanisms to bureaucratic mechanisms. And they focus not simply on providing public services, but on catalyzing all sectors—public, private, and voluntary—into actions to solve their community's problems."

4. For example, Janowitz (1976, 128-130) says:

> One central strategy for overcoming fragmentation and over specialization is to regroup agencies operating in a common geographic area. In a residential community, this would provide the organizational structure for the fusion of highly specialized agencies and for more effective access. The geographic dimension is also designed to contribute to a sense of group cohesion and

social solidarity of the citizenry involved, to inhibit excessive segregation of the welfare recipients, and to facilitate the institutional base for citizen participation.

5. Interviews with the pilot staff found the new units exhibited "improved worker morale" (Devitt 1992, 25). Improved morale, we hoped, could reduce the harmful aspects of worker turnover (Iglehart 1990) and provide more stability for the units .

# Chapter 8

1. Reform generally has different objectives and each are used as symbols that change is occurring. Czarniawska-Joerges (1989, 545–46) lists four objectives of reform and I have added two others:

> 1) Reform reshuffles power among bureaucrats. A new leader can elevate some and demote others. The public believes any new leader has the right to have his or her own "team." A new leadership team is often seen as a symbol of "reform" regardless of what they do.

> 2) Reform re-legitimates the institution. Public bureaucracies need to be perceived as being periodically "reformed" or they may lose public confidence. Reform of any type symbolizes that our institutions and social system are alive and, if not well, capable of getting better.

> 3) Reform re-socializes staff into the current political climate. The political landscape periodically changes and bureaucrats must become attuned to the new realities. Reform symbolizes to the bureaucracy that it must adapt to new political realities or face declining resources.

> 4) Reforms entertain some and threaten others. Reform can be a spectacle which causes some people to be energized and others enervated. Reform symbolizes that bureaucracies have a lively internal life with winners and losers in the constant struggle of individual bureaucats for advancement and prestige.

> 5) Reform can curtail legislative scrutiny. As long as "reform" is going on, legislative scrutiny is often relaxed and bureaucrats can maintain current budget levels and hide pet projects. Lack of "reform" sometimes angers overseers who then punish bureaucrats with budget cuts. Reform symbolizes to legis-

lators and taxpayers that bureaucrats are "doing something" about problems raised by constituents or the press.

6) Reform benefits "reformers." In the U.S. political system, elected officials appoint the heads of bureaucracies every few years and the new managers often prove themselves with "reform," adding to their résumés for their next job. Many reformers begin their administration, as we did, determined to "make a difference" to clients. But as the difficulty of change sinks in, cosmetic reforms are adopted because real change is just too hard. Reform symbolizes to elites and the public alike that there are professional "reformers" who can "take charge" of these bureaucracies and appear to make them work.

2. Even among social workers there is skepticism about more staff as a panacea. While a Milwaukee Department of Social Services survey found there was support to hire more social workers to adequately meet community needs, a majority of child welfare workers did not think "more staff" was DSS's main need (Hagedorn 1990).

3. We also found that the overload wasn't as bad as it seemed. "Cases" in foster care referred to parents and children, so a family of one mother and eight children would be reported as nine cases. The average number of families in a caseload of 100 might be no more than 20 or 25. Not all foster care cases are the same.

4. Galper (1975, 219) points out:

On the one hand, it is important to struggle for increased government spending for people in need. It is also important, however, to raise questions about the locus of control of these programs and the underlying purposes they serve.

5. There are other ways the councils may be used by the Department of Social Services for its own ends. By using the councils to sanction handing out contracts and favors to some providers, the councils can be used to quiet dissent from neighborhood providers dependent on County contracts (Galper 1975, 18). The councils' service delivery plans also provide a basis for the bureaucracy to claim new resources which might otherwise have gone directly to neighborhood providers. Sponsoring the Youth Initiative was seen as a reason for foundation, state, and federal funds to be sent under our bureaucracy's umbrella. As Cloward and Piven (1972, 207) said about the war on poverty: "Not only is citizen participation by and large a ritual conducted at the discretion of the public agencies, but it tends to become another vehicle for the extension of bureaucratic control" (see also Yates 1982, 98). The Department of Social Services

has tried hard to control the neighborhood councils with mixed results.

6. We did manage to secure a $50,000 per year commitment from the department for research and evaluation for the first three years and $25,000 for the next two, a not insubstantial sum. To measure neighborhood level changes, a second survey of residents in the two zip codes was intended to be administered in 1994, five years after the original research. Since our reform team left, the follow-up research was not implemented. An evaluation of the pilots found that it was impossible to measure the pilots' impact on clients due to data problems and difficulties in implementation (Pawasarat et al. 1993).

One fear I had was that the pilots and our new programs would become "innovation ghettoes" (Toch and Grant 1982, 133), isolated experiments allowed to die a slow and natural death. Rather, I hoped they would be "exemplars" (Kuhn 1970) , an example of what is to come, foreshadowing and providing a worked out structural solution if a shift in policy would occur (Rounds 1979, 50; 244). Simply put, I believed with Galper (1975, 220) "we must struggle to create, here and now, some examples, however modest, of a better way."

We also needed to know if our "better way" was any better and if it was having any impact on clients. We evaluated the "institutional impact evaluation" of the Youth Initiative by interviewing various stakeholders. We found that "important, but limited changes occurred; that institutionalization of some of these changes is beginning; but that these hard-won changes were still vulnerable" (Devitt 1992, 16). Devitt found that reform is precarious.

Finally, I am aware that formal evaluation is in the organizational interests of universities and the desire to please often guides even those "independent" efforts (Lincoln and Guba 1985). This does not diminish the need for independent evaluation.

7. This recalls Lindblom's (1959, 81) "successive limited comparisons" versus. rational comprehensive method. Good management, Lindblom said in the 1950s, was the result of the "science of muddling through."

8. Here are two stories which exemplify these qualities. The pilots were stalled by bureaucrats for over a year until a daring middle manager took matters into his own hands. We had to get an "official" memo out appointing line workers, who had already volunteered, to a pilot task force. Since the bureaucrat in charge kept putting it off, this determined manager finally forged the bureaucrat's name on the memo, and put the memo out himself. The workers' task force produced an exciting report defining what

ideal social service units would look like. The task force and report, along with pressure from the neighborhood councils, finally forced top managers to agree to form the new units. We then made sure we ran the selection process ourselves and got the pilot units running in about six months.

A second example is how the child welfare units got restructured. Unit integration was not part of the original Youth Initiative plan—none of us knew when we started what structural reform should look like. The plan for integrated units did not come from planning meetings, consultants, or studying books. Rather, one not-so-sober night, child welfare attorney Susan Hansen and I designed a detailed plan for unit integration on a napkin at Hooligan's bar. Sue then brazenly got Fuller and other top managers to admit at a Youth Initiative Committee meeting that such a restructuring could be completely accomplished in "six weeks." The plan on the napkin was rewritten into bureaucratic lingo and accepted in its entirety.

 In both examples, it was action implementing key chunks of an overall plan, combined with plenty of persistence, that was decisive in forcing change.

# Appendix 1

1. Mills declared there were three roles sociologists could play. Social scientists could aspire to become philosopher kings, basically seeking elected office themselves. Mills was skeptical of how many social scientists would be capable of benevolent rule. A more second role is "advisor to the king," more commonly known as consultant. Mills found distasteful the habit of social scientists selling their advice to the powerful and keeping quiet about the dirty laundry, or the king's lack of any clothes at all. Finally, Mills said social scientists could chose "to remain independent, to do one's own work, to select ones' own problems, but to direct this work at kings as well at to 'publics'" (Mills 1959, 181).

2. There is a Sociological Practice Association which encompasses applied research, evaluation, and clinical sociology, but its influence is small (Knudten 1990).

3. I didn't use only "involved observation" techniques in my participant observation. When going out on child abuse investigations with case workers I tried to be as unobtrusive as I could be to better observe the interaction between case worker and client. This implies "involved observation" techniques are more useful in some situations than others. Generally speaking, when the need is to understand a situation minus the influence of reform, it is better to have others do the observing. Once defined as a

reformer, some staff will always feel a "need for concealing, withholding, or distorting data" (Schwartz and Schwartz 1969, 95). The involved observer, on the other hand, may be in a better position than uninvolved observers to understand what is wrong with a bureaucratic system. Workers may be more likely to spill the beans about problems to someone they define as a change agent. As I said in my field notes:

> Can a partisan do objective research? A source of bias lies in how the observed reacts to the observer. If they think his role is to be non-partisan, not taking a side between the insanity of the system and the demand for reform... won't they respond in a biased manner also?
>
> *Field Notes, November 26, 1988*

4. Gouldner points out objectivity consists of three parts: 1) judgment between different versions of reality, 2) the capacity to admit the factuality of things that violate the researcher's own hopes and values, and 3) narrow technical concerns (Gouldner 1968, 113-16).

5. It would have been a violation of confidentiality for me to read the interview transcripts before I left my job, even though no names are listed.

6. Presentational data is necessary for street-level bureaucracies to assure the public they are doing some good. "In defense of the myth of altruism, street-level bureaucracies devote a relatively high proportion of energies to concealing lack of service and generating appearance of responsiveness." (Lipsky 1980, 76).

7. Elliot Liebow (1967, 12) also takes issue with Merton: "the timing of the hypothesis formulation is irrelevant...given the present state of the art, we can ill afford to look 'merely plausible' explanations of human behavior in the mouth" (see also Gans 1962).

8. In a way, my dissertation was like that. First data collection, analysis, exhausting study of several literatures, and writing occurred. The process of data analysis had given me a general idea of what this book would be about, but it was the act of writing, re-writing, and discussing the drafts with my colleagues that fashioned the final argument.

For example, Joan Moore read the second draft of the nearly complete dissertation and commented she could see why I made each point, but my main thesis shouldn't really come as a surprise to the reader. The reason the thesis was a surprise to the reader was that in a way it had also been a surprise to me. I had all the elements from my hard work, but I didn't clearly understand how the nature of real bureaucratic reform fit into my historical analysis and case study. It was only when I finished writing the entire book and listened to what others had to say, that I could be satisfied with a final rewrite. This has similarities with Weick's (1985) notion of "retrospective rationality." Grounded theory partisans need to address this issue.

# REFERENCES

Abraham, Katherine G.
   1983, "Structural/Functional vs Deficient Demand Unemployment:
   Some New Evidence." *The American Economic Review* 73: 708–24.

Adams,Paul and Karin Krauth
   1994, "Community-Centered Practice to Strengthen Families and
   Neighborhoods: The Patch Approach." *The Prevention Report.* The
   National Resource Center for Family Centered Practice. Fall.

Alinsky, Saul D.
   1949, *John L. Lewis: An Unauthorized Biography.* New York: Vintage.

Altshuler, Alan A.
   1970, *Community Control, The Black Demand for Participation in Large
   American Cities.* New York: Pegasus.

Arnstein, Sherry R.
   1969, "A Ladder of Citizen Participation." *AIP Journal* 35:216–224.

Axinn, June, and Herman Levin
   1982, *Social Welfare: A History of the American Response to Need.*
   Cambridge: Harper & Row.

Baird, Christopher, Deborah Neuenfeldt, Dennis Wagner and Richard Prestin
   1995, "Milwaukee Foster Care System." National Council on Crime and
   Delinquency.

Bandura, Albert
    1977, *Social Learning Theory*. Englewood Cliffs, New Jersey: Prentice-
    Hall.

Bargal, David, and Hillel Schmid
    1989, "Recent Themes in Theory and Reseach on Leadership and Their
    Implications for Management of the Human Services." *Administrative
    Leadership in the Social Services.*

Bateson, Gregory
    1980, *Mind and Nature: A Necessary Unity*. New York: Bantam Books.

Bath, Howard I., and David A. Haapala.
    1994, "Family Preservation Services: What Does the Outcome Research
    Really Tell Us?" *Social Service Review* 68 (3): 386–404.

Becker, Howard S.
    1986, *Writing for Social Scientists*. Chicago: University of Chicago.

Benson, J. Kenneth
    1981, "Organizations: A Dialectical View." In *Complex Organizations:
    Critical Perspectives,* ed. Mary Zey-Ferrell and Michael Aiken. Glenview,
    Illinois: Scott, Foresman, and Company.

Besharov, Douglas J.
    1986, "How Child Abuse Programs Hurt Poor Children: The Misuse of
    Foster Care." *American Enterprsie Institute for Public Policy*. Washington,
    D.C.

Block, Fred, Richard A. Cloward, Barbara Ehrenreich, and Frances Fox Piven
    1987, *The Mean Season: The Attack on the Welfare State*. New York:
    Pantheon.

Bluestone, Barry, and Bennett Harrison
    1982, *The Deindustrialization of America: Plant Closings, Community
    Abandonment, and the Dismantling of Basic Industry*. New York: Basic
    Books.

Bogdan, Robert, and Steven J. Taylor
    1975, *Introduction to Qualitative Research Methods*. New York: John Wiley & Sons.

Braverman, Harry
    1974, *Labor and Monopoly Capital*. New York: Monthly Review.

Cancian, Francesca M.
    1992, "Feminist Science: Methodologies that Challenge Inequality." *Gender and Society* 6: 623–42.

Center for the Study of Social Policy, The
    1988, "Claiming Available Federal Funds Under Title IV-E of the Social Security Act." Washington, D.C.: Center for the Study of Social Policy.

Chubb, John E., and Terry M. Moe
    1990, *Politics, Markets, & America's Schools*. Washington, D.C.: Brookings Institute.

Clark, Burton R.
    1972, "The Organizational Saga in Higher Education." *Administrative Science Quarterly* 17:178–84.

Clark, David L.
    1985, "Emerging Paradigms in Organizational Theory and Research." In *Organizational Theory and Inquiry*, ed. Yvonna S. Lincoln. Beverly Hills: Sage.

Clark, Kenneth
    1965, *Dark Ghetto*. New York: Harper & Row.

Cloward, Richard A., and Frances Fox Piven
    1966, "The Weight of the Poor: A Strategy to End Poverty." In *Blacks and Bureaucracy*, ed. Virginia B. Ermer and John H. Strange. New York: Thomas J. Crowell.

1972, "The Professional Bureaucracies: Benefit Systems as Influence Systems." In *Blacks and Bureaucracy: Readings in the Problems of Politics of Change*, ed. Virginia B. Ermer and John H. Strange. New York: Thomas Y. Crowell Company.

Cnaan, Ram A.
1991, "Neighborhood-Representing Organizations: How Democratic are They?" *Social Service Review* 65:614–34.

Cohen, Michael D., James G. March, and Johan P. Olsen
1972, "A Garbage Can Model of Organizational Choice." *Administrative Science Quarterly* 17:1–25.

Cohen, Stanley
1985, *Visions of Social Control*. Cambridge: Polity Press.

Curtis, Lynn A.
1985, *American Violence and Public Policy*. New Haven: Yale University Press.

Czarniawska-Joerges, Barbara
1989, "The Wonderland of Public Administration Reforms." *Organization Studies*. 10:531–48.

Dannenberg, Harry, Chris Deisinger, Shel Stromquist and David Weingrod
1970, "Strike at Allis-Chalmers, 1946-'47: Labor Radicalism Under Attack in the Post-war Period." Milwaukee: Milwaukee Independent School.

Danziger, Sheldon H., Robert H. Haveman, and Robert D. Plotnick
1986, "Antipoverty Policy: Effects on the Poor and Nonpoor." In Sheldon H. Danziger and Daniel H. Weinberg, ed., *Fighting Poverty: What Works and What Doesn't*. Cambridge, Mass.: Harvard University Press.

Dean, John P., and William Foote Whyte
1969, "How do You Know If the Informant is Telling the Truth." In *Issues in Participant Observation*, ed. George J. McCall and

J.L. Simmons. Reading, Massachusetts: Addison-Wesley.

Derthick, Martha
1975, *Uncontrollable Spending for Social Services Grants*. Washington, D.C.: Brookings Institute.

Devitt, Mary
1992, "Milwaukee County Youth Initiative Institutional Impact Evaluation." Milwaukee, Wisc.: University of Wisconsin-Milwaukee.

Downs, Anthony
1967, *Inside Bureaucracy*. Glenview,Ill: Scott, Foresman, and Company.

Drucker, Peter F.
1968, *The Age of Discontinuity: Guidelines to our Changing Society*. New York: Harper & Row.

1985, *Innovation and Entrepreneurship: Practice and Principles*. New York: Harper & Row.

Dryfoos, Joy
1988, "Bringing Children Out of the Shadows." *Carnegie Quarterly* 33:1–9.

Dugger, Celia W.,
1992, "Shortage of Trained Caseworkers Imperils Young Victims of Abuse." *New York Times*, December 28.

Duncan, Greg J.
1984, *Years of Poverty Years of Plenty: The Changing Fortunes of American Workers and Families*. Ann Arbor, Michigan: Institute for Social Research.

Economic Analysis, Bureau of
1988, "Total Transfer Payments: Table CA35." Washington D.C.: Regional Economic Information System.

Edin, Kathryn
    1991, "Surviving the Welfare System: How AFDC Recipients Make Ends
    Meet in Chicago." *Social Problems* 38:462–74.

Edna McConnell Clark Foundation, The
    1990, "Keeping Families Together: Facts on Family Preservation
    Services." The Edna McConnell Clark Foundation. New York.

Edwards, Richard
    1979, *Contested Terrain*. New York: Basic Books.

Ellwood, David T.
    1988, *Poor Support, Poverty in the American Family*. New York: Basic
    Books.

Emery, F.E., and E.L. Trist
    1965, "The Causal Texture of Organizational Environments." *Human
    Relations.* 18:21–31.

Erikson, Kai
    1990, "On Sociological Prose." In *The Rhetoric of Social Research
    Understood and Believed*, ed. Albert Hunter. New Brunswick: Rutgers.

Fein, Edith and Anthony N. Maluccio
    1992, "Permanency Planning: Another Remedy in Jeopardy." *Social
    Service Review.* 66:335–48.

Figueira-McDonough, Josefina
    1991, "Community Structure and Delinquency: A Typology." *Social
    Service Review* 65:68–91.

Fischer, Claude S.
    1990, "Entering Sociology into Public Discourse." In *Rhetoric of Social
    Research Understood and Believed,* ed. Albert Hunter. New Brunswick:
    Rutgers.

Foucault, Michel
    1979, *Discipline & Punish: The Birth of the Prison*. New York: Vintage.

Galper, Jeffrey H.
  1975, *The Politics of Social Services.* Englewood Cliffs, New Jersey:
  Prentice-Hall.

Gans, Herbert J.
  1962, *The Urban Villagers.* Glencoe: The Free Press of Glencoe.

Gerth, Hans, and C. Wright Mills
  1946, *From Max Weber.* Oxford: Oxford University Press.

Gilbert, Neil
  1977, "The Transformation of Social Services." *Social Service Review*
  51:624–41.

Glaser, Daniel
  1976, "Marginal Workers: Some Antecedents and Implications of an Idea
  from Shaw and McKay." In *Delinquency, Crime, and Society*, ed. James F.
  Short, Jr. Chicago: University of Chicago.

Golden, Olivia
  1990, "Innovation in Public Sector Human Services Programs: The
  Implications of Innovation by 'Groping Along.'" *Journal of Policy
  Analysis and Management* 9:219–48.

Goldstein, Arnold P.
  1991, *Delinquent Gangs: A Psychological Perspective.* Champaign, Illinois:
  Research Press.

Gordon, David M., Richard Edwards, and Michael Reich
  1982, *Segmented Work, Divided Workers.* Cambridge: Cambridge
  University Press.

Gouldner, Alvin
  1954, *Patterns of Industrial Bureaucracy.* Glencoe, Illinois: The Free
  Press.

  1957, "Cosmopolitans and Locals: Toward an Analysis of Latent Social
  Roles I and II." *Administrative Science Quarterly.* 2:281–306, 444–80.

1968, "The Sociologist As Partisan: Sociology and the Welfare State." *The American Sociologist*. May.

1970, *The Coming Crisis of Western Sociology*. New York: Basic Books.

Greene, Marcia Slacum,
  1989, "'Sitting on a Time Bomb Waiting for Kids to Die.'" Washington, D.C.: *Washington Post.*

Greenstein, Robert
  1991, "Universal and Targeted Approaches to Relieving Poverty." In *The Urban Underclass*, ed. Christopher Jencks and Paul E. Peterson. Washington, D.C.: The Brookings Institute.

Gusfield, Joseph R.
  1991, "Two Genres of Sociology: A Literary Analysis of the American Occupational Structure and Talley's Corner." In *The Rhetoric of Social Research Understood and Believed*, ed. Albert Hunter. New Brunswick: Rutgers University Press.

Hagedorn, John M.
  1988, *People and Folks: Gangs, Crime, and the Underclass in a Rustbelt City*. Chicago: Lake View Press.

  1989, "Study of Youth Released from Residential Treatment, Day Treatment, and Group Homes in 1989." Milwaukee: Milwaukee County Department of Health & Human Services.

  1990, "Survey of DSS Chips Staff: Final Report." Milwaukee: University of Wisconsin-Milwaukee.

  1991, "Gangs, Neighborhoods, and Public Policy." *Social Problems* 38:529–42.

Hagedorn, John M., and Deborah Schwartz
  1992, "Pilot Foster Care Analysis: Final Report." Milwaukee: Milwaukee County Department of Social Services.

Halpern, Robert

1990, "Fragile Families, Fragile Solutions: An Essay Review." *Social Service Review* 64:637–48.

1991, "Supportive Services for Families in Poverty: Dilemmas of Reform." *Social Service Review* 65:343–64.

Handler, Joel F., and Yeheskel Hasenfeld

1991, *The Moral Construction of Poverty: Welfare Reform in America.* Newbury Park, Calif.: Sage.

Hannan, Michael T. and John Freeman

1977, "The Population Ecology of Organizations." *American Journal of Sociology* 82:929–64.

Harding, Sandra

1987, "Is There a Feminist Method." In *Feminism and Methodology*, ed. Sandra Harding. Bloomington, Ind: Indiana University Press.

Hasenfeld, Yeheskel

1974, "Organizational Dilemmas in Innovating Social Services: The Case of Community Action." In *Human Service Organizations*, ed. Yeheskel Hasenfeld and Richard English. Ann Arbor: University of Michigan Press.

Herre, Ernest A.

1965, "Aggressive Casework in a Protective Services Unit." *Social Casework* 46:358–62.

Heydebrand, Wolf V.

1983, "Organization and Praxis." In *Beyond Method*, ed. Gareth Morgan. Newbury Park: Sage.

Hill, Robert B.

1981, "Multiple Public Benefits and Poor Black Families." In *Black Families*, ed. Harriettte Pipes McAdoo. Beverly Hills: Sage.

Hunter, Kathryn Montgomery
    1986, "'There was this one guy...': The Uses of Anecdotes in
    Medicine." *Perspectives in Biology and Medicine* 29:619–30.

Hyman, Herbert H.
    1954, *Interviewing in Social Research.* Chicago: University of Chicago.

Iglehart, Alfreda P.
    1990, "Turnover in the Social Services: Turning over the Benefits." *Social
    Service Review* 64:649–57.

Jacoby, Russell
    1987, *The Last Intellectuals, Amercan Culture in the Age of Decline.* New
    York: The Noonday Press.

Janowitz, Morris
    1976, *Social Control of the Welfare State.* Chicago: University of Chicago.

Jones, Stephen R.G.
    1992, "Was There a Hawthorne Effect?" *American Journal of Sociology*
    98:451–68.

Kamerman, Sheila B., and Alfred J. Kahn
    1989, "Social Services for Children, Youth, and Families in the United
    States." Greenwich, Connecticut: *The Annie E. Casey Foundation.*

    1990, "If CPS is Driving Child Welfare—Where Do We Go From Here?"
    *Public Welfare* 9–13.

Kanter, Rosabeth Moss
    1983, *The Change Masters.* New York: Simon & Schuster.

Katz, Michael B.,
    1986, *In the Shadow of the Poorhouse: A Social History of Welfare in
    America.* New York: Basic Books.

    1989, *The Undeserving Poor: From the War on Poverty to the War on
    Welfare.* New York: Pantheon Books.

Katznelson, Ira, and Margaret Weir
    1985, *Schooling for All: Class, Race, and the Decline of the Democratic Ideal.* Berkeley: University of California.

Knudten, Richard D.
    1990, "Sociological Practice: Scope and Content." *Wisconsin Sociologist* 27:4–5.

Kuhn, Thomas S.
    1970, *The Structure of Scientific Revolutions.* Chicago: University of Chicago.

Ladner, Joyce
    1973, *The Death of White Sociology.* New York: Vintage.

Lawrence, Paul R., and Jay W. Lorsch
    1969, *Organization and Environment: Managing Differentiation and Integration.* Homewood, Illinois: Richard D. Irwin.

Lieberson, Stanley
    1980, *A Piece of the Pie: Blacks and White Immigrants Since 1880.* Berkeley: University of California.

Liebow, Elliot
    1967, *Tally's Corner.* Boston: Little, Brown, and Co.

Lincoln, Yvonna
    1985, "The Substance of the Emergent Paradigm: Implications for Researchers." In *Organizational Theory and Inquiry,* ed. Yvonna Lincoln. Beverly Hills: Sage.

    1985, *Organizational Theory and Inquiry: The Paradigm Revolution.* Beverly Hills: Sage.

Lincoln, Yvonna S., and Egon G. Guba
    1985, *Naturalistic Inquiry.* Beverly Hills: Sage.

Lindblom, Charles E.
    1959, "The Science of 'Muddling Through.'" *Public Administrative Review* 19:79–88.

Lindsey, Almont
    1942, *The Pullman Strike.* Chicago: University of Chicago.

Lipsky, Michael
    1972, "Street-Level Bureaucracy and the Analysis of Urban Reform." In *Blacks and Bureaucracy: Readings in the Problems of Politics of Change,* ed. Virginia B. Ermer and John H. Strange. New York: Thomas Y. Crowell Co.

    1980, *Street-Level Bureaucracies: Dilemmas of the Individual in Public Services.* New York: Russell Sage.

    1984, "Bureaucratic Disentitlement in Social Welfare Programs." *Social Service Review* 58:3–27.

March, James G., and Johan P. Olsen
    1976, *Ambiguity and Choice in Organizations.* Bergen, Norway: Universitetsforlaget.

Markoff, John,
    1991, "IBM Announces a Sweeping Shift on its Structure." New York: *New York Times.*

Markowitz, Laura M.
    1992, "Making House Calls: Family Preservation Goes Beyond Office-bound Therapy." *Networker* July/August.

Marris, Peter, and Martin Rein
    1967, *Dilemmas of Social Reform, Poverty and Community Action in the United States.* Chicago: University of Chicago.

McKnight, John L.
    1987, "The Future of Low-Income Neighborhoods and the People Who

Reside There." Evanston, Ill.: Northwestern University Center for Urban Affairs and Policy Research.

Merton, Robert K.
1968, *Social Theory and Social Structure*. New York: The Free Press.

Meyer, John M., and Brian Rowan
1981, "Institutionalized Organizations: Formal Structure as Myth and Ceremony." In *Complex Organizations: Critical Perspectives*, ed. Mary Zey-Ferrell and Michael Aiken. Glenview, Illinois: Scott, Foresman, and Company.

Meyer, Marshall W., and Lynne G. Zucker
1989, *Permanently Failing Organizations*. Newbury Park: Sage.

Meyers, Marcia K.
1993, "Organizational Factors in the Integration of Services for Children." *Social Service Review* 67:547–75.

Michels, Robert
1915, *Political Parties: A Sociological Study of the Oligarchical Tendencies of Modern Democracy*. New York: The Free Press.

Midwest American Assembly
1990, "The Future of Social Welfare in America." Madison, Wis.: *The Robert M. La Follettee Institute of Public Affairs*.

Miller, S.M.
1969, "The Participant Observer and "Over-Rapport." In *Issues in Participant Observation*, ed. George J. McCall and J.L. Simmons. Reading, Massachusetts: Addison-Wesley.

Mills, C. Wright
1959, *The Sociological Imagination*. London: Oxford University Press.

Milofsky, Carl
1990, "Writing and Seeing: Is There Any Sociology Here?" In *Rhetoric*

*of Social Research Understood and Believed,* ed. Albert Hunter. New Brunswick: Rutgers University Press.

Milwaukee County Department of Social Services
1962–1988, "Facts and Figures." Milwaukee.

1988, "Youth Initiative Committee Final Report." Milwaukee.

*Milwaukee Journal*
1992, January 8, "Jackson Doubts Welfare Fraud Story." Milwaukee.

1992, March 13, Editorial, "Learnfare Tripped up by Facts." Milwaukee.

Mintzberg, Henry
1979, "An Emerging Strategy of "Direct" Research." *Administrative Science Quarterly* 24:582–89.

Minuchin, Salvador
1991, "Family Abuse and Neglect...Child Welfare System Indicted." *The Prevention Report* 7-8.

Moore, Joan
1977, "A Case Study of Collaboration: The Chicano Pinto Research Project." *Journal of Social Issues* 33:144–58.

1989 "Is There an Hispanic Underclass?" *Social Science Quarterly* 70:265–84.

Moore, Joan W., and Ronald Edari
1990, "Survey of Chips Clients: Final Report." Milwaukee: UWM Urban Research Center.

1990, "Youth Initiative Needs Assessment Survey: Final Report." Milwaukee: University of Wisconsin-Milwaukee.

Moore, Joan W. and Raquel Pinderhughes
1993, *In the Barrios: Latinos and the Underclass Debate.* New York: Russell Sage Foundation.

Morgan, Gareth
    1986, *Images of Organization.* Beverly Hills: Sage.

Moynihan, Daniel P.
    1969, *Maximum Feasible Misunderstanding, Community Action in the War on Poverty.* New York: The Free Press.

Murray, Charles
    1984, *Losing Ground: American Social Policy 1950–1980.* New York: Basic Books.

    1994, *The Bell Curve: Intelligence and Class Structure in American Life.* New York. The Free Press.

Murray, Charles, and Deborah Laren
    1986, "According to Age: Longitudinal Profiles of AFDC Recipients and the Poor by Age Group." Paper presented at The Working Seminar on the Family and American Welfare Policy.

Nathan, Richard P.
    1988, *Social Science in Government.* New York: Basic Books.

National Commission on Child Welfare and Family Preservation,
    1990, "A Commitment to Change: Interim Report." Washington, D.C.: American Public Welfare Association.

Nelson, Douglas
    1988, "Recognizing and Realizing the Potential of "Family Preservation." Washington, D.C.: Center for the Study of Social Policy.

    1991, "The Public Policy Implications of Family Preservation." In *Family Preservation Services*, ed. Kathleen Wells and David E. Biegel, Newbury Park, Calif.: Sage.

Nelson, Kristine, Miriam J. Landsman, and Wendy Deutelman
    1990, "Three Models of Family-Centered Placement Prevention Services." *Child Welfare* LXIX:3–21.

North City Area-Wide Council, Inc., as told to Sherry R. Arnstein
     1972, "Maximum Feasible Manipulation." In *Blacks and Bureaucracy:
     Readings in the Problems and Politics of Change*, ed. Virginia B. Ermer
     and John H. Strange. New York: Thomas Y. Crowell.

Oakley, Anne
     1981, "Interviewing Women: a contradiction in terms." In *Doing
     Feminist Research*, ed. Helen Roberts. London: Routledge and Keegan
     Paul.

Orfield, Gary
     1991, "Cutback Policies, Declining Opportunities, and the Role of Social
     Service Providers." *Social Service Review* 65:516–30.

Orloff, Ann Shola
     1988, "The Political Origins of America's Belated Welfare State." In *The
     Politics of Social Policy in the United States,* ed. Margaret Weir, Ann Shola
     Orloff and Theda Skocpol. Princeton, New Jersey: Princeton University
     Press.

Osborne, David, and Ted Gaebler
     1992, *Reinventing Government: How the Entrepreneurial Spirit is
     Transforming the Public Sector*. Reading, Mass.: Addison-Wesley.

Osterman, Paul
     1991, "Gains from Growth? The Impact of Full Employment." In *The
     Urban Underclass,* ed. Christopher Jencks and Paul E. Peterson.
     Washington, D.C.: The Brookings Institute.

Park, Robert
     1969, "Human Migration and the Marginal Man." In *Classic Essays on the
     Culture of Cities*, ed. Richard Sennett. Englewood Cliffs: Prentice-Hall.

Patterson, James T.
     1986, *America's Struggle Against Poverty 1900–1985*. Cambridge,
     Massachusetts: Harvard University Press.

Patti, Rino
> 1975, "The New Scientific Management: Systems Management for Social Welfare." *Public Welfare 33*:23–31.

> 1974, "Organizational Resistance and Change: The View from Below." *Social Service Review* 48:367–83.

Patti, Rino J., and Herman Resnick
> 1972, "Changing the Agency from Within." *Social Work* July: 48-57.

Pawasarat, John
> 1989, "Youth Initiative Research and Evaluation Project." Milwaukee,Wis.: University of Wisconsin-Milwaukee Employment & Training Institute.

> 1991, "Identifying Milwaukee Youth in Critical Need of Intervention: Lessons from the Past, Measures for the Future." Milwaukee, Wis.: University of Wisconsin-Milwaukee Employment and Training Institute.

Pawasarat, John and Lois Quinn
> 1990, "Youth Initiative Report." Employment & Training Institute. Milwaukee: University of Wisconsin-Milwaukee.

Pawasarat, John, Lois Quinn, Norma Wright, and Manual Chavez
> 1993, "Evaluation of Child Welfare Pilot Units." Milwaukee, Wis.: University of Wisconsin-Milwaukee University Outreach. Employment and Training Institute.

Pelton, Leroy H.
> 1989, *For Reasons of Poverty: A Critical Analysis of the Public Child Welfare System in the United States.* New York: Praeger.

Perrow, Charles
> 1978, "The Short and Glorious History of Organizational Theory." In *Classics of Organization Theory*, ed. Jay M. Shafritz and Philip H. Whitbeck. Oak Park, Ill.: Moore Publishing Company.

> 1979, *Complex Organizations: A Critical Essay.* New York: Random House.

1986, *Complex Organizations: A Critical Essay*. New York: Random House.

Peters, Thomas J. and Robert H. Waterman Jr.
1982, *In Search of Excellence: Lessons from America's Best Run Companies*. New York: Warner Books.

Pfeffer, Jeffrey
1982, *Organizations and Organizational Theory*. Boston: Pitman.

Pfeffer, Jeffrey and Grald R. Salancik
1978, *The External Control of Organizations: A Resource Dependence Perspective*. New York: Harper and Row.

Pfohl, Stephen J.
1977, "The Discovery of Child Abuse." *Social Problems* 24: 310–23.

Phillips, Kevin
1990, *The Politics of Rich and Poor: Wealth and the American Electorate in the Reagan Aftermath*. New York: Harper Perennial.

Piven, Frances Fox
1973, "The Urban Crisis: Who Got What and Why." In *1984 Revisited*, ed. Robert Paul Wolff. New York: Alfred A. Knopf.

Piven, Frances Fox, and Richard A. Cloward
1971, *Regulating the Poor: The Functions of Public Welfare*. New York: Pantheon.

1980, *Poor People's Movements: Why they Succeed, How they Fail*. New York: Vintage.

1982, *The New Class War: Reagan's Attack on the Welfare State and its Consequences*. New York: Pantheon.

1987, "The Contemporary Relief Debate." In *The Mean Season: The Attack on the Welfare State*, ed. Fred Block, Richard A. Cloward, Barbara Ehrenreich and Frances Fox Piven, New York: Pantheon.

1988, *Why Americans Don't Vote*. New York: Pantheon Books.

1993, *Regulating the Poor: The Functions of Public Welfare*. New York: Vintage.

Planning Council for Mental Health and Social Services
1986, "Access to the Service System: The Race/Heritage Status of Developmentally Disabled Persons Serviced by CCSB Funded Programs." Milwaukee, Wis.: The Planning Council for Mental Health and Social Services.

1990, "Final Report of the RFP Project Committee." Milwaukee, Wis: Milwaukee County Department of Health and Human Services.

Platt, Anthony M.
1969, *The Child Savers: The Invention of Delinquency*. Chicago and London: University of Chicago.

Pressman, Jeffrey L., and Aaron Wildavsky
1973, *Implementation: How Great Expectations in Washington are Dashed in Oakland or Why it is Amazing that Federal Programs Work at All.* Berkeley: University of California Press.

Quinn, Lois
1991, Personal Communication. to author.

Rai, Gauri S.
1983, "Reducing Bureaucratic Inflexibility." *Social Service Review* 57:44-58.

Reason, Peter.
1994, "Three Approaches to Participative Inquiry." In *Handbook of Qualitative Research,* ed. Norman K. Denzin and Yvonna S. Lincoln. Thousand Oaks: Sage, 1994.

Roethlisberger, F. J. and William J. Dickson
1947, *Management and the Worker.* Cambridge, Mass.: Harvard University Press.

Rosenthal, Stephen R.
    1989, "Mandatory or Voluntary Work for Welfare Recipients? Operations
    Management Perspectives." *Journal for Policy Analysis and Management*
    8:293–303.

Rothman, David J.
    1971, *The Discovery of the Asylum: Social Order and Disorder in the New
    Republic*. Boston: Little, Brown and Co.

    1980, *Conscience and Convenience: The Asylum and its Alternatives in
    Progressive America*. Boston: Little, Brown and Co.

    1981, *Doing Good: The Limits of Benevolonce*. New York: Pantheon.

Rounds, James Harry
    1979, "Social Theory, Public Policy and Social Order." Unpublished
    Ph.D. dissertation. University of California-Los Angeles.

Schorr, Lisbeth
    1988, *Within our Reach*. New York: Doubleday.

Schwartz, Morris S., and Charlotte G. Schwartz
    1969, "Problems in Participant Observation." In *Issues in Participant
    Observation*, ed. George J. McCall and J.L. Simmons. Reading,
    Massachusetts: Addison-Wesley.

Schwartz, Peter, and James Ogilvy
    1979, *The Emergent Paradigm: Changing Patterns of Thought and Belief*.
    Menlo Park, California: SRI International.

Schwartzman, Helen B.
    1993, *Ethnography in Organizations*. Newbury Park, Calif.: Sage.

Schwendinger, Herman, and Julia R. Schwendinger
    1974, *The Sociologists of the Chair*. New York: Basic Books.

Selznick, Philip
    1949, *TVA and the Grass Roots: A Study of Politics and Organization*.
    Berkeley and Los Angeles: University of California Press.

1957, *Leadership in Administration: A Sociological Interpretation.*
Berkely and Los Angeles: University of California.

Senge, Peter M.
1990, "The Leader's New Work: Building Learning Organizations."
*Sloan Management Review.* Fall: 7–22.

Simon, Herbert
1956, *Models of Man.* New York: John Wiley and Sons.

Sjoberg, Gideon, Richard A. Brymer and Buford Farris
1966, "Bureaucracy and the Lower Class." *Sociology and Social Research*
50:325–37.

Sjoberg, Gideon, and Roger Nett
1968, *A Methodology of Social Research.* New York: Harper and Row.

Slessarev, Helene
1988, "Racial Tensions and Institutional Support: Social Programs
During a Period of Retrenchment." In *The Politics of Social Policy in the
United States,* ed. Margaret Weir, Ann Shola Orloff, and Theda Skocpol.
Princeton, New Jersey: Princeton University Press.

Sosin, Michael R.
1990, "Decentralizing the Social Service System: A Reassessment."
*Social Service Review* 64:617–36.

Spear, Allan H.
1967, *Black Chicago: The Making of a Negro Ghetto, 1890–1920.*
Chicago: University of Chicago.

Specht, Harry and Mark Courtney
1994, *Unfaithful Angels: How Social Work Abandoned its Mission.* New
York: The Free Press.

Spitzer, Stephen
1975, "Towards a Marxist Theory of Deviance." *Social Problems*
22:638–50.

Stack, Carol B.
    1974, *All Our Kin*. New York: Harper.

Stagner, Matthew, and Harold Richman
    1986, "Help-Seeking and the Use of Social Service Providers by Welfare
    Families in Chicago." Chicago.

Steinberg, Stephen
    1981, *The Ethnic Myth*. Boston: Beacon Press.

Strauss, Anselm L.
    1987, *Qualitative Analysis for Social Scientists.* Cambridge: Cambridge
    University Press.

Streeter, Calvin L.
    1992, "Redundancy in Organizational Systems." *Social Service Review*
    66:97–111.

Suttles, Gerald D.
    1968, *The Social Order of the Slum*. Chicago: University of Chicago.

Toch, Hans, and J. Douglas Grant
    1982, *Reforming Human Services: Change Through Participation.*
    Beverly Hills: Sage.

Trattner, Walter I.
    1979, *From Poor Law to Welfare State: A History of Social Welfare in
    America*. New York: Free Press.

U.S. Advisory Board on Child Abuse and Neglect, The
    1990, "Child Abuse and Neglect: Critical First Steps in Response to a
    National Emergency: Key Excerpts." Washington, D.C.: The U.S.
    Advisory Board on Child Abuse and Neglect.

Van Maanen, John
    1979, "The Fact of Fiction in Organizational Ethnography."
    *Administrative Science Quarterly* 24:539–50.

1979, "Reclaiming Qualitative Methods for Organizational Research: A Preface." *Administrative Science Quarterly* 24.

Van Maanen, John
1988, *Tales of the Field: On Writing Ethnography*. Chicago: University of Chicago.

Wald, Michael S.
1988, "Family Preservation: Are we moving too fast?" *Public Welfare* 33–38.

Walmsley, Gary L.
1969, *Selective Service and a Changing America*. Columbus, Ohio: Charles E. Merrill Publishing Co.

Webb, Eugene, and Karl E. Weick
1979, "Unobtrusive Measures in Organizational Theory: A Reminder." *Administrative Science Quarterly*. 24:650–59.

Weick, Karl E.
1976, "Educational Organizations as Loosely Coupled Systems." *Administrative Science Quarterly* 21:1–19.

1985, "Sources of Order in Underorganized Systems: Themes in Recent Orghanizational Theory." In *Organizational Theory and Inquiry: The Paradigm Revolution*, ed. Yvonna S. Lincoln. Beverly Hills: Sage.

Weir, Margaret, Ann Shola Orloff, and Theda Skocpol
1988, "The Future of Social Policy in the United States: Political Constraints and Possibilities." In *The Politics of Social Policy in the United States*, ed. Margaret Weir, Ann Shola Orloff and Theda Skocpol. Princeton, New Jersey: Princeton University Press.

Wells, Kathleen, and David E. Biegel
1991, *Family Preservation Services*. Newbury Park, Calif.: Sage.

1991, "Introduction." In *Family Preservation Services*, ed. Kathleen Wells and David E. Biegel. Newbury Park, Calif.: Sage.

White, Sammis, John F. Zipp, Peter Reynolds, and James R. Paetsch
    1988, "The Changing Milwaukee Industrial Structure." *University of
    Wisconsin-Milwaukee Urban Research Center*. Milwaukee.

Whyte, William Foote
    1943, *Street Corner Society*. Chicago: University of Chicago.

    1984, *Learning from the Field*. Beverly Hills: Sage.

    1991, *Participatory Action Research*. Beverly Hills: Sage.

Wilensky, Harold L., and Charles N. Lebeaux
    1965, *Industrial Society and Social Welfare*. New York: Free Press.

Williams, Celeste,
    1992, "Report Decries State of Juvenile Justice." Milwaukee, Wis.: *The
    Milwaukee Journal*.

Wilson, James Q.
    1989, *Bureaucracy: What Government Agencies Do and Why They Do
    Them*. New York: Basic Books.

Wilson, William Julius
    1978, *The Declining Significance of Race*. Chicago: University of
    Chicago.

    1987, *The Truly Disadvantaged*. Chicago: University of Chicago.

    1991, "Poverty, Joblessness, and Family Structure in the Inner City: A
    Comparative Perspective." Paper presented at Chicago Urban Poverty
    and Family Life Conference. Chicago, Illinois.

Wulczyn, Fred
    1991, "Caseload Dynamics and Foster Care Reentry." *Social Service
    Review* 65:133-156.

Wulczyn, Fred H., and Robert M. Goerge
    1992, "Foster Care in New York and Illinois: The Challenge of Rapid
    Change." *Social Service Review* 66:278-294.

# AUTHOR INDEX

Abraham, Katherine G., 109
Adams, Paul, 130
Alinsky, Saul D., 84
Altshuler, Alan A., 150
Analysis, Bureau of Economic, 184
Arnstein, Sherry R., 150, 152
Axinn, June, 28, 31, 32, 46, 82, 85, 86, 88, 100, 101, 191n.5
Baird, Christopher, 137
Bandura, Albert, 126
Bargal, David, 158
Bateson, Gregory, 181
Bath, Howard I., 129
Becker, Howard S., 179
Benson, J. Kenneth, 163
Berger, Michael A., 158
Besharov, Douglas J., 47
Biegel, David E., 35, 37, 154
Block, Fred, 104, 185
Bluestone, Barry, 104, 105
Bogdan, Robert, 162
Braverman, Harry, 79
Brymer, Richard A., 96, 124
Cancian, Francesca M., 165
Center for Study of Social Policy, The, 34
Chubb, John E., 51
Clark, Burton R., 181
Clark, David L., 105, 195n.11
Clark, Kenneth, 16, 161, 163
Cloward, Richard A., xi, 16, 17, 18, 78, 84, 85, 87, 90, 91, 94, 104, 108, 109, 110, 111, 112, 113, 173, 185, 199n.5, 191n.1, 192n.8
Cnaan, Ram A., 153

Cohen, Michael D., 50, 194n.10
Cohen, Stanley, 78, 144
Courtney, Mark, 14
Curtis, Lynn A., 107
Czarniawska-Joerges, Barbara, 145, 198n.1
Dannenberg, Harry, 192n.6
Danziger, Sheldon H., 187n.4
Dean, John P., 169
Deisinger, Chris, 192n.6
Denton, Patricia, 193n.5
Derthick, Martha, 34, 35, 100, 193n.7
Deutelman, Wendy, 126
Devitt, Mary, 51, 56, 132, 133, 187n.2, 189n.2, 198n.5, 200n.6
Dickson, William J., 224
Downs, Anthony, 134, 193n.8
Druck, Peter F., 105
Dryfoos, Joy, 60
Dugger, Celia W., 146
Duncan, Greg J., 185
Edari, Ronald, 62, 70, 71, 134, 183, 190n.5
Edin, Kathryn, 108, 196n.15
Edna McDonnell Clark Foundation, The, 35, 126
Edwards, Richard, 79, 80, 81, 82, 84, 86, 87, 88, 91, 93, 108, 189n.1, 190n.4, 191n.3, 192n.7
Ehrenreich, Barbara, 104, 185
Ellwood, David T., 196n.15
Emery, F. E., 192n.2
Erikson, Kai, 179
Farris, Buford, 96, 124
Fein, Edith, 63

Figueira-McDonough, Josefina, 190n.6
Fischer, Claude S., 179
Foucault, Michel, 79, 191n.3
Freeman, John, 97, 192n.2
Gaebler, Ted, 51, 122, 143, 153, 197n.3
Galper, Jeffry H., 8, 32, 78, 123, 152,
    199n.4, 199n.5, 200n.6
Gans, Herbert J., 202n.7
Gerth, Hans, 193n.8
Gilbert, Neil, 31, 33, 100
Glaser, Daniel, 164
Goerge, Robert M., 147
Golden, Olivia, 155
Goldstein, Arnold P., 190n.3
Gordon, David M., 79, 81, 82, 84, 86,
    87, 91, 93, 108, 190n.4
Gouldner, Alvin, 8, 164, 169, 173,
    190n.4, 193n.5, 202n.4
Grant, J. Douglas, 200n.6
Greene, Marcia Slacum, 31
Greenstein, Robert, 14
Guba, Egon G., 170, 171, 176, 177,
    200n.6
Gusfield, Joseph R., 179
Haapala, David A., 129
Hagedorn, John M., 53, 66, 148,
    190n.5
Halpern, Robert, 14, 45, 46, 48, 56, 60,
    95, 103, 121, 129
Handler, Joe F., 78
Hannan, Michael T., 97, 192n.2
Harding, Sandra, 172
Harrison, Bennett, 104, 105
Hasenfeld, Yeheskel, 78, 102
Haveman, Robert H., 187n.4
Herre, Ernest A., 33
Heydebrand, Wolf V., 197n.2
Hill, Robert B., 153, 190n.4
Hunter, Kathryn Montgomery, 181
Hyman, Herbert H., 170

Iglehart, Alfreda P., 198n.5
Jacoby, Russell, 165, 178
Janowitz, Morris, 60, 72, 90, 95, 113,
    197n.4
Jones, Stephen R. G., 84
Kahn, Alfred J., 14, 29, 30, 32, 34, 41,
    44, 46, 47, 100, 103
Kamerman, Sheila B., 14, 29, 30, 32,
    34, 41, 44, 46, 47, 100, 103
Kanter, Rosabeth Moss, 54, 124, 125,
    182
Katz, Michael B., 37, 79, 80, 81, 83, 84,
    85, 88, 89, 100, 103
Knudten, Richard D., 201n.2
Krauth, Karin, 130
Kuhn, Thomas S., 195n.11, 200n.6
Ladner, Joyce, 171
Landsman, Miriam J., 126
Laren, Deborah, 108, 185
Lawrence, Paul R., 45, 48, 94
Lebeaux, Charles N., 45, 77, 80, 90, 94,
    102, 124, 144, 191n.5
Levin, Herman, 28, 31, 32, 46, 82, 85,
    86, 88, 100, 101, 102, 191n.5,
    193n.9
Lieberson, Stanley, 82, 185
Liebow, Elliot, 202n.7
Lincoln, Yvonna S., 170, 171, 176, 177,
    195n.11, 200n.6
Lindblom, Charles E., 200n.7
Lindsey, Almont, 80
Lipsky, Michael, 6, 8, 16, 44, 46, 49, 51,
    53, 54, 61, 122, 131, 145, 146, 154,
    189n.5, 193n.6, 197n.2, 202n.7
Lorsch, Jay W., 45, 48, 94
Maluccio, Anthony N., 63
March, James G., 50, 143, 157,
    194n.10, 197n.2
Markoff, John, 196n.13
Markowitz, Laura M., 14

Marris, Peter, 16, 17, 18, 61, 154, 193n.4
McKnight, John L., 153
Merton, Robert K., 8, 175, 176, 177, 202n.7
Meyer, John M., 48, 145, 153, 172
Meyer, Marshall W., 48, 95, 97, 102, 189n.5
Meyers, Marcia K., 78, 125
Michels, Robert, 173
Midwest American Assembly, 14
Miller, S. M., 162, 172
Mills, C. Wright, 164, 172, 178, 193n.8, 201n.2
Milofsky, Carl, 180, 181
Milwaukee County, 95, 107
Milwaukee Journal, 109, 110
Mintzberg, Henry, 177
Minuchin, Salvador, 30, 188n.2
Moe, Terry M., 51
Moore, Joan W., 62, 70, 71, 134, 165, 183, 190n.5
Morgan, Gareth, 79, 86, 124, 125, 193n.5, 194n.10, 195n.11
Moynihan, Daniel P., 16, 150, 164, 165, 187n.2
Murray, Charles, 104, 108, 185
Nathan, Richard P., 164, 165
National Commission on Child Welfare and Family Preservation, 30
Nelson, Douglas, 37, 50, 126, 128
Nelson, Kristine, 126
Nett, Roger, 166, 169, 173
Neuenfeldt, Deborah, 137
North City Area-Wide Council, Inc., 150
Oakley, Anne, 171
Ogilvy, James, 195n.11
Olsen, Johan P., 50, 143, 157, 194n.10, 197n.2

Orfield, Gary, 113, 196n.17
Orloff, Ann Shola, 89, 109, 112, 191n.1, 192n.8
Osborne, David, 51, 122, 143, 153, 197n.3
Osterman, Paul, 185
Paetsch, James R., 183
Park, Robert, 173
Patterson, James T., 83, 88, 89, 90
Patti, Rino J., 48, 78, 127, 193n.3
Pawasarat, John, 6, 30, 35
Pelton, Leroy, 29, 32, 33, 34, 35, 36, 63, 143, 144
Perrow, Charles, 84, 94, 97, 99, 123, 143, 181, 191n.3, 193n.5
Peters, Thomas J., 84, 105, 106, 143, 149, 155, 157, 180, 181, 186, 192n.1, 195n.12, 196n.13
Pfeffer, Jeffrey, 192n.2, 196n.16
Pfohl, Stephen J., 32
Phillips, Kevin, 104
Piven, Frances Fox, xi, 16, 17, 18, 78, 84, 85, 87, 90, 91, 94, 104, 108, 109, 110, 111, 112, 113, 173, 185, 191n.1, 192n.8, 199n.5
Planning Council for Health and Human Services, 65, 72
Platt, Anthony M., 37, 78, 82, 83, 173
Plotnick, Robert D., 187n.4
Pressman, Jeffrey L., 143
Prestin, Richard, 137
Quinn, Lois, 30, 109
Rai, Gauri S., 78
Reason, Peter, 165
Reich, Michael, 79, 81, 82, 84, 86, 87, 91, 93, 108, 190n.4
Rein, Martin, 16, 17, 18, 61, 154, 193n.4
Resnick, Herman, 78
Reynolds, Peter, 183

Richman, Harold, 72
Rivest, Michelle, 129, 154
Roethlisberger, F.J., 84
Rosenstein, Carolyn, 192n.2
Rosenthal, Stephen R., 45, 95
Rothman, David J., 77, 78, 79, 80, 81, 82, 83, 191n.3
Rounds, James Harry, 200n.6
Rowan, Brian, 48, 145, 153, 172
Salancik, Gerald, 196n.16
Schmid, Hillel, 158
Schorr, Lisbeth, 14, 15, 16, 44, 55, 56, 60, 129, 141, 189n.2
Schwartz, Charlotte G., 162, 202n.3
Schwartz, Deborah, 148
Schwartz, Morris S., 162, 202n.3
Schwartz, Peter, 195n.11
Schwartzman, Helen B., 172, 181
Schwendinger, Herman, 163
Schwendinger, Julia R., 163
Selznick, Philip, 97, 100, 125
Senge, Peter, 49, 54
Simon, Herbert, 195n.11
Sjoberg, Gideon, 96, 124, 166, 169, 173
Skocpol, Theda, 109, 112, 191n.1
Slessarev, Helene, 196n.14
Sosin, Michael R., 47, 66, 102, 124
Spear, Allan H., 82
Specht, Harry, 14
Spitzer, Stephen, 90
Stack, Carol B., 71, 91
Stagner, Matthew, 72
Steinberg, Stephen, 183
Strauss, Anselm L., 174, 175, 177
Streeter, Calvin L., 124
Stromquist, Shel, 192n.6
Suttles, Gerald D., 194n.6
Taylor, Steven J., 162
Toch, Hans, 200n.6

Trattner, Walter I., 85
Trist, E. L., 192n.2
U.S. Advisory Board on child Abuse and Neglect, The, 31
Van Maanen, John, 175, 181
Wagner, Dennis, 137
Wald, Michael S., 37, 129
Walmsley, Gary L., 193n.5
Waterman, Robert H., Jr., 84, 105, 106, 124, 143, 149, 155, 157, 180, 181, 186, 192n.1, 195n.12, 196n.13
Webb, Eugene, 168
Weick, Karl E., 106, 143, 155, 168, 194n.10, 203n.8
Weingrod, David, 192n.6
Weir, Margaret, 109, 112, 191n.1
Wells, Kathleen, 35, 37, 154
White, Sammis, 183
Whyte, William Foote, 162, 165, 168, 169, 176
Wildavsky, Aaron, 143
Wilensky, Harold L., 45, 77, 80, 90, 94, 102, 124, 144, 191n.5, 193n.9
Williams, Celeste, 34
Wilson, James Q., 25, 120, 121, 124, 126, 154, 197n.2
Wilson, William Julius, 16, 55, 61, 62, 82, 108, 109, 130, 135, 143, 185, 189n.2
Wulczyn, Fred H., 147
Yates, Douglas, 199n.5
Yin, Robert K., 181
Yuan, Ying-ying T., 129, 154
Zakhar, Arlene A., 187n.2
Zald, Mayer N., 158
Zelditch, Morris, Jr., 167, 169
Zipp, John F., 183
Zucker, Lynne G., 48, 94, 97, 102, 189n.5, 192n.2

# SUBJECT INDEX

academic research,
    involved observers in, 161–82
ADC, 91
Adoption Assistance and
    Child Welfare Act of 1980, 188n.4
AFDC
    caseload increase after Black
        migration, 94–95
    conservative threats to abolish, 104
    increase in rolls of, 31
    informal income required
        to survive on, 196n.15
    Learnfare program for, 109
    percentage of African Americans
        in Milwaukee on, 183–85
    recipients less likely to know
        about social services, 71
    as substitute of low-wage
        menial employment, 108
    welfare caseworkers' control
        over, 46, 101
African Americans, 183–85
    denied benefits as agricultural
        workers, 91
    faring poorly despite New Deal, 90
    formation of northern ghettoes, 82
    ignored in Progressive era, 82
    kinship ties among, 70, 71
    lack of commerce and services
        in neighborhoods of, 72, 190n.5
    in low-wage jobs, 108
    in manufacturing industries, 91
    migrating north with no accrued
        benefits, 91, 93
    percentage on AFDC in
        Milwaukee, 183–85

rebellions of the 1960s, 93
social service focus
    on children of, 100
agricultural workers, 91
Allis-Chalmers, 191n.6
American Civil Liberties Union, 137
Annie E. Casey Foundation, 13–14
authoritarianism, 111–13
battered child syndrome, 32
Behavioral Science Institute, 125
Betty (social worker), 12–13
bias of limited location, 167–68
bias of personal distortion, 167, 169
Black Panther Militia, 5
Brophy, Tom, 110, 127, 128
bureaucracies
    academic treatment of, 78
    administrative costs, 103
    aligning themselves with Reagan
        budget cuts, 107–11
    as amoral, 159
    anti-poor rhetoric adopted by, 112
    assembly line nature of, 15, 95
    bureaucratization correlated
        with expansion, 193n.8
    cannot be final arbiter of
        community needs, 130
    in Child Protective Services, 41–44
    civil servants defending their
        jobs in, 97–98
    competing with community-based
        programs, 102
    controlling community-based
        programs, 103
    divergent goals among
        bureaucrats, 142

emergence of, 79–80
evolution during Progressive era, 83
expansion due to New Deal, 89–91
expansion of child abuse
    bureaucracy, 31–35, 48–49
in factories, 79
in formation of the underclass, 67
fragmentation as component of
    control in, 189n.1
gaining by punishing
    the poor, 36–37, 90
growth during Reagan era, 107
historical context of reform
    of, 75–114
how bureaucracies became
    fragmented, 45–49
institutionalization of, 97–99
lives of the poor dominated by, 6
minority participation in, 18
neighborhood-based programs
    as alternatives to, 48
objectives of reform and, 198n.1
outside reformers resisted by, 16–17
as over-centralized, fragmented,
    and ineffective, 17
periodic reorganizations for, 149
as permanently failing
    organizations, 97–99
puppet view of bureaucrats, 159
pushing control out of and into
    the community, 197n.3
redundancy eliminated by, 124
reforming local bureaucracies,
    158–60
reform resisted by, 16–17
reforms adding specialized
    layers to, 47
in search of a new mission, 103–4
self-interest of misdirecting
    reform, 78

social work bureaucracies fitting
    legal bureaucracies, 48
specialization in, 41, 45–47, 101–2
stock sets of solutions used by, 50
as unresponsive to their minority
    clients, 96
War on Poverty as fund-raiser
    for, 187n.4
War on Poverty's attempt to
    bypass, 96
See also civil service; street-level
    bureaucracies
business
    attributes of excellent companies,
        195n.12
    contingency theory and reform of,
        94–96
    downsizing and decentralizing,
        6, 105
    drive system, 81, 84
    factory system development, 79
    IBM, 195n.13
    McDonald's, 196n.13
    Packard on organization charts, 106
    restructuring of during Reagan era,
        104–7
    scientific management, 80–81,
        193n.3
    Taylorism, 80–81, 191n.3, 193n.3
    team approach in, 125
    as technical organizations, 193n.6
    unions contesting organizational
        goals with management, 86
Chicago Area Project, 164
Chicago School of sociology, 164
child abuse and neglect
    battered child syndrome, 32
    becoming a national issue, 32
    definition of broadened, 36, 144
    expansion of bureaucracy for,
        31–35, 48–49

federal social service funds
    used for, 103
increase in referrals, 30, 33, 188n.4
number of DHHS referrals, 6
poverty correlated with, 63
preoccupation with fitting the ethos
    of the age, 113–14
safe house for abused children,
    148–49
transferring responsibility for to
    police proposed, 143–44
*See also* Child Protective Services;
    child sexual abuse
Child Protective Services (CPS)
    bureaucratic labyrinth of, 41–44
    burn-out factor in, 51
    child welfare system driven by, 30
    control of AFDC grants, 46–47
    daily routine of social workers,
        25–26
    a day's cases for, 67–69
    emergency plan for, 118, 148–49
    growth of, 32–33
    increase in referrals after staff
        expansion, 33
    job satisfaction by seniority, 53
    problems in, 24
    referrals divided into "good" and
        "bad" addresses, 190n.2
    requirement to investigate referrals
        within 24 hours, 24, 25
    state of emergency declared for, 118
    vacant positions in, 118–19
    workers transferring to juvenile
        probation, 52–53
child sexual abuse
    lack of training for investigators,
        9–10
    pressures on intake workers, 12–13
    a "second sexual assault" by the
        investigator, 9, 10

    trying to get dolls for
        victims of, 11–12
child welfare system
    Adoption Assistance and Child
        Welfare Act of 1980, 188n.4
    Child Protective Services driving, 30
    court domination of, 29–31
    dual function of, 143–44
    integrated units in, 201n.8
    liberal call for more
        resources for, 141
    as means of resisting budget cuts, 34
    more staff as need of, 199n.2
    percentage of cases tied
        to courts, 30, 188n.3
    *See also* Child Protective Services;
        family preservation; foster care
citizen control, 151–52
civil service
    allowing job transfer throughout
        Milwaukee County, 53
    civil servants defending their jobs
        in the bureaucracy, 97–98
    employees benefiting from
        New Deal, 89
    lifetime jobs created by, 51
    regulations making experimental
        units difficult to staff, 130
    workers with seniority transferring
        to specialty positions, 51–52
classlessness, myth of, 63
Clinton, Bill, 112
Cloward, Richard, 164
color maps, 61
community-based programs. *See*
    neighborhood-based programs
community control, 60–61, 150
Congress of Industrial Organizations
    (CIO), 84
conservatives
    adoption advocated by, 113–14

big government conservatives, 141
blaming social workers
for system failures, 50
reform having different meanings
for liberals and, 8, 14
threats to abolish welfare, 104, 108
welfare reform called for by, 141
workfare supported by, 108–9, 112
contingency theory, 94–96, 195n.11,
196n.13
courts
child welfare dominated by, 29–31
family preservation replacing
time in, 126
percentage of child abuse cases
tied to, 30, 188n.3
percentage of foster children
who become delinquent, 35
social workers becoming used
to the routine, 28
social workers not having time
to study cases, 27
social workers waiting for hearings,
26, 29, 176
transferring responsibility for
foster care to proposed, 143
CPS. *See* Child Protective Services
Daisy (teenager), 43
Debs, Eugene, 80
deindustrialization of America, 104–5
Department of Health and Human
Services (DHHS)
child abuse referrals, 6
decision to not invest in
central city, 65
Fuller appointed director, 4, 5–6, 117
Fuller leaves, 24, 137
Fuller's reorganization of, 149
mandate for change for, 117
number of employees, 7

percentage of child welfare cases
tied to courts, 30, 188n.3
percentage of county youth
as clients, 6, 187n.1
request for 675 new
social workers, 119
*See also* Child Protective Services;
Department of Social Services
Department of Social Services (DSS)
administrative cost increases
during Reagan era, 107
American Civil Liberties Union
suit, 137
decentralization of, 73
exemplifying punitive state of
social services, 113
neighborhood council coordinators
funded by, 133
neighborhood councils used for
its own ends, 199n.5
resisting family preservation pilot,
127–28
Youth Initiative's attempt to
reduce hostility between
public schools and, 39
*See also* Youth Initiative
DHHS. See Department of Health
and Human Services
Dickinson, Emily, 177
Dinkins, David, 146–47
drive system, 81, 84
DSS. *See* Department of Social Services
emergent organizational school,
176, 180, 195n.11
evaluation, 152–54
factories, 79
family preservation
cost of, 126
defined, 125
failure of attempts to shift
resources to, 144

Homebuilders program, 125
  integrated unit for, 121
  performance measures for, 154
  pilot program for, 127–28
  social service as removing
    children from their home
    rather than, 37, 48–49, 103
  social service bureaucracy
    preserving itself rather than, 114
  as structural change of
    social work, 125–29
family values, 141
FAWs. *See* financial assistance workers
Federal Emergency Relief
  Administration (FERA), 85–86
feminism, 171–72
financial assistance workers (FAWs)
  assembly line nature of
    departments, 45
  lack of communication with
    social workers, 42
  social services separated from,
    46, 101–2
  social worker cooperation with,
    188n.1
Ford Foundation
  award for neighborhood
    councils, 135
  "grey area" grants, 16–17
foster care
  adding more staff for, 147–48,
    199n.3
  contradiction between removing
    children and family preservation,
    37, 48–49, 103
  as core task of social work, 36
  daily routine of social workers, 26
  family income as predictor of
    removal of a child, 63
  increase in placements,
    30, 35, 188n.4

minorities as more likely
    to be placed in, 35
  multiple moves and no permanent
    ties for foster children, 35
  percentage of foster children
    who become delinquent, 35
  percentage of public spending
    increases going to, 34–35
  permanency plans, 44
  PL96-272, 44
  transferring responsibility for
    to the courts proposed, 143
  workers having little contact
    with their clients, 44
Frank (social worker), 139–40
Fuller, Howard, 3
  appointed director of DHHS,
    4, 6, 117
  DHHS reorganized by, 149
  emergency plan for Child
    Protective Services, 118, 148–49
  family preservation pilot
    supported by, 127–28
  Greater Milwaukee Committee
    support for, 58, 59
  Hagedorn's controversial
    strategy memo to, 23
  Hagedorn's dependence on as
    possible source of bias, 173
  on Hagedorn's dissertation
    committee, 176
  leaves DHHS for public schools,
    24, 137
  neighborhood service delivery
    plans funded by, 134–35, 150
  safe house proposal, 148–49
  transformational style of leadership,
    158
  on unit integration plan, 201n.8
  veteran social workers on, 8
Gault decision (U.S. Supreme Court), 46

Great Depression, 84
Greater Milwaukee Committee (GMC),
    57–59
Hagedorn, John M., 3, 161–62
    appointed Youth Initiative
        coordinator, 4, 5–6, 23
    controversial strategy memo
        to Fuller, 23
    Daisy's case, 43
    dependence on Fuller as possible
        source of bias, 173
    Fuller on dissertation
        committee of, 176
    at Greater Milwaukee Committee
        presentation, 57–59
    leaves Youth Initiative, 137
    *People & Folks,* 162
    unit integration plan, 201n.8
    veteran social workers on, 8
Hansen, Susan, 24, 201n.8
Hawthorne effect, 84
Heisenberg's uncertainty principle, 170
Homebuilders program, 125
Hopkins, Harry, 85, 89
human relations school, 84, 87, 192n.1,
    195n.11
IBM, 195n.13
*In Search of Excellence: Lesson's from
    America's Best-run Companies*
    (Peters and Waterman), 105
institutionalized organizations, 97, 114,
    193n.6
involved observers, 161–82
    bias of the paycheck, 172–74
    criticism of, 163–66
    as more useful in some situations
        than others, 201n.3
    practical problems of, 166–67
    problem of analyzing the data,
        174–77

    problem of bias in data gathering,
        167–69
    problem of taking sides in, 161–67
    problem of writing for
        the audience, 177–79
iron law of oligarchy, 173
job ladders, 86–87
job security, 86–87
Kempe, Harry, 32
Kennedy, John F., 100
King, Martin Luther, 183
kinship ties, 70–71
labor
    agricultural workers, 91
    common purpose with
        management, 88
    deindustrialization's effect on, 104–5
    division of in factory system, 79
    increase of supervisors, 87
    job ladders and job security, 86–87
    primary labor markets, 94
    secondary labor market, 87, 88, 104,
        108, 196n.13
    segmentation of, 84, 87, 88, 89
    underclass as result of
        segmentation of, 90
    under scientific management, 80–81
    *See also* unions
Learnfare program, 109
Lewis, John L., 84
liberals
    calling for more resources for
        child welfare, 141
    on the Reagan revolution, 104
    reform having different meanings
        for conservatives and, 8, 14
    workfare supported by, 108–9, 112
McDonald's, 196n.13
McGee, Michael, 3–4, 5, 159
Medicaid, 196n.14

Miller Brewing Company, 121
Mills, C. Wright, 164, 201n.1
Milwaukee
    African Americans in, 183–85
    Black Panther Militia, 5
    Brophy, 110, 127, 128
    concentration of poverty in, 58, 61
    Greater Milwaukee Committee,
        57–59
    increased welfare caseload and
        costs during 1960s, 95
    loss of manufacturing jobs in, 183
    new administration elected, 3–4
    Schulz, 5–6, 59, 117, 118, 119
    an underclass in, 61
    welfare fraud in, 110
    zip code map of, 64
    *See also* civil service; Department of
        Health and Human Services;
        Milwaukee Public Schools
Milwaukee Public Schools (MPS)
    collaboration in family
        preservation services, 127
    Fuller becomes superintendent,
        24, 137
    Peterkin's reforms, 58
    Youth Initiative's attempt to reduce
        hostility between DSS and, 39
minorities
    bureaucracies as unresponsive to, 96
    commerce and services in
        neighborhoods of, 190n.5
    exclusion from modern economy, 96
    ignored in Progressive era, 82
    in low-wage jobs, 108
    as more likely to be placed in
        foster care, 35
    New Deal benefits for, 91
    participation in bureaucracies, 18
    percentage of funds allocated to

    minority-run agencies, 65
    rebellions of the 1960s, 93
    social problems concentrated
        in communities of, 63
    subsidized housing cuts, 108,
        196n.14
    workfare for minority women, 108–9
    *See also* African Americans
Moore, Joan, 162, 165, 202n.8
Moynihan, Daniel P., 164
myth of classlessness, 63
National Commission on Children, 14
*Naturalist Inquiries* (Lincoln and
    Guba), 170
neighborhood-based (community-
    based) programs
    accused of not being effective, 66
    as alternative to centralized
        bureaucracies, 48
    bureaucracies competing with, 102
    bureaucracies controlling, 103
    decline with demise of OEO, 66
    empowering poor neighborhoods,
        129–35
    representativeness and influence
        questioned, 153–54
    social control promoted by, 190n.6
    War on Poverty's funding of, 96
    Youth Initiative commitment to, 60
neighborhood councils, 132–35
    budget process, 134
    coordinators funded by DSS, 133
    Ford Foundation award, 135
    functions of, 132
    monthly meetings of, 133
    neighborhood service delivery plans,
        133–35, 150
    real influence of, 150, 152
    struggling to remain independent
        of bureaucracy, 136

used by DSS for its own ends,
    199n.5
in Youth Initiative program, 62–63
new authoritarianism, 111–13
New Deal, 88–89
    African Americans faring poorly
        during, 90
    civil service employees
        benefiting from, 89
    expansion of bureaucracies
        due to, 89–91
    Federal Emergency Relief
        Administration, 85–86
    half-way policies of, 192n.8
    minority benefits from, 91
    the poor benefiting from, 88, 90
    private social agencies on, 191n.5
    response to Great Depression,
        84–86
    Social Security, 88, 89, 91
    social service specialization
        deriving from, 45
New York City, 146–47
Nixon, Richard M., 32, 100
objectivity, 173, 202n.4
Office of Economic Opportunity
    (OEO), 66, 101
organizations
    bureaucracies as permanently
        failing organizations, 97–99
    businesses as technical
        organizations, 193n.6
    causal textures of organizational
        environments, 192n.2
    changing structure as key
        to reform, 123–25
    collegial model of, 124
    contingency theory of, 94–96,
        195n.11, 196n.13
    emergent organizational school,
        176, 180, 195n.11

garbage can model of, 194n.10
geographical dimension of, 197n.4
holograph model of, 194n.10
human relations school on,
    84, 87, 192n.1, 195n.11
informal organizations, 195n.11
institutionalized organizations,
    97, 114, 193n.6
organizational fluidity, 106
Peters and Waterman's stages
    of organizational theory, 186
population ecology approach to,
    192n.2
rationalization of, 83, 105, 195n.11
soccer match model of, 194n.10
Tennessee Valley Authority, 97
tool view of, 159
See also bureaucracies; business
Packard, David, 106
participant action research (PAR), 165
participant observers, 162, 163, 167–68
People & Folks (Hagedorn), 162
permanency plans, 44
Peterkin, Bob, 58
Philip Morris Company, 127, 131
Piven, Frances Fox, 164
PL96-272, 44
police
    altering core tasks as means
        of reform, 197n.1
    growth during eighties and
        nineties, 112–13
    the poor turning to for social
        services, 71, 72
    social worker cooperation with,
        188n.1
    social workers needing police
        powers, 27
    transferring responsibility for
        child abuse to proposed, 143–44

poor, the
benefit cuts during Reagan era, 108
bureaucracies dominating life of, 6
bureaucracies gaining by
punishing, 36–37, 90
child abuse correlated with
poverty, 63
the "deserving" and "undeserving"
poor, 89
deteriorating conditions for, 34
empowering poor neighborhoods,
129–35
family values for, 141
funds spent on decreasing, 103
increasing poverty increasing
social service caseload, 36
New Deal benefits for, 88, 90
as not having won much from
War on Poverty, 17
poorhouses, 79–80
Reagan revolution's effect on, 104
social isolation of, 61–62, 72
social service bureaucracy adopting
anti-poor rhetoric, 112
turning to police for social services,
71, 72
undermining poor neighborhoods,
57–73
under-utilization of social services,
71–72
writing off the "undeserving" poor,
59
*See also* underclass, the
poorhouses, 79–80
post factum theorizing, 176–77
post-positivist research, 170–72
primary labor markets, 94
probation and parole, 81–82
Progressive movement, 80–82, 83, 90
public service unions

child protection bureaucracies
as suiting, 48
as obstacles to creating
effective organizations, 51
regulations making experimental
units difficult to staff, 130
resistance to reforms aimed
at worker performance, 98
Pullman strike, 80
Reagan, Ronald
business restructuring and, 104–7
lack of opposition to welfare
cuts by, 111, 112
social service bureaucracies and
Reagan era cuts, 107–11
reform of social services, 13–15
action more important than the
plan in, 155–56
as adding more staff, 93, 146–48
as adding specialized layers
to bureaucracies, 47
altering core tasks of social
workers, 120–29
bureaucracies resistant to, 16 17
changing organizational structure
as key to, 123–25
conservative calls for welfare
reform, 141
contingency theory and, 94–96
for controlling and dividing
the working class, 78
cooptation of, 173
defeatism in movement for, 142–44
different meanings for liberals
and conservatives, 8, 14
direction and misdirection of,
115–60
as diversion from structural
change, 148–50
empowering poor neighborhoods,
129–35

evaluation process required for,
  152–54
family preservation as structural
  change to social work, 125–29
Ford Foundation "grey area"
  grants for, 16–17
frustration of, 77–91
groping along and policy
  planning models of, 155
historical context of, 75–114
integrated units as means of,
  121, 201n.8
of local bureaucracies, 158–60
as matter of daring leaps rather
  than careful steps, 142
misdirected by bureaucracies, 78
notions of as too rational, 155
objectives of, 198n.1
outside reformers resisted
  by bureaucracies, 16–17
as phony participation, 150–52
Progressive movement, 80–82,
  83, 90
public service unions' resistance
  to, 98
punishment and, 93–114
real reform, 117–37
requiring its supporters in positions
  of authority, 18
restructuring work at street level
  required for, 49
ritual significance of, 145
scientific reform as more
  supervision, 80–82
as seizing opportunities as they
  present themselves, 154–57
social workers on Youth Initiative
  reform, 7–9, 130
social workers' skepticism
  regarding, 12

of street-level bureaucracies,
  49, 197n.1
structural change of social work
  required for, 37, 49, 53
symbolic reform versus real support
  for social services, 139–60
taking advantage of divergent goals
  among bureaucrats, 142
team approach as means of, 121–22
as threatening the myths that
  define the institution, 99
as a typical governmental
  activity, 145
welfare reform act of 1967, 32
welfare reform called for by
  conservatives, 141
welfare reform under Gingrich-led
  Congress, 111
Wisconsin's welfare reforms, 109–10
research, involved observers in, 161–82
Reuther, Walter, 191n.6
Rockefeller, John D., 14
Roosevelt, Franklin Delano, 85, 89
Schulz, David, 5–6, 59, 117, 118, 119
secondary labor market, 87, 88, 104,
  108, 196n.13
social learning theory, 126
Social Security, 35, 88, 89, 91
social welfare. *See* welfare
social work (social services)
  administrative costs increasing, 103
  avoiding budget cuts for, 141
  confronting unique client
    problems, 125
  contradiction between removing
    children and family preservation,
    37, 48–49, 103
  core tasks of, 23–37
  expansion with War on Poverty
    funds, 93

family preservation as
structural change to, 125–29
financial assistance separated
from, 46, 101–2
fragmented structure of, 39–56
funds allocated to private
providers of, 65–67
geographical basis of funding
of, 62–67
historic view of, 32
increasing poverty increasing
caseload, 36
left-wing critique of, 32
location of agencies as cause
of under-utilization, 72
the myth of doing good, 98–99
as nobody's job to look at a
family's problems as a whole, 40
as patronage before Progressive
era, 81
private agencies during the
Great Depression, 191n.5
privatization of services, 28, 114
public spending increase
between 1903 and 1928, 81
public spending increase of
1960s, 31
punitive functions stressed in, 49
social services component
expanded, 99–101
support networks and, 67–73
three factors in crisis of, 36
three perspectives on history
of, 77–78
as unable to cope with the
Great Depression, 84–86
under-utilized by the poor, 71–72
*See also* bureaucracies; child welfare
system; neighborhood-based
(community-based) programs;

reform of social services; welfare
social workers
agencies with whom social workers
cooperate best, 188n.1
altering core tasks of, 120–29
bidding for better jobs through
seniority system, 51–52
blamed for system failures, 50–55
as burnt out on clients, 28
civil service creating lifetime
jobs for, 51
daily routines of, 25–29
DHHS request of 675 new, 119
expanding employment in
Great Depression, 85–86
investigation and paperwork
replacing services, 25
not turned to by people in need, 71
number of in 1930, 81
police powers needed by, 27
on real problems of social work,
9–13
salary increases during 1960s, 95
salary increases from federal funds,
100–101
skepticism regarding reform, 12
spending their time in court, 26, 27,
28, 29, 176
on staff increases, 199n.2
on Youth Initiative reforms, 7–9, 130
*See also* civil service; public service
unions
Sociological Practice Association,
201n.2
sociology
activism in, 163–64
Chicago School, 164
Mills on the sociologist's roles,
201n.1
positivist and naturalist approaches
in, 170–72

stories in, 180
writing in, 178–79
specialization in social service
    bureaucracies, 41, 45–47, 101–2
stories, 180–81
street-level bureaucracies
    altering core tasks as means
        of reform, 197n.1
    concealing their lack of service,
        202n.6
    defined, 6
    lack of discretion by, 189n.5
    persisting regardless of quality
        of services, 193n.6
    reform requiring restructuring
        of work in, 49
    as winners of War on Poverty, 17
subsidized housing, 108, 196n.14
support networks, 67–73
Taylorism, 80–81, 191n.3, 193n.3
Tennessee Valley Authority (TVA), 97
Thompson, Tommy, 109–10
Title IV of Social Security Act
    of 1961, 35
underclass, the
    gangs as problem of, 162
    in Milwaukee, 61
    public bureaucracies contributing
        to formation of, 67
    as result of labor segmentation, 90
    social isolation of, 72
    writing off, 59
unions
    Allis-Chalmers strike, 191n.6
    Congress of Industrial
        Organizations, 84
    contesting organizational goals
        with management, 86
    failing to expand into small firms,
        87, 192n.7

labor segmented by, 87
Pullman strike, 80
taking root in large mass
    production industries, 86
turning on communists, 87, 191n.6
United Auto Workers, 191n.6
worker demand for, 84
See also public service unions
United Auto Workers, 191n.6
War on Poverty, 15–18
    attempt to bypass service
        bureaucracies, 96
    as campaign for public
        employment, 95
    community control concept, 60–61
    as fund-raiser for bureaucracies,
        187n.4
    lasting successes of, 193n.4
    maximum feasible participation
        requirement, 102, 150, 199n.5
    neighborhood-based programs
        funded by, 96
    Nixon's curtailment of, 32
    Office of Economic Opportunity,
        66, 101
    the poor not winning much from, 17
    programs evolving from response
        to opportunity, 154–55
    social service expansion with
        funds from, 93
    specialization in programs of, 45
    street-level bureaucracies as
        winners of, 17
Weber, Max, 45, 193n.8, 195n.11
welfare
    ADC, 91
    additional recipients in early 1960s,
        100
    Clinton on ending, 112
    conservative calls for reform of, 141

conservative threats to abolish,
104, 108
as institutionalized from the 1930s,
90
lack of opposition to Reagan cuts in,
111, 112
Medicaid, 196n.14
reform act of 1967, 32
reform under Gingrich-led
Congress, 111
the safety net, 111
as social control mechanism, 111,
112
"spells" on, 185
spending increases in 1930s, 88
subsidized housing, 108, 196n.14
welfare dependency, 108
welfare fraud, 110, 196n.15
Wisconsin's reform program,
109–10
See also AFDC
West Allis, Wisconsin, 191n.6
Wisconsin
Allis-Chalmers strike, 191n.6
Learnfare program, 109
welfare reform in, 109–10
See also Milwaukee
workfare, 108–9, 112
Youth Initiative
agencies with whom social workers
cooperate best, 188n.1
attempt to institutionalize
change, 125
attempt to reduce hostility between
DSS and the public schools, 39
as bureaucratic insurgency rather
than mass movement, 158
commitment to neighborhood
agencies, 60
decentralized pilot units, 130–32

empowering client
neighborhoods, 130
as ending in failure, 137
evaluation process for, 152–54,
200n.6
geographical focus of, 62
Greater Milwaukee Committee
presentation, 57–59
Hagedorn appointed coordinator,
4, 5–6, 23
Hagedorn leaves, 137
as innovation ghetto or exemplar,
200n.6
neighborhood councils formed by,
62–63, 132–35
reform plan of, 55–56, 73
reforms stifled by bureaucracy, 136
Schulz's attitude toward, 118
social workers on reform of, 7–9,
130
Youth Initiative Committee
composition of, 59
Final Report of, 61, 62
reading Schorr and Wilson
for theoretical base, 55, 189n.2
zip code maps, 58, 62–67

## About the author

John M. Hagedorn spent two years as a leader of a reform of Milwaukee County's child welfare system, serving as the coordinator of its Youth Initiative. He had already established his reputation as a sociologist with his book *People and Folks: Gangs, Crime and the Underclass in a Rustbelt City*, an influential work on street gangs which challenged assumptions about gangs widely accepted in the media, law enforcement and criminology. *Forsaking Our Children* is a continuation of years of research as an "involved observer" in Milwaukee's poverty neighborhoods.

Hagedorn is now co-principal investigator in a major study of gangs, drugs, and female gang members at the Urban Research Center of University of Wisconsin-Milwaukee. His work focuses on humanizing gang members and the underclass to both academics and the public. He and his partner, Mary Devitt, have six children.